Aspirations for Modernity and Prosperity

Text copyright © 2014 remains with the authors and for the collection with ATF Theology. All rights reserved. Except for any fair dealing permitted under the Copyright Act, no part of the publication may be reproduced by any means without prior permission. Inquiries should be made in the first instance with the publisher.

Text copyright © 2014 remains with the authors and for the collection with ATF Theology. All rights reserved. Except for any fair dealing permitted under the Copyright Act, no part of the publication may be reproduced by any means without prior permission. Inquiries should be made in the first instance with the publisher.

A Forum for Theology in the World
Volume 1, Issue 1, 2014

A Forum for Theology in the World is an academic refereed journal aimed at engaging with issues in the contemporary world, a world which is pluralist and eucumenical in nature. The journal reflects this pluralism and ecumenism. Each edition is theme specific and has its own editor responsible for the production. The journal aims to elicit and encourage dialogue on topics and issues in contemporary society and within a variety of religious traditions. The Editor in Chief welcomes submissions of manuscripts, collections of articles, for review from individuals or institutions, which may be from seminars or conferences or written specifically for the journal. An internal peer review is expected before submitting the manuscript. It is the expectation of the publisher that, once a manuscript has been accepted for publication, it will be submitted according o the house style o be found tat the back of this volume. All submissions to the Editor in Chief are to be sent to: hdregan@atf.org.au.
Each edition is available as a journal subscription, or as a book in print, pdf or epub, through the ATF Press web site - www.atfpress.com. Journal subscriptions are also available through EBSCO and other library suppliers.

A Forum for Theology in the World
Volume 1, Issue 1, 2014
Editor in Chief
Hilary Regan, ATF Press

A Forum for Theology in the World is published by ATF Theology and imprint of ATF (Australia) Ltd (ABN 90 116 359 963) and is published twice or three times a year.
ISSN 1329-6264

ATF Press
PO Box 504
Hindmarsh SA 5007
Australia
www.atfpress.com

Subscription rates 2014/2015

Print	Online	Print and online
Aus $65 individuals	Aus $55 individuals	Aus $75 individuals
Aus $90 institutions	$80 institutions	Aus $100 institutions

Aspirations for Modernity and Prosperity: Symbols and Sources Behind Pentecostal/Charismatic Growth in Indonesia

edited by Christine E Gudorf, Zainal Abidin Bagir and Marthen Tahun

ATF Theology
Adelaide

2014

A Forum for Theology in the World Vol 1 No 1/2014

Table of Contents

Preface   Zainal Abidin Bagir   v

Chapter One Introduction:
  Pentecostalism Amid the Late Modern Shifts
  in Indonesian Society   1
  Christine E Gudorf

Chapter Two 'Here I Am to Worship':
  Professionalisation and Emotional Needs
  Fulfillment in Pentecostal and Charismatic
  Worship in Indonesia.   15
  Johanes Louis M Lengkong

Chapter Three The Spiritual Experience of Pentecostal
  and Charismatic Church Members   39
  Y Agus Heru Santoso

Chapter Four Class, Status and the Theology of Success Among
  Indonesian Pentecostals and Charismatics   53
  Ubed Abdilah Syarif

Chapter Five Modifying Christian Sexism:
  Gender and Modernity Among Indonesian
  Pentecostals and Charismatics   85
  Christine E Gudorf

Chapter Six Autonomy, Splintering and Growing Ecumenism:
  Governance and Organisation in Pentecostal and
  Charismatic Synods in Indonesia   111
  Angie Olivia Wuysang and Marthen Tahun

Chapter Seven Fractured Ecumenism and the Attempts at Fence-
　　　　Mending: Relations Between Pentecostals and
　　　　Non-Pentecostal Christians in Indonesia　　　139
　　Marthen Tahun

Chapter Eight Pentecostal-Muslim Relations in Indonesia:
　　　　Indifference, Potentials for Conflict,
　　　　and Prospects for Harmony　　　171
　　Zainal Abidin Bagir

Appendix A　List of the churches observed, interviewed,
　　　　　and/or surveyed.　　　195

Appendix B　Member survey questions.　　　203

Appendix C　Frequencies for member survey responses.　　　209

A Forum for Theology in the World Vol 1 No 1/2014

Preface

Researching Pentecostalism in a Majority Muslim Country

One of the very first questions asked about the research from which this book comes about was why we, working in an academic center at a 'secular,' state university, were interested in doing it. This question came from a number of the people we interviewed. It was not surprising. It came from the way religion is commonly understood and the social and political sensitivity of anything related to religion in Indonesia. Indonesia is a majority Muslim country but one that has a long history of the presence of other religions, the interactions among whom were not always friendly.

The Center for Religious and Cross-cultural Studies (CRCS), established in 2000, is located at Gadjah Mada University, the largest and oldest university in Indonesia. It offers a Master of Arts degree in religious studies and has been involved in many research projects on religion and culture. It was unique in Indonesia in the sense of being the only graduate program in a non-religiously affiliated university offering a degree in religious studies. 'Science of Religion,' as the official Indonesian nomenclature refers to the discipline, used to mainly refer to the disciplines studied in a confessional context in Islamic universities, Christian theological seminaries, or Hindu and Buddhist colleges. In the past few years academic study of religion has developed well in those higher education institutions, yet the idea that religion is studied for religious reasons is still prevalent and poses a challenge as reflected in the above question.

In general, religion is always a politically delicate issue in Indonesia and as such, under the previous authoritarian regime, was not a favored topic of research. The democratisation that started in 1998 created a new atmosphere of freedom, including freedom to do research on religious issues. This new situation also contributed to the possibility of establishing CRCS, two years after that historical turning point. Even in this new atmosphere, some of the research we did, especially on relations between religious communities and the issue of religious freedom, were still regarded as sensitive.

CRCS has been involved in many research topics, including contemporary issues that affect religious communities, such as religion and ecology, science and religion, religion and disaster, indigenous religions, and interactions between religions and local cultures. For the past six years we have also published annual reports on Indonesian religious life which look at issues around religious freedom, religion and public policies and religious conflicts. With regard to Pentecostalism, our main interest was first of all to understand it as a contemporary expression of religiosity, a phenomenon of the resurgence of religions, with its many implications for inter-religious relations, gender issues, and its encounter with local cultures.

For CRCS, the research on Pentecostalism was rather special in terms of the magnitude of research (conducted over a period of two years in five disparate areas in Indonesia simultaneously) and its focus on one particular religious community. Consistent with our main interest in inter-religious relations, though, we also paid close attention to relations between Pentecostals and other religious communities, including non-Pentecostals Christians. In terms of inter-religious, more particularly Muslim-Christian, relations, which shows a long history of mutual suspicions, this research became more challenging.

With the background as described above, we did expect that there would be some difficulties to access the subjects we wanted to learn about. Further, when observing, interviewing and engaging them, the field researchers (two Protestants, a Catholic and two Muslims, including a woman wearing a head scarf) came with their own personal identities which clearly affected the way the research is conducted. Suspicions were not only directed to the Muslim researchers; other researchers also had to work hard to gain trust from pastors before the questionnaire could be distributed and some of them interviewed.

In the end, with the perseverance of the researchers and the help of many people, including mostly the Pentecostals themselves, we managed to finish this two-year study, getting 3748 members of

Pentecostal churches to fill in our questionnaire, around 100 pastor interviews in 270 different churches in five areas in Indonesia. We also undertook interviews with non-Pentecostal Christian scholars and leaders. Conversations with them had shed important lights on many topics.

Our first words of gratitude thus have to go to them, without whose openness it was simply impossible to have this book. We sincerely hope that in turn they can take benefits from this study. It is noteworthy that this study on Pentecostalism was the first relatively large research on a particular religion, more especially Christianity, we ever did at CRCS.

Not less important were the two conferences we held during the period of this study, 2010-2012. In the first conference, held in January 2011, we mostly listened to the many invited speakers who helped us to understand Pentecostalism and the conceptual and practical difficulties in doing this kind of research. We thank all the speakers and participants whose enthusiasm was a source of motivation for us to do better. Many of the papers presented during the first conference will be included in the book that we will publish in Bahasa Indonesia after the publication of this book. A number of speakers from the first conference also came for the second conference in May 2012, to comment on our final findings. These comments were helpful for us in writing the final report and the articles in this book.

This project was fully funded by and a part of the larger global program of the Pentecostal and Charismatic Research Initiative (PCRI, crcc.usc.edu/initiatives/pcri/) at the University of Southern California. In general this research program was aimed to understand the growth of Pentecostal and Charismatic movements in the world, with researchers doing their research in over 20 countries. In general the research addresses questions about the characteristics of Pentecostalism, explanations for its growth, and its social and political consequences. Each of the research projects in particular countries then chose its own focus, and developed independently in response to a call for proposals. We especially thank Donald Miller of PCRI who led the project and managed to visit us once in Indonesia. We are happy that we had full freedom and support to carry out this research. The researchers from all around the world met twice in Quito and Nairobi; the discussions there helped us further to interpret the results of our research.

From our side, the idea for this project was conceived in a series of discussion between Christine E Gudorf of Florida International University, Zainal Abidin Bagir and Marthen Tahun from CRCS. Since 2002 Chris has always been a big support for CRCS, spending a few semesters and Summers to teach courses, and serving as the host and mentor for a number of our students who got grants to take courses at FIU as part of our exchange programs. Her support was very central not only in this research but more broadly in the development of CRCS for more than a decade. Other than the three of us as Principal Investigators, the central parts of this research has been the field researchers: Y Agus Heru Santosa (working in Medan), Johanes Louis M Lengkong (Jakarta), Haryani Saptaningtyas (Yogyakarta), Ubed Abdillah Syarif (Surabaya) and Angie Olivia Wuysang (Manado). They contributed their own chapters in this book, except Yani, whose chapter will appear in the Indonesian book that will be published after this. We are happy that, as they narrated at the 2012 conference, this research, with all its difficulties, has benefitted them, not only in gaining more knowledge about the issues, but also in enriching their personal understanding and awareness of the work as researchers which at times could be transformative. Not less important at all, at every stage of this research since day one until it was finished, the administrative and academic staffs at CRCS have been very supportive. We hope they share our delight in finally seeing the publication of this book.

Finally we would like to express our gratitude to the ATF Press (Adelaide), especially Hilary Regan, who has been our colleague and with whom CRCS has had several joint publication projects before this one.

Zainal Abidin Bagir
Center for Religious and Cross-cultural Studies
Graduate School, Gadjah Mada University

… Chapter One:
The Pentecostal/Charismatic Movement in Indonesia

Christine E Gudorf

What did we find out about Indonesian Pentecostalism/Charismaticism in our two year research study? Our findings were both similar and dissimilar to other research on Pentecostalism in the developing world. Unlike most of the Latin American research done on Pentecostalism in the 1980s–1990s, Indonesian Pentecostals/Charismatics are not usually the poor, and are even less likely to be the poorest of the poor, though, as in Latin America, there is a female majority.[1] Like much of African Pentecostalism, Pentecostalism/Charismaticism is making huge inroads into the membership of other Christian denominations, though not so much into indigenous religions as in Africa. As in both Latin America and Africa, as it has grown, it has become a more and more public phenomenon, increasingly involved in national politics and debates, though in Indonesia, political involvement is most often found in areas of Christian majority.

One of the more interesting findings was that while Indonesian Pentecostalism/Charismaticism continues the Pentecostal emphasis on morality, it has a somewhat different focus in Indonesia, and is not such a prominent part of the Pentecostal brand as in other parts of the world. We suspect that this is because the high moral road for religions in Indonesia is already taken by the Islamic revival of the last generation or so. While some parts of traditional Pentecostal morality—honesty in business and personal life, no recourse to bribery, bans on alcohol and smoking, opposition to pornography—are still central to the moral teaching of Pentecostal

---

1. Paul Freston, 'Pentecostalism in Latin America: Characteristics and Controversies,' *Social Compass* 45.3 (September 1998): 335-358.

and Charismatic churches, there is little of the traditional patriarchal assumptions on sex/gender. Sex is not a prominent topic at all, and despite the general recourse to biblical literalism, the New Testament restrictions on women (subjection to husbands as heads of families, silence in church, etc) are seldom, if ever, preached. The general message on women is one of equality—equal education, equal job opportunity, and equal—though sometimes distinctly different—roles in the family. Where there are obstacles to women becoming pastors, these are not generally preached, though the practice of the Tiberias churches of men only distributing communion—even when the pastor is female—seems to be known and perhaps accepted far beyond the Tiberias synod.

If original American Pentecostalism held inclusivity as a mark of the church, as it clearly did in integrating blacks and whites in their congregations decades before that became even marginally acceptable in the American South,[2] Indonesian P/C churches are inclusive in a slightly different way. The P/C churches in Indonesia do still appeal to persons status-deprived; they were originally inclusive in taking in persons of mixed European/Indonesian ethnicity (who had often been ignored by other Christian churches), as well as many Indonesians of Chinese descent, despite the widespread animosity towards those of Chinese descent. In urban areas, they have also grown by taking in persons who have emigrated from their ethnic villages. Partly out of this experience, partly out of the need for unity in mega-churches, the general trend in P/C churches is to attempt to rise above ethnicity, and bond together based on shared experience of global citizenship, the support of the Holy Spirit, and the community of the saints.

Perhaps the most striking thing we found was that Indonesian Pentecostal/Charismatic (P/C) churches present, on the whole, a very late-modern face. That face is high tech in its worship, high tech in its communications. It deliberately utilises a great deal of English in its songs, it banners and slogans, as an emblem of modernity—even though most of their membership seems to have little or no English. The P/C face is full of young people, and energy. The energy of the young, and their hopes and expectations for the future, are seen as

---

2. Howard Elinson, 'The Implications of Pentecostal Religion for Intellectualism, Politics and Race Relations,' *American Journal of Sociology* LXX.4 (January 1965): 403.

evidence of the Holy Spirit. Worship is loud (at least for Indonesians) and typified by rock bands. Indonesian P/C churches prize good management, and have in some ways managed to put a personal face on what are in many ways corporate management practices.

The image of P/C churches (though not nearly yet the norm) is that of a mega-church, and increasingly the fact of that mega-church is a massive, luxurious, modern building. This image clearly corresponds to the aspirations of many Indonesians, who have seen their nation take great strides in education, economic development, and political democracy in the last generation, and who expect that progress to continue. When many Indonesians look at the P/C churches on Sunday mornings, they see a church of well-dressed persons, many carrying smart phones or Ipads on which they have digital bibles to follow the bible readings. They see banners announcing events, often in English. They see parking lots full of motorcycles and cars, symbols of prosperity.

These late modern characteristics present a sharp distinction from traditional Indonesia, the Indonesia of villages, rice fields and palm plantations, of hundreds of distinct ethnicities, complete with their own language and culture, most of whom had synthesised tribal tradition with Islam over the last six centuries. There are over 13,000 inhabited islands comprising the nation of Indonesia, and six recognised religions: Islam, Hinduism, Buddhism, Catholicism, Protestant Christianity, and Confucianism (not added until the *reformasi* period of democracy which began in 1998). Though Muslims make up 89% of Indonesian citizens, both Hinduism and Buddhism preceded Islam in Indonesia. Christianity arrived with Dutch colonialists, who only left after the war for independence, which lasted from 1945-1949. Chinese immigration also largely began under the Dutch, and continued into the 20th century, with the Dutch East Indies Company using the Chinese as trading intermediaries. However, for much of the last few centuries Chinese Indonesians have not only been the target of discriminatory laws,[3] but also periodic targets of mass violence.

---

3. Though there is still some discrimination against the Chinese Indonesians, most of the discriminatory laws have gradually been dismantled, and Confucianism became recognised as one of the six Indonesian religions, since the country became democratic in 1998.

Religious Tensions and Suspicions

Thus religious and cultural diversity have been constant in Indonesia for many centuries, but that diversity has not always been harmonious. Religious suspicion can run high, depending on the location and current events. In our two year research study of Pentecostal and Charismatic churches in five major urban areas of Indonesia, we encountered some criticism, even hostility, towards P/C churches on the part of non-P/C Christians and some Muslims, and we encountered the resulting suspicions that members of P/C churches feel as a result of widespread criticism and hostility. Progress was very slow during the first six months; suspicions were high on the part of the church staffs that we were not being open about our agenda: 'Gadjah Mada University is a state university—why is it researching in religion?' 'We can't let you have any data on our church, as it could be used against us'. This last was sometimes aimed at the Christian field workers, who were either Catholic or mainstream Protestant, both groups historically hostile to the Pentecostal /Charismatic churches to whom they had lost significant numbers of members. At other times these rebuffs were aimed at our Muslim field workers, because radical Muslims since the colonial period had regularly accused Christians, and sometimes especially Pentecostals, of proselytisation, which is technically illegal. Any signs of growth (such as building new churches) were interpreted as evidence of proselytisation. We explained that while the grant for the research had been given to the Center for Religious and Cross-cultural Studies at Gadjah Mada University for its researchers to carry out, the project was a part of the program of the Pentecostal and Charismatic Initiative at the University of Southern California, which had authorised and supported sixteen different research projects to investigate Pentecostal and Charismatic churches throughout Asia, Africa, Latin America and the former Soviet Union. The PCI wanted to document the growth and strength of the Pentecostal and Charismatic movement, its trends and innovations. It was a slow process overcoming the skepticism about our intentions, because religious suspicion between Christians and Muslims, and P/C and non-P/C Christians, has long existed, and periodically becomes political, even violent.

The Question of Growth

In other global contexts, especially Latin America and Africa, there have been extensive controversies about both how much growth has occurred in Pentecostal churches and what credence to give to membership numbers claimed by Pentecostal churches. In Latin American research, the highest membership numbers came from the church rolls themselves, with some evidence of significant numbers of Pentecostal 'floaters' who move from church to church and are counted in more than one. By contrast, our Pentecostal sample claimed to be rather stable. Ninety and six-tenths percent claimed to be registered only in the church in which they were surveyed.

At the same time, when we queried pastors, some admitted that their membership rolls were sadly out of date; some stated that they had as many as ten times the number of registered members as attended even holiday services. This was confirmed in the pastor surveys. One pastor, who reported that he had pastored his church for all of its 45 years, reported that it had 4500 members on the rolls, but that 500 was the average Sunday attendance. Another church, 65 years old, reported a membership of 12,000 and an average Sunday attendance rate of 1500. In general, the older the church, the larger the discrepancy between the number registered and the number attending. For this reason, we have not attempted to put a number to the Pentecostal/Charismatic presence in Indonesia. While the Ministry of Religion requires registration of church synods, it does not track membership, and the only other source of numbers, the churches themselves, admit the inadequacy of their records. Evidence of growth is thus both anecdotal, and based on the numbers of new churches, the size of many of these churches, as well as the size of crowds that turn out for church events. Estimates by others of the Pentecostal/Charismatic presence in Indonesia vary from 8 million to 23 million.

Fervor for Growth: Advantages and Disadvantages

P/C churches, because of their growth, are objects of suspicion by both other Christians and sometimes by Muslims (though as we see in Chapter Eight, many Muslims do not distinguish P/C churches from other Christian churches, recognising only the distinction enshrined in Indonesian law between Protestant Christian and Catholic churches). Pentecostal growth is obvious to all observers of the religious scene in Indonesia and has gotten great play in the media over the last decade or so both with the construction of megachurches in a number of cities and with news stories of stadiums that fill to hear the most popular Pentecostal preachers. The argument from growth is that if Pentecostals are growing so swiftly that they are building new and larger churches, and drawing many thousands to their events, then they *must* be illegally proselytising.

Pentecostals/Charismatics do seem to rank making converts as very important. Among our respondents, 82.1% said that it was very important for their church to grow, with 16.3% reporting that it was somewhat important for the church to grow. Asked if they were personally active in spreading the gospel, 91.8% said yes. Nevertheless, the mainstream Christian charge that Pentecostals arouse Muslim wrath against Christian groups in general by proselytising seems overblown, since very few conversions seem to have been of Muslims. About half the conversions in our Pentecostal/Charismatic sample were from other Protestant Christian churches, which does not challenge the law, since it does not change the legal designation of a person's religion.

Buying converts? Another charge sometimes heard from some Muslims is based on an understanding of Christian churches—and especially Pentecostal churches, for those Muslims that recognise distinctions between Christian sects—as buying converts, usually with funds imported from outside Indonesia. With this criticism in mind, we asked our respondents if they had ever received financial support from their church. Slightly over 79% responded that no, they had never received support from their church. Almost 16% said that yes, they did receive support, and another 8.2% had received support in the past, but no longer did. When these responses are crossed with those detailing previous religious affiliation, it turns out that each group that converted from another church or religion is getting roughly the same proportion of aid as it represents in the total membership—a slight bit more for lifelong Pentecostals and Muslims, and a slight bit less than their proportion for Catholics, non-Pentecostal Christians, Buddhists, Hindus, and Confucians.

As for the sources of this funding the churches were distributing, the pastors we interviewed laughed at the idea that they had foreign sources of aid. 'From where would we get such aid?' they asked. They explained that in the beginnings of Pentecostalism in Indonesia, foreign missionaries had been able to get some support from their home missions or churches in Europe or the US, but that virtually all Pentecostal churches in Indonesia were now pastored by native Indonesians who do not have such international contacts.

Permission to build. Are the charges of buying converts simply a carryover from the missionary period of Indonesian Pentecostalism? Probably not. As part of the process for gaining approval to build houses of worship, the government has required permit-seeking religious communities to show the local Forum for Interreligious Harmony, a local government-mandated committee with proportional representation of all the religions in the locality, signature support from the neighborhood in which they wish to build. The idea is that the church must demonstrate that it will be a good neighbor, and to do that it must meet with both individual neighbors and neighborhood associations. One of the most common ways for churches to demonstrate good will is to invite the neighbors to Christmas and Easter celebrations complete with gift giving, to contribute to local *Idul Fitri* celebrations, and to offer services, such as schools or health services, to the local community. Gift-giving and service provision can be yet another cause of charges of attempting to 'buy' converts. But at the same time, any Christian church which does not do this, especially in a poor neighborhood that sees Pentecostals showing up for worship driving cars and motorcycles, is almost certain to be accused of being stingy, as well as discriminating against other religions in its charity.

The Problem of Access

Our team waded into this morass of suspicion, charge and counter-charge. We consisted of three PIs—Zainal Abidin Bagir, Christine E Gudorf, and Marthen Tahun—and five fieldworkers—Haryani Saptaningtyas (Yogyakarta), Johanes Lengkong (Jakarta), Agus Heru (Medan), Ubed Abdillah (Surabaya), and Angie Wuysang (Manado). Our work began in June 2010. When we met at the end of the first six months of fieldwork, spirits were low. We were far from meeting our six month targets in either pastor interviews or member surveys. Field workers were discouraged; they had been repeatedly turned away, visit after visit, from many churches. They could usually go to observe Sunday worship, but beyond that, the doors closed. Yet field workers continued to try to make appointments to see pastors. On those rare occasions when they succeeded, it was usually only after weeks or months of visits, sometimes being screened numerous times by secretaries and assistant pastors. Field workers' interest and sincerity gradually won over a few pastors, who agreed to grant them access to survey and/or interview pastoral staff.

At the end of the second six months, the rate of interviews and surveys began to pick up as one pastor reported to another about the project and their positive experience with the field workers. At the end of this first year, however, we realised that we had made much more progress gaining access to the Old Pentecostal churches than to the Neo-Pentecostal/Charismatic churches, and had been especially unsuccessful at gaining access to mega-churches, most of which were Neo-Pentecostal/Charismatic. We decided to concentrate on access to mega-churches in the second and final year, enlisting the help of the PIs and any prominent figures whom they knew who might help us gain access. The PIs met with officials of the synods, of the Ministry of Religion, and of the Forums on Interreligious Harmony (FKUB) during the second year of the project, and this also helped accelerate the rate of interviews and surveys in the mega-churches. In the end our field workers surveyed 3748 members of Pentecostal and Charismatic churches, interviewed 100 pastors, and observed a wide variety of services—cell meetings, baptisms, weddings, revivals, as well as regular Sunday worship services, special services for youth, children, and adults—in 270 different churches. (See Appendix A for a list of the churches.)

On Separating Pentecostal from Charismatic

One of the first questions we had to answer once the churches began to consider giving us access was: 'What do you mean by Pentecostal/Charismatic movement? There are Pentecostal churches, and there are Charismatic churches, but they are not the same.' Many pastors and synod officials expressed irritation at our 'lumping' these different churches together as parts of this same general movement. To them, some churches are clearly Pentecostal, and others clearly Charismatic, though they all admit that some churches not only have elements of both in their theology and practices, but also have associations with both types of churches. At the 2011 and especially our 2012 conference at CRCS, both church and synod officials expressed disappointment that our research did not lead to drawing clearer lines between who were Pentecostals and who were Charismatics. They had clearly hoped that 'outsiders' would have more luck at drawing hard and fast lines and producing clarity than they had from the inside.

Yet our research has shown that in all of these churches, regardless of the theology of the pastor, the age of the church, its ecumenical memberships, or even the synod to which it belongs—the usual indices for deciding identity—there are significant numbers of members, sometimes even a slight majority, who claim a religious identity at odds with that of the pastor/church/synod. Overall, our respondents divided roughly into thirds, with the largest group identifying as Charismatic, a slightly smaller group as Pentecostals, and a yet smaller group, but still almost 27%, identifying as both Pentecostal and Charismatic. Four percent of respondents identified themselves as Evangelical, and 7% as Other—but all these respondents were scattered among many churches, with no church having more than 10% identifying as neither Pentecostal nor Charismatic. As you will see in the later chapters, these divisions between those who claim to be Pentecostal, or Charismatic, or both, persist not only in the group as a whole, but also within particular synods. Since the congregations of all churches are themselves very divided about their individual religious identity, it would be impossible for any study to draw hard and fast lines between the churches themselves in terms of which are Pentecostal, which are Charismatic, and which have elements of both. As we conclude in later chapters, this makes perfect sense, in that the original Charismatic movement (within mainstream Protestant and Catholic churches—before separating into Charismatic churches) consciously adopted some Pentecostal practices (eg, tongues) and once the Charismatic/Neo-Pentecostal church movement became very successful, many (Old) Pentecostal churches adopted some practices of the Charismatics, especially around worship, but also in other fields, such as administration.

Our research showed that the P/C churches had made very few inroads into Islam—although Islam is the religion of 89% of Indonesians, less than 4% of our P/C church members report converting from Islam. Yet the image of the P/C church members as global citizens, tied by the latest technology into global networks of P/C churches, is so clearly attractive to all Indonesian youth, and correlates so closely with the aspirations of many Indonesian Muslims, that Muslim suspicion of P/C (often simply understood as Christian) churches as actively proselytising Muslims is difficult to overcome, especially when the evidence of new church building is so common.

In the following chapters, we assemble a sketch of Indonesian P/C churches today, based on our observations, pastor interviews and member surveys in P/C churches. In order to better understand relations of P/C churches with other Christians and with Muslims in Indonesia, we also interviewed officials of the governmental Ministry of Religion, officials of mainstream Christian churches, and Muslim and other religious officials in various interreligious organisations.

Chapter Two, by Johannes Lengkong, surveys P/C worship, which demonstrates a number of trends. Old Pentecostal worship style was quieter, used many traditional hymns, and seldom manifested speaking in tongues or other exuberant practices. Its congregations were and are smaller. But the exuberant, tongues-speaking, rock band, large scale LED screen worship services of the Neo-Pentecostal or Charismatic churches became so effective in drawing youth that they are increasingly imitated, where resources allow, by Old Pentecostal churches. Around this new worship style an entire music industry has grown up, which is global. This music is spreading outside P/C churches to more mainstream and Catholic worship as well. Chapter Two introduces you to the performers on the altar, their instruments and electronic equipment, and in the P/C music industry that is taking over the Christian music market around the world.

Chapter Three, by Agus Heru, examines the spiritual experience of members of P/C churches, which is focused around experience of the Holy Spirit, both of the Spirit as generally present in the congregation during worship, and the intense individual awareness of the indwelling of the Holy Spirit that is present in Holy Spirit baptism, which is for P/C churches the sequel and completion of the baptism by water shared with other Christian churches. Members of P/C churches are taught to see all the ordinary experiences of everyday life as an engagement with the Holy Spirit, as a response to God, but generally defer to pastors as those who have the most experience of the Holy Spirit, and are expected to share that experience through sermons. Members share their testimonies about experience of the Holy Spirit, which often concern gaining help in such everyday matters as jobs, business success/failure, sickness and personal relationships. Our surveys show that the historical marker of Pentecostalism, the gift of tongues, is relatively rare among those who identify as Pentecostals, but very common among those who identify as either Charismatic or Pentecostal and Charismatic.

Chapter Four, by Ubed Abdillah, examines class and status among believers. Indonesians in P/C churches come from all economic classes, though their average income is significantly above the national average. Members of P/C churches are on the whole much better educated than most Indonesians—the rate of post-secondary education among them is eight times the national rate. This is, of course, related to the fact that so many of their members are young. The focus of this chapter is the relationship between these demographics and the theology of success in P/C churches. There is a great deal of criticism of the prosperity gospel/theology of success of P/C churches both in Indonesia and in other areas of the world. This chapter examines the issue from the side of many P/C churches, who argue that they do not promise riches, but satisfaction and happiness emanating from closeness to God. The chapter also deals with their charge that traditional Christianity understood rich persons as evil, while the interpretation dominant in Neo-Pentecostal/Charismatic churches is that God rewards the good in many ways, including earthly possessions. Those who are still poor? Our time is not God's time, they say; deliverance may be at hand yet.

In Chapter Five, by Christine E Gudorf, we examine the issue of sex/gender in P/C churches, including the puzzling question of why there are more women than men in the P/C churches of Indonesia when the standard reasons given in other nations for female majorities do not seem to apply in Indonesia. The chapter also deals with the question of how the P/C churches are dealing with the women's movement in Indonesia, and finds that despite a certain level of literalism in the general approach to scripture in the P/C churches, the anti-female verses of the New Testament are seldom used against women. While P/C churches have a much lower rate of women pastors than mainstream Protestant churches, they do have some, and most P/C members understand that there are no restrictions against women holding any position in their institutions. In general, the churches seem to understand that the role of women in society and family has undergone rapid, ongoing changes in the previous generation, and are unwilling to come down on the side of tradition when that might put them at odds with the future, already present in their large youth membership. There are anomalies in our data, some of which seem to result from some churches following somewhat exclusionary practices against women without mandating them. There are also some interesting differences between what men report of their church's policy on women's service, and what women report.

Chapter Six, by Angie Wuysang and Marthen Tahun, focuses on four of the major P/C synods in Indonesia: the Pentecostal Church of Indonesia, Bethel Church Indonesia, Bethany Church Indonesia, and the International Full Gospel Fellowship—GISI. A brief organisational history of these synods demonstrates the tendency among P/C churches to splinter and form new synods from old ones, a tendency which is supported by the autonomy granted each church under the congregational system of organisation that is typical of most P/C synods. The chapter also details the growing ecumenism of P/C churches, which is somewhat of a break with Pentecostal history.

Chapter Seven, by Marthen Tahun, begins with the process of recognising the Pentecostal/Charismatic movement as an integral part of global Christianity, a process that has occurred over the last decades, accelerating as we approach the present due to the undeniable growth and spread of the P/C movement. The chapter then turns to the attempts to mend the relationships between P/C churches and other Christian churches in Indonesia, and gives numerous examples of successful ecumenism involving the P/C churches in Indonesia.

Chapter Eight, by Zainal Abidin Bagir, focuses on Pentecostal-Muslim relations in Indonesia, examining the patterns in the incidence of violence against Christian churches, including Pentecostal/Charismatic ones, by extremist Muslims. Bagir explores both the criticisms of Pentecostal/Charismatic churches by more moderate

Muslims—proselytising, evading the laws requiring permits to build houses of worship, noisy worship—and more tolerant responses from other Muslims, who equate loud P/C music with mosque loudspeakers broadcasting calls to prayer. There are some grounds for optimism regarding the prognosis for tolerance, in the surprising agreement of P/C members with various moral stances of Muslims, even when those stances are part of a Muslim political agenda of which one might expect Christian suspicion. On issues such as pornography and bribery, the historic Pentecostal insistence on righteousness before God prevails in Indonesia, providing some common ground. Also hopeful, is the finding that over 60% have no problems when the teachers of their children are Muslim, or members of any other religion, though they are, by a slight margin, most comfortable with P/C or non-P/C Christians as the teachers of their children.

Chapter Two
'Here I Am to Worship'[1]
Professionalisation and Emotional Needs Fulfillment in the Worship of Pentecostal and Charismatic Churches in Indonesia.

Johanes Louis M Lengkong

There was a conversation between two young men actively involved in youth service of a mainstream church. The one young man said to his fellow, 'Last Sunday I met A in the mall in Central Jakarta. He was with his girlfriend, attending church X in the 5th floor of the mall. A has not been seen in our youth service recently, although his parents are elders in our church.' A few weeks later these two young men visited their friend, A, in his house. They each talked to him and then eventually came up with the question,'Sorry to ask, but why don't you show up in our youth service anymore?' A replied calmly to his two fellows, 'Sorry, my friends, I didn't attend because I don't feel comfortable anymore at our youth worship. I am more comfortable in church X. I can be more expressive because their songs are more personal and vibrant: I can flow with them. The music is pleasing and festive, and is professionally produced. Initially, I just wanted to come because my friend invited me. I didn't intend to leave our church. But it turns out that I found more joy there than I've ever felt before in our church. I feel that X is the church that helped me find my true self.'

When I was a youth activist in a mainstream church in Tangerang, just west of Jakarta, I participated in this very conversation. Similar conversations are often heard among my writer friends who moved from mainstream Protestant churches to Pentecostal and Charismatic

---

1. The title of this chapter takes its title from a Christian pop song by Tim Hughes. This song is very famous and topped the music charts of Christian Copyright Licensing International for two consecutive years. This song is oftenly sung in worship in Pentecostal and Charismatic church. Source: http://en.wikipedia.org/wiki/Here_I_Am_to_Worship_(song)

(P/C) churches. The main reason they always give for their 'conversion' is that the worship service in P/C churches is always spirit-filled, aimed at youth, with religious pop music by skillful musicians. These accounts pushed me to investigate more deeply into the worship services of P/C churches, which nowadays seem to grow so rapidly. Much of that growth is commonly attributed to the great number of young people attending these churches. Within our research project at the Center for Religious and Cross-Cultural Study at Gadjah Mada University on factors in P/C church growth in Indonesia, I worked principally in Jakarta, with special attention to worship services. Through the experience of attending various P/C churches, I came to see a strong correlation between the professionalism and creativity in contemporary P/C church worship, especially music, and the growing number of people attending P/C churches, in particular, large numbers of youth.

Professionalism and Technology Fetishism in Holy Space

Dietrich Bonhoeffer, in his writings in *Letters from Prison*, concluded that a living church is a church capable of making its presence felt in the world today.[2] For the sake of its great mission, the church should be able to live within a changing community. Contextualisation has been done in the past in order to avoid a separation of the church from the world. Theological formulations and understandings of the faith, which led to the amendment of church governance, were revised. Pentecostal and Charismatic Christianity, originally separated from the development of the world, has become engaged to it. In fact, the P/C churches have begun to open up to modern technology and science, utilise them, and even to support the development of technology and modern science.

Many churches, whether in big cities or small towns, have begun to utilise, even to rely on, technology, both simple, old fashioned technology and high-tech, whose use is still limited to certain privileged circles. In my observation of the P/C churches, I find that these churches are very close to technology, especially information

---

2. Dietrich Bonhoeffer. *Letters and Papers from Prison. Dietrich Bonhoeffer Works, Volume 8.* John W de Gruchy, Editor. Translated by Isabel Best; Lisa E Dahill; Reinhard Krauss; Nancy Lukens. Fortress Press, 2009.

and communication technologies. There are many applications of technology, especially in the construction[3] of worship. A few of the technologies that can be encountered when entering P/C churches are multimedia, music, and the interior design of the worship space.

Multimedia[4]: Sophistication in the Presentation of God's Word in Worship Services. P/C churches, both the 'old' traditional churches and the more recent Charismatic Neo-Pentecostal churches, have flocked to use multimedia in their worship. The size varies; a church with a small chapel occupying a shophouse unit as a place of worship, may only use a small projector that reflects onto a small- sized white screen. But a church with a large and magnificent worship space will use a large projector, whose images are projected onto very large screens. In fact, 42-50 inch LED televisions are often placed in every corner of the room so that the images can reach all the people who sit at the back of the worship space. A mega-church located in Kemayoran, Central Jakarta, even uses a giant LED screen of 3 x 10 meters, so that the picture display is extremely clear from any vantage point. Not only are these images large, but they are varied. Small churches tend to use more conventional software which is only capable of producing a static image that does not move, with the text of the song stuck at the bottom of the picture. But other churches have started using animated images in their presentation. Animation obviously makes the worship more interesting and less boring. The attention of the congregation can focus on the display screen presentation. In addition to its advantage in centering audience attention, a multimedia presentation on a projector also allows the worshipers to reflect on the understanding of the Christian faith contained in the songs sung and the sermon—they are not intent on finding the song lyrics in a song book, or repeatedly glancing down to see the words of the next stanza.

One of the Bethel churches in Jakarta, as a matter of guidance for the officers of the Multimedia and Information Department, implemented the theory of communication expert, Edgar Dale, in his book, *Audio Visual Method in Teaching*, which says that people

---

3. The term construction is meant to convey the understanding that worship is a production process, involving both workers and capital.
4. Multimedia is a combination of audio, text, still image, animation, video, which are connected to one another.

can only remember 10% of what is read, 20% of what they hear, 30% of what they see, 50% of what is heard and seen at once, but 90% of what is simultaneously seen, heard, and acted out.[5] Multimedia is thus believed to be an effective learning tool for the church. In fact, multimedia is believed to be the main attraction to bring urban congregations.

LED monitor owned by Bethel PRJ. With its huge size and the production of large, clear images, the monitor is able to reach all of the congregation that sits around the room, regardless of their location.

Without wishing to imply that large churches are necessarily more multimedia techno-literate than small churches, I saw a strong tendency for the churches with better multimedia technologies to be churches with sizeable congregations of largely Neo-Pentecostal (Charismatic) character.[6]

The use of projection screens also includes the use of video cameras to cover and broadcast directly onto those projection screens. Initially, the use of video cameras had a practical purpose, so that the people

---

5. Edgar Dale, *Audiovisual Methods in Teaching*. 3rd Ed (New York: The Dryden Press, 1969).
6. Churches categorised as megachurches typically use multimedia technologies very well. Small churches usually only use a simple model. For example, Indonesia Bethel Church—Praise Revival for Jesus (GBI-PRJ), Jakarta Praise Community Church (JPCC), and Bethany Indonesian Church Nginden are all in the megachurch category, and all have excellent multimedia. They not only use animation, but also videos taken by professionals like those who cover a professional musical performance.

sitting in the back could see clearly the worship leader and preacher who serve in front. The video camera is connected directly to the computer that regulates the display image reflected by the projector to the screen. The actors in front can be seen clearly on the screen, even if the church uses only one camera and one angle. From some of my observations, some churches have started using multiple cameras in their video process. Multiple camera angles capture the moment in the same chronology but with different angles. In fact, a *jimmy jib*[7] is often used to take pictures from above with a moving effect. Image processing is the duty of an editor who sees all the camera visuals simultaneously and determines which point of view (camera image) will be aired on the projector for the next seconds or minutes. With such techniques, the congregation witnesses a projector that 'masters' the entire room, thus eliminating worry about being stuck in the back of the room or on the balcony. With the multi-camera technique, a large room feels smaller and a smaller room feels bigger.

Professional Musicians in a Worship Service. Music gets the most attention in worship services in P/C churches in Indonesia. The music that flows continuously from the beginning to the end of the worship service is believed to be an important attraction for the growth of P/C churches. Moreover, the appearance of the often very excellent sound apparatus makes worship truly an entertaining show, while at the same time both invigorating and soothing the members of the congregation who are tired from all the events in their lives during the previous week. The importance of music in P/C churches can also be seen from the percentage of time given over to music in the worship service. In almost all the P/C churches we surveyed (270), 65% percent of the worship hour is given over to song.[8] Worship begins with a welcome by the worship leader who then invites the congregation to 'enter into the presence of God' by singing. This musical activity continues, stopping only just before the sermon is delivered by the preacher—although there are some churches in which preachers

---

7. A jimmy jib is a camera mounted on a moveable crane that travels on an overhead track.
8. This figure is based on the percentage in a worship service of average duration: generally, two-hours. Only about 35% (40 minutes) does not have music, and this time is most often monopolised by the sermon.

continue a soft background music as they preach.⁹ After the sermon, musical activity resumes when the preacher invites the congregation to pray in song, to be more open to God's loving words as delivered by the preacher. At the end of worship, the preacher or a pastor delivers the blessing and closes the worship with more songs to accompany the congregation as they begin to move out of the worship space.

One thing that is always mentioned in reports of observing P/C worship is that the musicians who serve in that worship seem to be very professional ones. That is, the musicians who play in the worship are highly trained and many of them are said to make their living just by playing music in churches. In several interviews with P/C church musicians, they said that they are given an 'honorarium' every time they play somewhere. Although they mentioned that the wages they receive are not huge and cannot be called wages in the real sense, these 'rewards' are much greater than those earned by musicians in the mainstream churches, some of whom are not paid at all. This remuneration seems to make musicians in P/C churches more responsible towards their duties. In an interview with a group of musicians from a mega-church,[10] they said that they make themselves available at least twice a week to assemble and rehearse the program that will be performed at the next worship service, and are required to work full time on Sundays, when they are on duty from morning til night.

This demanding professionalism, oddly enough, does not make them bound to this church full time. Many of them 'travel' to other churches (sometimes in the same city) to play music as well. The musicians in the church sometimes play in other P/C churches which may lack musicians, or may exchange places with the musicians of other churches on a given Sunday, or just fill in when other musicians are ill or travelling. In some large churches, some of the musicians are not members of the church in which they are regularly professionally engaged. This happens not because no one in that congregation can

---

9. The keyboard is the principal instrument used. When other instruments accompany the keyboard, they, too, have typically been soft, not loud. Melodies used were usually simple melodies, which is the key 1, 4, and 5 in the major scale.
10. Interviews with LGLP (Loving God, Loving People), a band of Christian musicians whose first worship services took place at GBI Praise Revival for Jesus (GBI-PRJ).

play a musical instrument such as guitar, bass, keyboards, or drums, but because of the professional demands placed on these musicians, who are required to play every song in the church's repertoire perfectly, but also uniquely and creatively. These are not amateurs; they are not easily located, and must be taken as they are.

I am well acquainted with a group of church musicians who come from various churches and denominations. They play in a specific church on Sunday, but they can also play in other churches for services on other days of the week. The professionalism demanded of them in the P/C churches is very useful when they are engaged to play outside of their band, as in another church. It allows them to adapt to other professionals quickly, and to produce excellent sound with minimal practice. A group of well-trained musicians cannot only play well with minimal practice, but can also improvise and innovate together in ways that keep their music fresh. Like a mosaic, each musician who may be a permanent member of another musical group, gathers with others and performs the music in a worship service. They are able to achieve professional standards—to play perfectly, creatively, and uniquely, even though they have only gathered once or twice for practice. Although each has a different musical background, they agree on a basic pattern as the arrangement for each song. Musical freedom, carried by the very Spirit in Pentecostalism, is still a central part of the musical traditions of the P/C churches.[11]

These professional musicians are also supported with sophisticated sound systems like the ones found in music concerts or theatre buildings. Big speakers are placed on all sides of the worship space, resulting in booming voices from the back to the front. The placement is not random, but rather follows the pattern of the room's acoustics, also designed by an interior acoustics professional. The operators of the sound system are always in the back of a mixer in order to adjust the sound of each instrument and vocals to create an equilibrium.

---

11. Related to this basic pattern, the musicians say that it is easier for them to practice there, especially when they have to meet other people in connection with upcoming services. In addition, the basic pattern also allows the church to recognise the songs played by the musicians. For example, contemporary pop repertoire is usually played on a major scale, with four per four-bar, tap tempo more than 110 per minute, and avoid the dissonance (two notes are sounded together and create disharmony in harmony structure of main stream).

Sound system operators are often employed full-time by the church, especially in large churches which have numerous events each week. They regulate the sound levels and mix in the worship space each day.

The professional who designs the acoustics in the worship space is not only seeking a clear sound, controlled reverberation and balance, but is also seeking soundproofing power. Loud, especially explosive, sound can be properly mitigated by attention to soundproofing in the design of worship space. Whether it is mega-church or a small one which occupies a shop, all use soundproofing technology as much as possible. In some parts of Indonesia, the noise generated by a church can be a very sensitive matter, especially for a church located in the middle of a non-Christian residential area, because the music can disturb the public and potentially create conflicts with the locals.

Decoration and Lighting. Room decor is an important matter. Worship is presented as a divine entertainment: it is not only as entertaining as virtually any commercial entertainment, but is also able to bring the congregation into 'God's presence' so that the service is an encounter with the Divine. The congregation must be made comfortable with the atmosphere of the church, in particular the worship space. Some churches make the room like a theatre, with a large stage at the front. Some churches hold worship in a hotel ballroom or a shopping center auditorium, so the decor of the worship space follows the existing decor of the room, which is somewhat anonymous, but usually luxurious. Thick carpets, soft and comfortable seats, and air conditioning are selling points for the church.[12] In addition, small portable pulpits showed the face of Pentecostalism as flexible and open to changes. There are often (temporary) banners strung across the front of the stage, with either the name of the church, or ads for some upcoming church event. The stage can be decorated with various

---

12. Indonesia has a tropical climate; though the humidity is very high during the rainy season (80-95%), and high (64-75%) the other half of the year, the daytime high temperature only ranges from 83 degrees F to 88 degrees F. Virtually no private homes have A/C, and many traditional commercial buildings do not, either. Air conditioning is one of the reasons for the popularity of malls in Indonesia, though many people, accustomed to the heat and humidity, complain that A/C is too cold, when it is, in fact, kept 5-8 degrees higher than commercial space in the US.

forms of ornaments without having to interfere with the presence of the 'rooted' pulpit in the middle of the stage.[13]

One of the important things in the worship space is the lighting. Almost all P/C churches we observed rely heavily on artificially generated light from electric lamps.[14] The lighting is largely stage lighting, under which the musicians, singers, and preachers perform. According to J Michael Gillette, stage lighting is used to stimulate feelings and evoke the emotions of the audience.[15] In P/C worship, lighting can assist the music in developing mood. For example, in singing slow, mellow songs aimed at lifting the heart, the lamp used is a combination lamp that produces soft calm shades, while more lively music that encourages the congregation to hop and twist is accompanied by bright blinking lights. In addition, several youth-oriented churches commonly use laser lights and fog machines, which make the worship space atmosphere more lively and sparkling, like a night club, a place where the young people are looking for novelty. The social life represented by nightclubs carries the value of liberalism, humanism and romanticism, thereby become also part of the image of the church.

Professional Church Leaders: The Marriage of Theocracy and Corporate Management. When the church began to make technology an important element in achieving its mission of outreach and growth, both technocrats and technologists became necessary. Technocrats are people who have expertise in economics and administration, while technologists are those who master the technology, especially the latest technology. Some P/C churches have even begun to integrate principles of corporate management into the life of the

---

13. Calvinist mainstream church pulpits are placed in the middle of the stage; this symbolises Calvin's theological understanding that the God's Word is the center of worship.
14. Most of these churches do not have an adequate window for the entry of sunlight into the room, especially churches that use the ballroom or convention room as a worship space. Even churches that build their own building for worship, for example, Bethel Sharon Rose Jakarta, and Bethany Church Nginden Indonesia in Surabaya, do not construct big windows for the entry of sunlight. If there are windows, they are usually closed with a curtain.
15. Gillette, J Michael. *Designing With Light: An Introduction to Stage Lighting, Fourth Edition.* (New York: McGraw Hill, 2003), 12.

church. Pastors appoint technocrats and technologists to assist them in running the ministry of the church. The congregational system adopted by Pentecostalism has helped to enable this implementation, because each local church is responsible for the management of their own respective activities, and does not have bishops or other administrators above the congregational level who must approve of all new initiatives with the church. (However, a church may have many congregations in different locations, and decisions made at the church level—often with participation of representatives from all the congregations— will usually be implemented in all the locations. The chapter on synods will deal with this in more detail.)

Interestingly, the governance of the Pentecostal and Charismatic church services is currently displaying a new trend, which is to rely on professionals who have background knowledge and skills in secular work, who also demonstrate interest and aptitude in church work, and to invest these persons with the title of 'pastor.' In fact, in the P/C churches of Indonesia, many pastors came from the secular world. They were most often professionals in various fields of work. They were spiritually called, often following invitations from church leaders to participate in church ministry, and bring their professional skills to a new field, a non-profit field but one blessed with plenty: the P/C churches of Indonesia.

Through interviews with pastors, we learned that most of them came from the secular[16] world where they held good positions. For example, the Indonesia Tiberias Church pastor, Reverend Yesaya Pariadji, was a corporate leader before he took on shepherding the church. Rev.erend Ir Niko Njotorahardjo, pastor of Bethel Gatot Subroto, was formerly an agricultural engineer. Pastor Abraham Alex Tanusaputra, chairman of the Synod of Bethany Church Indonesia, has a contracting company that took over the construction of the mega-project, Jakarta Tower, a building that will function, according

---

16. This word secular is often used to describe the world outside the church, illustrating that the dichotomy between secular and religious continues and creates negative stereotypes of everything that smells secular. Ambivalence was unavoidable when, on one side, the church should be, holy and separate from the world. Recently the concept of the godly secular has appeared in some Pentecostal and Charismatic churches, as a reconciliation between the two.

to its publicity, as the 'prayer tower of Jakarta' and will be the tallest building in not only Jakarta, but in all of Indonesia. Pastor Josafat Messach, pastor of Bethel Petamburan, is a physician, as was the founder of the Bethel Synod, Reverend HL Senduk. Pastor Jimmy Oentoro, founder of the International Full Gospel Fellowship (IFGF-GISI), has an undergraduate degree in economics from the United States and also works as a consultant in business and leadership formation. These pastors, and many like them, went into the world of the church without first having any formal theological training. Their theological education was on-the-job training; at most they may have taken a short course of study at a bible college, often part-time. This also affects the way they run the church itself, as a company belonging to the Lord, with them as its Chief Executive Officer.

This is very different from what happens in the mainstream Protestant Church in Indonesia, where a church is usually shepherded by a pastor appointed by the synod. In these churches those desiring to be pastors are required to have formal theological education above the undergraduate level. Theological education long ago became the basis for the ordination required to lead the congregation. Pastors in the mainstream churches have been principally trained in biblical, systematic and historical theology, with some attention to homiletics and ecclesial polity, and call upon these to lead their congregations, while their colleagues in the P/C churches, many of whom do not have formal theological education, use practical methods of modern organisation in leading their congregations. Even those P/C pastors who graduated from schools of theology eventually take on the professional management skills of their brethren, sometimes as a requirement of self-defense and church survival.[17]

Methods of modern organisational management, the hiring of professionals who have mastered technology and administration, and an organisational climate that is open to change and adjustment, have all contributed to making professionalism central to the identity of P/C churches in Indonesia today.

---

17. This freedom fostering the spirit of Pentecostalism is evident in the secular priests of Neo-Pentecostalism. A spiritual leader is a person who lives holy, has divine visions, and is able to be a role model—not just one with a degree in theology.

Well-managed churches usually increase congregational participation in terms of both attendance and involvement. Professionalism is thus considered a necessity and its high costs are deemed worthwhile. A euphemism famous in the ecclesiastical world— 'Serve the Lord that He will replenish all'—is successfully paired with the phrase 'God will bless them that bless the church' to produce exceptional loyalty in terms of the congregation's financial participation in the church. The Christian value of giving is successfully internalised in members who then entrust some of their wealth to the church, understanding it as investment that will pay off in the future. Expensive development of the physical plant and infrastructure can be managed when the congregation has confidence in the professional management of the church. A well-managed church which has big 'capital' tends to get bigger, while a small church with voluntary management principles and less 'capital' often gets smaller.[18]

Corporate management has even become a commodity in the church. Bethel Glow Fellowship Center (Glow), a mega-church, offered to cooperate with smaller churches under the term 'church network' if those churches were willing to walk together according to the vision and mission of GBI Glow. GBI Glow shares not only its vision and mission, but also the Glow church management system, which follows general principles of corporate management. This 'franchising' is expected to increase participation, and thus the membership of the local church, which then leads to an increase in church finances. The benefit for Bethel Glow is the franchise tributes given at the beginning of the contract, and every month thereafter.[19] Another indication of the corporate management style is the

---

18. Based on my observations at two small churches with less than 30 members of the congregation after ten years of existence, small numbers of people and a small chapel causes the church to not grow both in size and financially. One church uses an attic space as a place of worship, and the other uses a two-storeys hop house unit. Limitations of space and facilities for worship makes new congregants reluctant to join. Moreover, there are many larger and more magnificent churches near. Yet, the number of church members has remained stable and not lessened because the pastor is able to provide good attentive care to his congregation.
19. Based on interviews with representatives of Bethel Glow FC pastor, the Rev Anthony Julius, October 11, 2011.

frequent seminars and public speakers on leadership in the church. Well-known national and international speakers are brought in to demonstrate the status and depth of the church, and its interest in improving the quality of its human resources. These seminars and speeches are not free, and the fees paid constitute another source of income for the church.

Pop Music and the Band in the Church: A Marriage Between Altar and the Market. It is undeniable that music plays a principal role in the development of the P/C churches in Indonesia. The lively music serves as an icon, indicating the existence of P/C churches. In fact, in a survey of more than three thousand five hundred respondents, they say that one of the most compelling reasons for them to join P/C churches is the lively music.

This lively music with full band and contemporary rhythms first appeared in the United States in the late 1960s and early 1970s in the Jesus Movement, a movement initiated by Chuck Smith, a pastor at Calvary Chapel, Costa Mesa, California, in order to bring young people back to worship in the church. The hippie lifestyle and rock & roll music were thought responsible for young people pulling out of worship in the church, which at that time still relied on traditional songs from a hymnal, many of them composed during the Reformation of the 16th century. This youth movement then created music and songs in the style of rock & roll, creating an alternative to traditional worship music. As a result, many young people began to return to worship. Spiritually-oriented pop music exploded, with more available every day. The field was not limited to specialists; many people were able to create a simple and easy listening song, without fear of violating rules for composing a hymn. The most important rule was simply that the song must express a deep desire to praise God. Gradually the organ and the piano were abandoned, and the guitar, bass, and drums were more often played in worship—instruments that had previously been considered taboo in church.

During two years of observation at several churches in Indonesia, I found virtually no P/C church that relies only on the organ or piano in worship, without a band. Some churches even use a large band, in which two or more musicians may play the same musical instrument (for example, three guitarists) and there are also some additional instruments, such as trumpet, saxophone, violin, acoustic percussion, and so forth. The author Greg Scheer has written that a band can function as well today as an organ of fifty years ago.[20] It is the band that makes praise & worship style authentic for today, as it is derived from the pop and rock genres. A band also functions, like the organ of the past, to lead the congregation in singing in the praise & worship style. Rhythm, syncopation, and the variety of forms of music that characterise contemporary songs can be performed well only with band accompaniment.

Romance and Contemporary Spiritual Songs. The lyrics of contemporary gospel music revolve most often around love: how God loves people, and invites people to love God. Limited human depictions of God, the transcendent and infinite, take on shape from prevailing terms in human culture, especially in the realm of romance. The Divine is regarded as a lover or groom who comes to the bride (the people), and then saves and brings people with Him to eternal happiness. These lyrics, which invite members into infinite happiness, makes the congregation, especially young people, more open and emotionally committed to God in the worship.

The surge of numbers of youth in P/C churches was greatly influenced by the song lyrics familiar to young people. Lyrics with shades of romance tend to be more easily understood than the lyrics of hymnal songs based in theological formulations, which may be more rich and structured, but are also more difficult for modern laity to understand. These contemporary songs, rather than being foreign to the spirit of Pentecostalism, reflect its traditional spirit of simplicity. The phrase 'for God nothing is impossible, for God nothing is impossible' is more easily understood and accepted than 'We Praise Thee happily, God is great; like flowers on the day, our hearts were in bloom.' Lyrics which use familiar language and phrasing from everyday life are becoming a powerful tool for P/C churches to use evangelising outside the church, either to the mainline Protestants, Roman Catholics, or even people of other faiths, including Islam. Not only that, but these new types of songs are also a means of internal conversion. Pastors in old Pentecostal churches regularly complained

---

20. Anthony Giddens, The Consequences of Modernity (Stanford: Stanford University Press, 1990), 64.

about the reduced number of young people at their services because so many had moved to a new P/C church. From the interviews with pastors who had lost 'young sheep' we learned that pastors understood that young people moved to such new places of worship which made them feel more alive, whose new songs connected to their own experience, and whose lyrics are simple and attractive. So these pastors were pushing their remaining congregations in the direction of this new music and new style of service in hopes of retaining, even recovering, young people.

However, simplicity in music does not produce a small repertoire. There is a multitude of songs available for an English-speaking worship. Most of Indonesia's contemporary Christian songs are imported from America and Australia. Names like Hillsong Music Australia, Michael W Smith, Don Moen, Ron Kenoly, Israel Houghton and Chris Tomlin are familiar in P/C churches; they are the composers and world class singers of contemporary Christian songs. Their work has been used in almost all P/C churches who use English in their services, including those in Indonesia. Swift currents of globalisation and the high standard of English education in middle class urban communities across Asia has made English a second language for many, although many worshipers seem to have limited understanding of the meaning of songs in English (another reason for the success of simplicity in lyrics).

In the post-colonial frame, the use of imported English songs without translation is thought to add status, to indicate a kind of global Christian citizenship as well as to connect to young people's image of the western world as better. The stereotype that the western world is more Christian, more advanced, and promises a better life, makes English-language products, including contemporary Christian songs, regarded as better products than the compositions of local musicians, both in the song lyrics, as well as the arrangements of songs (melody and accompaniment).

I have categorised a small sample of contemporary Christian songs that contain an element of romance and are often used in worship in the P/C churches of Indonesia, some in English and some in the Indonesian language. My selections used the categorisation created by Jenell Williams Paris, that this music exudes both emotionally intimate language and physically intimate language.[21] The indicators of romance are located in all or part of the lyrics in the song, especially the refrains, and include words and phrases that explicitly demonstrate emotional and or physical intimacy.

Divine Romance in P/C Service Music

Song Title	Lyrics Indicator
With All I Am	'You're the reason that I live, the reason that I breathe.'
Here I Am To Worship	'Beauty that makes this heart adore You / Hope of a life spent with You.'
Heart Of Worship	'Longing just to bring something that's of worth that will bless Your heart.'
Yesus Kekasih Jiwaku	'*Yesus Kekasih jiwaku, sungguh ku percaya pada-Mu.*'
Love You From The Inside Out	'My heart, my soul, Lord I give you control.'
You're my all in all / Engkaulah S'galanya	'You're my strength when I am weak. You are the shelter that I seek.'
Karya Terbesar	'*Yesus, Engkau kukagumi.*'
Tetap Setia	'*Selidiki aku, lihat hatiku / Kau dapati aku tetap setia*'
Above All	'Like a rose trampled on the ground / You took the fall and thought of me.'

According to Jenell Williams Paris, these romantic songs create an image of the relationship of God and His people as that of a man and a woman who are in love. The Lord is the man who takes the role as leader and protector, and who protects and keeps the people that are His. Meanwhile, the people take the feminine role which is described as weak, passive, overtly dependent on God, and needing

---

21. Jenell Williams Paris, 'I Could Sing Of Your Love Forever: American Romance in Contemporary Worship Music' in Robert Woods & Brian Walrath (eds), *The Message in The Music: Studying Contemporary Praise and Worship* (Nashville: Abingdon Press, 2007), 45-46.

help.[22] However, the reader will see in the chapter on gender, P/C churches in Indonesia are adapting to the changing education, careers and domestic roles of women by reframing what were in the past understood within the church as gender roles. The power and leadership within the God/believer relationship are seldom referred to as masculine, and the submission of the people is not referred to as feminine; they are simply understood as the appropriate relationship between the divine and the human. On the one hand, this shift is freeing women from roles of submission to men; on the other hand, it is calling men, too, to submission/surrender—and promising both men and women great reward for submitting to God's plan.

Romance between God and the people contained in these songs gradually creates an atmosphere of intimacy through congregational singing. The formality that reigns from seeing God as the Supreme Being who reigns in heaven disappears when God 'comes down' and embraces individuals in His arms of love. The intimate atmosphere created from theological romance is seen in the very way people worship. People no longer sit quietly when coming into the presence of God, but they sway and dance, welcoming their true lover, Jesus Christ. The people cheer, instead of quietly brooding in silence. Christ came to pick up His bride; together they move into the wedding banquet.

True Worshippers: A Trendsetter Within Contemporary Christian Music. True Worshippers (TW) is an Indonesian band known for its Christian spirituals, whose songs are widespread among Christians in Indonesia. Their songs are often used in the worship in P/C churches. Since its founding in 1996, TW has continued to grow. In 1999, TW increasingly spread its wings and began a production house that also houses the band Giving My Best (GMB), Sidney Mohede, Sari Simorangkir, Nindy Ellesse, Kiddy TW, TW Youth and, of course, True Worshippers itself.[23] Through the end of 2010, TW has produced thirty-two albums by eight different bands and soloists.

---

22. *Ibid*, page 47.
23. The Christian spiritual artists mentioned are all members of the band True Worshippers. Quoted from http://youngstersquat.wordpress.com/2010/07/19/true-worshippers/.

Most individual TW members shelter under the roof of the same church, Jakarta Praise Community Church (JPCC), a mega-church which focuses its service on youth. This church was pioneered in 1996-1997, along with the establishment of TW. The relationship between the two is very close; the two mutually influence each other and cannot be completely separated, even though they are two different things: TW is JPCC, JPCC is TW. TW has highly colored the style of praise and worship at JPCC. In fact, almost all the songs sung in every worship at JPCC are TW's songs. The music team, including the singers and worship leaders at JPCC, are also part of TW, along with the band. When we speak of professionalism in the P/C churches, TW is perhaps the outstanding Indonesian example of professionalism in P/C music.

JPCC, where the standard of praise and worship music was raised directly by TW, is a trendsetter for the P/C churches in youth-oriented services these days. In several interviews with youth pastors, parish pastors, and youth congregations in Jakarta, the explicit message was that JPCC and TW are the model for excellence in youth worship.[24] TW consists of many personnel divided into singers, worship leaders and musicians who play various musical instruments. The singers have recognised vocal skills; one of them, Ruth Sahanaya, is even considered a diva in Indonesia. Interestingly, most of the singers are capable of taking on the role of the worship leader who invites the congregation to enter into worship, and then serves as master of ceremonies during the service. The result is that a number of different people take turns at leading the worship on different days, sometimes even within different sections of the service.

The trend of churches having large musical groups whose music is known and sold outside the church is well established. Tiberias Church of Indonesia (GTI) has a popular music team called

---

24. In our pastor interviews, a question that arises is what is the main attraction of their respective churches. Some of the pastors said, 'the warmth of the fellowship is the appeal of our church. We do not have a team like JPCC music and outstanding facilities. ' There is a general agreement among pastors that JPCC was capable of organising big church praise and worship very well. From some congregations, I got an answer that JPCC worship is very different from worship at their church (read: Old Pentecostal churches). JPCC is more energetic and interesting, while at the old Pentecostal church worship seems a bit monotonous though there is some attempt to encourage spontaneity.

Boanerges.[25] They actively accompany the worship service dedicated to youth every Sunday afternoon at Balai Sarbini. Bethel PRJ also has a successful music team called Loving God, Loving People (LGLP), which serves, like TW, in worship at the Bethel PRJ.[26]

TW's affiliation with JPCC creates a symbiotic mutualism between the two. TW may be a servant of the larger church in worship—though a servant-leader at that—but they have also become the official icon of JPCC. JPCC advertises itself through TW as part of 'God's company'. At the same time, TW needs JPCC in order that their songs continue to be sung and spread to other churches. JPCC also becomes a place for them to practice every week and hone their creativity to create and arrange new songs. In fact, three of its members, Sidney Mohede, Jussar Badudu, and Alvi Radjagukguk, are also entrusted with leadership roles as youth pastors in JPCC. The church needs the brand (read: the TW band) as a means of promoting its congregation; but the brand also needs to be rooted in the church if it is to be successful in selling the work.

Many Christian bands as well as soloists in Indonesia are not rooted in or affiliated with any church. As a result, the songs they create have not sold well, and are much less likely to become a song of praise and worship in church services. One interesting fact is that virtually all the songs by TW, unlike those by other groups, do not need to go through church censors to become songs of praise and worship in a P/C church. From interviews with LGLP and a music department chairman from a P/C church in Yogyakarta, it was found that there is a censorship process for new songs that is usually conducted by a music pastor or the pastor who supervises the music department. The selection of (approved) songs for worship is then left entirely to the worship leader in consultation with the music pastor. TW products seem to have an unwritten license for use in worship from all the P/C churches in Indonesia, whether in general public worship or in youth worship. The fact that many TW albums are produced in live praise and worship sessions is one factor that makes audiences, including pastors, believe that these songs are appropriate

---

25. Information about Boanerges can be found on the official website of the Church of Tiberias Indonesia http://www.tiberias.or.id/page.php?linkid=44
26. Information about LGLP can be found in their official website http://lglpmusic.com/home.

for worship. TW makes every concert promoting the album seem like a praise and worship session, complete with reverent discourse. The stage decoration is attractive, with colorful stage lights, laser lights, fogging, and a multimedia display on a projector to make this concert display all the trappings that appeal to young people who are familiar with the urban atmosphere of 'sparkle' (clubbing). The concert is then recorded and then produced as a live album recording. The audience at the concert does not only listen, but they also can see how praise and worship can being produced, and then copy it in their respective churches. The replication process may include several areas, including stage design, arrangements of songs, musicians' and singers' compositions, and even costumes.

English Language and Global Pentecostal Network

When one views the list of songs by TW, one sees immediately that approximately fifty percent of them are in English. Since TW is regarded as a trendsetter in contemporary praise and worship, their songs, including their songs in English, are widely known and sung in worship. Their songs are sung both within the general congregation's public worship and in that of the youth organisations.

The use of songs in English, both Indonesian English[27] and American English, has become ubiquitous in many P/C churches, especially the Charismatic/Neo-Pentecostal ones. Advances in information and communication technologies have prompted the formation of a global Pentecostalism that inevitably colors Pentecostalism in Indonesia. Anthony Giddens says that globalisation is a global intensification of social relations, in which the events that take place in one particular area are also related to situations and events in another hemisphere.[28] Global Pentecostalism has emerged as part of globalisation; the rise of Pentecostalism in the rest of the world, for example, also influences the development of the church in Indonesia, including both the style of worship as well as choices of songs during praise and worship. Songs in English are regularly sung in churches with Indonesian-speaking congregations.

---

27. This term refers to English songs created by the people of Indonesia.
28. Giddens, 64-65.

Hillsong Music Australia has now become a major production center for English language service music sung in P/C churches around the world, including Indonesia. Every year, Hillsong produces a live-recorded album which will be played in many churches, a practice which has lately been followed by True Worshippers (TW) in Indonesia, whose songs are sung in English in P/C churches without being translated into Indonesian. The selection of Hillsong songs and other English songs, such as those by TW, for Indonesian P/C praise and worship demonstrates that, in the eyes of Indonesians, the West is still superior. The West is still regarded as the center of technological advance as well as the font of the dream for a better life. In the Pentecostal context, the West (read: America) is an area where the the Holy Spirit's outpouring happened for the first time in the modern era (Azusa Street), and the place where Pentecostalism first flourished, as evidenced by the many churches that have sprung up there, from small churches to mega-churches. For urban youth, the use of English shows that they are 'modern', 'technology literate', and highly educated. For this reason, English is used in almost every aspect of youth worship and fellowship. For example, the Jakarta Praise Community Church (JPCC) and the Army of God (youth movement of Sharon Rose Church) both not only have English as the dominant language in song lyrics, but also use English in event banners, newsletters, and multimedia news. They also use the English term 'pastor' for pastors and church leaders in youth ministry. Efforts at mimicry, to borrow a phrase from Homi Bhabha, are massive on the part of these churches today.

In addition, the use of English is also an attempt to symbolise participation in a global network of Pentecostal and Charismatic churches. In terms of praise and worship, churches in Indonesia use songs of singers and contemporary music groups from the United States and Australia, including Don Moen, Michael W. Smith, Ron Kenoly, Israel Houghton and Hillsong Music Australia. In addition, local musicians create works that have recently been picked up in foreign countries. One of these is the song 'Hosanna' by Sidney Mohede that has been sung by Israel Houghton on his last album and was awarded a Grammy Award in 2011. Hillsong Music Australia has also launched the Global Project, which is translating some of their most famous songs into nine languages, with the aim of making their songs better known around the world and expanding the network of praise and worship.²⁹ This project involves local musicians from each country, and TW is believed to be working on one such project in the Indonesian language.

Intensification of cooperation and networking among churches in Indonesia can be seen also from the frequency with which preachers from abroad come and preach in Indonesia. They are welcomed and 'hailed' by the church; the number of people attending even increases when great preachers from abroad come to Indonesia, whether they be Benny Hinn,³⁰ Kong Hee,³¹ or Joseph Prince.³² In early 2013, Joyce Meyer, a very well known preacher and televangelist of the United States, came to Indonesia and brought with her Darlene Zschech, worship leader and songwriter from Hillsong Music Australia, as well as the True Worshippers. Meyer pointed out that Pentecostalism in Indonesia is in the process of building a network with Pentecostalism across the world. This can be seen from several successfull global-scale events hosted in Indonesia, such as the World Prayer Assembly 2012 at the Sentul International Convention Center, the building owned by Bethel Gatot Subroto Church.

Conclusion

The growth of P/C churches currently cannot be separated from the professionalisation of all areas of church ministry, the most important areas of which deal with worship. Worship is organised very efficiently to produce an integration of multimedia, music, decor

---

29. http://au.hillsongmusic.com/hillsong-global-project-indonesian/
30. Benny Hinn has several times come to Indonesia and held a revival accompanied by healing miracles. His last visit was 14 to 22 September 2012 in Surabaya and Jakarta. In previous visits, his sermons were held in a public open area, the Taman Impian Jaya Ancol complex, and attracted public attention because of the many people who attended the service.
31. Pastor of the largest church in Singapore, City Harvest Church, Kong Hee very often comes to Indonesia and has preached in many churches in various areas, such as Jakarta, Surabaya and Medan. Kong Hee's preaching schedule for the next year can be seen in http://edition.konghee.com/Itinerary/
32. Joseph Prince is the pastor of New Creation Church in Singapore. The church has been growing rapidly into a number of congregations since his appointment as pastor in 1990. Quoted from http://www.josephprince.org/About_Joseph_And_Wendy.html?active=about.

and lighting that forms an atmosphere in which people experience an encounter with the Divine. Church management imbued with the principles of corporate management has also made the church grow measurably. The workers live out the church work ethic: 'give the best, certainly be blessed abundantly.' Well-managed churches have increased congregational participation in worship, service areas, as well as participation in supporting the financial needs of the church that lead to a well-developed physical infrastructure.

A 'resurrection' within contemporary Christian music was perhaps the primary driver for the speed of Pentecostal growth, especially among urban youth. Pop and rock music carry the theme of freedom, which brings fresh air for renewing worship stuck repeating traditional, staid and outdated hymns. The passion and free spirits brought by Pentecostalism have found their true partner in pop and rock music. The lyrics, laden with romantic themes, make the songs memorable and support the emotional atmosphere inherent to the congregation. Jesus is considered the lover and the bridegroom of the people, who promises comfort and help to people facing everyday problems that they feel unable to face alone. The romantic lyrics are able to bring people to a satisfying feeling of intimacy with God, enabling them to take a break from the world and their burdens, in the hope that when they land back in material reality their heavy burdens and distress will be diminished, if not overcome. Many critics of these songs maintain that they contribute to an individualistic attitude and naive way of viewing life, that the theology underlying them is shallow, and that important Christian themes such as cross and asceticism have been omitted. Critics think the lyrics imply that each person only needs God in his/her life, not others or a community, and that they promise an easy life because God will lift all the burdens of life. The regular repetition of these ideas, say the critics, internalises them in the understanding of the faith of the people in church. But much of this criticism is dismissed as sour grapes; defenders of P/C theology say that people do not need to be reminded of the reality of suffering and cross, that they live these themselves, and reach out to help others touched by suffering. But their principal *riposte* to their critics is that the P/C churches continue to grow, indicating that they are meeting at least some important human needs.

The development of contemporary Christian music has also been accompanied by the appearance of new bands and singers who have created and sing Christian pop songs. Those songs became best known in churches as praise and worship songs. They started from the United States, and then spread throughout the world through sophisticated information technology. In Indonesia today many pop bands or singers have emerged who sing Christian pop songs, including the True Worshippers, LGLP, Boanerges, Giving My Best, Sidney Mohede, and others. These bands not only create and sing Christian pop songs, but they are affiliated with a particular church, serving in that church's worship, as well as constituting a think tank around praise and worship services at the church. They were, in the beginning, simply that church's musicians and singers. With strong financial support from the church they made recordings that reached out to other churches and were marketed widely. These band became well-known and also made known their supporting churches. The bands managed to make money from album sales, and the church with which they are affiliated was able to gain new souls who wanted to see their musical idols leading the praise and worship services. These new recruits can become lost in emotional and spiritual ecstasy when they can sing along with band songs that they already liked and were familiar with. There can be no doubt that the band and singers became a brand of the church: an icon for marketing and selling a commodity of proven value. In the end, people are vying to get in and swim in the religiosity of the market, where the search for God is also the search for pleasure and sensual satisfaction.

Chapter Three
The Spiritual Experience of Pentecostal and Charismatic Church Members

Y Agus Heru Santoso

The Pentecostal/Charismatic (P/C) movement has rapidly grown and spread across the globe in the last fifty years. In Indonesia, the first Pentecostal movement was centred in Java—Cepu, Surabaya, Temanggung, and Bandung—but local missionaries quickly spread the movement across Indonesia. At first, the movement attracted Indo-Europeans and Tionghoa (those of Chinese descent in Indonesia) then it gradually reached out to the native peoples. The Holy Spirit, a prominent aspect in the Pentecostal credo, was a cultural bridge for the movement, because the natives generally regarded the human-divine relationship as very important. For example, most Indonesians believe that spirits play roles in securing good and bad things in human lives. Hence, this concept of an active Holy Spirit attracted local people to join the church. Clapping hands, vigorous music and enthusiastic choirs also created a new and invigorating atmosphere for those who came from mainstream churches whose liturgies were more staid and formal.[1] In the 1970s the Evangelical and Pentecostal movement in Indonesia started to bloom, yet the burgeoning of the Pentecostal and Charismatic movement was even more marked in the 1980s–1990s. There are, however, no reliable

---

1. Georg Kirchberger & John Mansford Prior (eds), *Kekuatan Ketiga Kekristenan, Seabad Gerakan Pantekostal 1906-2006* (Ledalero-Candradita, Maumere, 2007).
2. Bambang Budijanto, 'Evangelicals and Politics in Indonesia: The Case of Surakarta,' in David Halloran Lumsdaine, Ed, *Evangelical Christianity and Democracy in Asia* (UK: Oxford University Press, 2009),164-165.

statistics on membership during these years, merely an explosion of new congregations.²

In line with Kirchberger's thesis,³ my observations suggest that the P/C churches predispose their congregations to see their daily spiritual experience as a response to God's will. The characteristics peculiar to their spirituality are intuition, direct communication and literal interpretation. Their spirituatility emphasises supranatural roles, such as casting out demons, encounters with divinity through dreams, speaking in tongues, prophecies, wisdom and interpretation of tongues. Their spiritual experience and reflection on their spirituality are not only expressed inside the church, but also outside. The spiritual experience of members is also manifested through the church's response toward social issues, both immediate and long-term issues. Immediate issues are those such as natural disasters—earthquakes, volcanic eruptions, tsunamis, and floods are regular occurances in Indonesia—while long term issues include legal advocacy for the poor, free/low cost health care, and building schools at all levels of education. Such responses from the P/C churches are varied, depending on the scale and availability of human resources in each church.

According to the surveys we conducted in five large cities in Indonesia, namely Jakarta, Surabaya, Yogyakarta, Medan, and Manado, there are several compelling reasons why people join P/C churches. Fifty-six percent of respondents report being attracted by sermons and fifty-one percent by fellowship. Support from the church, both emotional and material, was also prominent in reasons for joining. Other reasons were music (38%), miracle healing (35%), leadership and organisation training (30%), and the urging of family and friends (24%). As seen in both surveys and interviews, the sermon was the greatest attraction, even though other factors such as fellowship, church support, and music are also important.

Sermon

The finding on the importance of the sermon in attracting new church members can be a stepping stone to see how church members understand what an interesting sermon is. According to one of the

---

3. Kirchberger, 6.

respondents, a good sermon is one that is simple and talks about daily life as experienced by the church members or pastors. Pastor interviews reported the same understanding of good sermons: they are simple and understood by the listener because they concern daily life struggles.[4]

A pastor is expected to be open (in sermons) about receiving particular messages through divine interventions; these messages can be manifested through dreams, visions, lights, or even specific feelings. Whenever a pastor receives these divine interventions, she/he needs to share them, even though she/he may have prepared a different sermon. During observation conducted in churches in Medan, one pastor shared his experience receiving God's 'visit' in which he was asked to deliver a specific message to the church members.[5]

Similar testimonies of direct experiences of the divine have also been shared by church members; testimony plays an important role in their spirituality and marks their spiritual maturity. In one service, a church member testified to his experience overcoming financial crisis:

> ... When the business was down, I was very frustrated and thought of leaving Christ. I sought an escape by practicing rituals like *mandi kembang* and visiting shamans in order to revive my business. After some time, my business still did not improve, so I returned to church, joined the services and asked for prayer from the pastors. Step by step I received the blessings and my business started to grow again ...[6]

Church members perceive pastors as persons who most often receive divine visions, even though the Holy Spirit can be manifest to anyone in the church. Therefore, the pastors' opinions play an important role in heated discussions around important policy issues. Unlike democratic institutions where most decisions are based on a negotiation process

---

4. Interviews with a pastor and church member in Medan.
5. Observation in some P/C churches in Medan in 2010.
6. Observation: sermon in a Charismatic church in Medan. *Mandi kembang* is a local ritual practised by some ethnics in Indonesia; this ritual is considered a mystical cleansing of a person both spiritually and physically.

or on a decision by the majority, many P/C churches give great weight to pastors' opinion. For example, consider the disaster relief efforts following the eruption of Mt Merapi in Yogyakarta in October 2010. The eruption had caused thousands of people to flee their homes seeking safer places. Many humanitarian organisations, including churches, were involved in organising aid, which was either directly distributed to victims or distributed through other humanitarian organisations. One of the Pentecostal churches in Yogyakarta helped build, organise and run a public kitchen for the victims; the initiative for this activity came from the pastor of the church, who claimed he had received God's vision right after the eruption. Using the church's network in other surrounding cities, the church quickly gathered a very large amount of initial funding to build a public kitchen for the victims.[7]

Preachers in the P/C churches are usually the pastors of the church or guest pastors from the same synod; sometimes they are from different P/C churches. The visits of guest pastors, both domestic and international, are possible due to the churches' affiliation and the pastors' networking. Some morning newspapers, weekend edition, publicise church schedules, including the names of the pastors who will preach. Among those names are listed some popular preachers, who preach in a number of different churches on the same day. Sometimes, the intervals between one service and another are very brief. Generally, such preachers only come to the church to preach. Until the guest pastor arrives, the worship leader has the extra job of extending the worship time until she receives a sign from others that the guest pastor has come. Soon after the sermon is finished guest pastors leave to preach in other churches even though the service is still going on. Church members are aware of the situation; they patiently wait until the pastor comes and are not surprised to see the pastor leave shortly after the sermon. Usually departing pastors will say 'sorry and goodbye' to the congregation as they leave.

The reasons why some pastors are very popular are diverse. Apart from their distinctive appearances and personalities, popular pastors also emphasise particular aspects of the sermon; some stress

---

7. Observation in Kemah Daud Church and other Pentecostal churches in Yogyakarta.

miracle healing; others emphasise praise and worship, or a distinctive sermon structure, or testimonies. These popular pastors' presence and sermons are thought to affect the members' growth in spirituality as well as attracting more people to come to the service. Thus one church management strategy has been to invite popular pastors to either regular Sunday services or to other services, especially revival services.

Technology and Spirituality

P/C churches have been at the forefront in using information technology and modern communication to support their activities. Information distribution is digital through the internet; e-bible applications in many gadgets replace the printed bible; musical instruments are parts of complete sound systems; multimedia record the service as a real time service; and satellite broadcasting streams live-video of the service from one location to others.

P/C churches adapt the forces of modernity to support the churches' development and services. This strategy is in line with the interests of youth, who are the largest demographic within P/C churches. As a consequence, P/C churches are always in transition. In many cases, the changes/adaptations are based in pragmatic decisions to meet current needs. Even the theological aspects in some policy-making are based on pragmatism, instead of the reverse. The mega-church Tiberias Indonesia Church offers an example. The church uses satellite broadcasting to air services in the main church to the branch churches in other cities. In the communion service, for example, Mr Pariadji, the senior pastor and the founder of the church, leads the communion service in Jakarta and the service is simultaneously aired in branches in other cities. When the bread and the wine are distributed, the church members, both in Jakarta and other cities, together take the bread and the wine for communion. In other words, not only did Pastor Pariadji serve the communion in Jakarta but also in Tiberias churches in other cities through the live-streaming video. For the main church, the live streaming video has effectively helped the church spread the services to others, while the branch churches feel connected to a larger community. In this case, technology not only provides the all the congregations with a 'spiritual communion with

Jesus Christ,' but also does this within a late modern technological mode that also conveys the power of the church.

Traditional P/C Sunday services have lasted two or more hours. The growth of many congregations has outstripped their seating capacity, leading them to arrange two to four or even more Sunday services and thus necessitating shortening the normal service in order to give parking around the church—whether their own lot or on-street parking—time to clear and then refill. But even churches who are able to accommodate all members at two hour services have sometimes shortened services to accomodate those who are busy, allowing them to join the service despite their tight schedules and activities. One church in Surabaya observed this 'busy-ness' of members phenomenon and in response initiated a one hour service. The church rents a room in one of the hypermarts to serve fifty people at a time in a one hour service. The service is called 'one hour church' and the church provides ten services each Sunday, beginning in the morning and extending until evening. The pastor told me:

> My experiences as a pastor/evangelist, especially in big cities, told me that many church members are reluctant to go to church on Sunday because the service is too long; the sermon, praise and worship, testimonial session, and prayers consume lots of time. Knowing that, I developed the concept of a one hour service where everything is shortened, including the sermon, prayers, praise and worship etc, yet the core of the service remains.[8]

Information about the service is advertised both through pamphlets and flyers around the service location and by the church staff, which actively invites newcomers. There is as yet no research examining how participants at the one hour services differ from those at the longer services, or even whether there is significant movement of participants between the longer and shorter services.

This flexibility in offering the one hour service also serves as strategy to respond the needs of the people in the cities who have high mobility. This pragmatic decision in limiting the service into one hour is also a response to the felt needs of contemporary people, who

---

8. Interview with Pastor Samuel Gunawan, January 2012.

are easily bored. Another way to accommodate urban populations is by locating services in the city center, even in shopping malls, so people can continue activities such as shopping or restaurant meals nearby right after services end.

In addition to being physically present to hear sermons, church members can listen to the sermon by radio and even watch and hear the sermon on VCD/DVD compilations of sermons. Megachurches tend to record sermons of pastors or popular guest pastors and compile them into VCD/DVD, which they then sell to church members. Stories and life experiences of the pastors or other role models in the church are also recorded and sold to the members.[9] Many of the stories are about typical pastor experiences, including accounts of their downfalls and feelings of repentance giving way to miracles, healing, and other examples of God's providence, as well as accounts of pastors' trips abroad (such as pilgrimages to Israel to visit biblical sites) and of pastors' later spiritual experience.

Baptism and Spiritual Strength

In P/C churches, baptism is by immersion, but the immersion can be done in rivers, swimming pools (either public or hotel), or in a pool specially constructed for a revival service. The location is chosen based on practical considerations such as distance, accessibility, and comfort. Some churches who meet in hotels use the hotel swimming pool for the baptism. However, some churches which already own their own church buildings rent swimming pools, either in a hotel or a public swimming pool, on a specific day for performing baptisms. Other churches whose location may even be far from a river insist on baptising people in the river so that the baptism can also serve as a vacation for church families. Differing from normal immersion baptism, baptisms within revival services are meant to serve those who receive a calling of repentance during the revival service. The pool for this type of baptism is usually smaller and portable, specially prepared for that revival service.

I attended baptism rituals in Medan. In one church, the pastor and those who were about to be baptised wore white robes. Another group

---

9. See MH Ribah, *Before 30: Kisah dan Prinsip Kehidupan Philip Mantofa* (CV Pustaka Rajawali, Surabaya, 2008).

of people from the church sat separately and prayed; their duty was to support the baptism process through prayer. The pastor and people in charge for the baptism prepared the baptism while the prayer group kept praying until the pastor finished the preparations. The pastor completely immersed each of the persons awaiting baptism in the pool three times, pronouncing the ritual words. Afterwards, all the church members congratulated the new members and all of them went to a restaurant to celebrate their new status.

I attended another immersion baptism which was done in a river. The environment was quite shady and the water was crystal clear so the river was a good spot for family outings. Not only had the pastor, the persons to be baptised, and the church staffs arrived at the spot, but all the church members came with their lunch-boxes and picnic baskets. Before the baptism began, they all prayed, led by the pastor, and ate together. The atmosphere was relaxed, warm and friendly, reflecting how close the relationship was between pastor and church members on the one hand, and on the other hand, among church members themselves. After eating, they conducted a short service followed by the baptism in the river. Those to be baptised wore white robes and the pastor wore a black cassock. The pastor was assisted by church members who stood behind the persons to be baptised. All of them went to the deeper part (hip level of adult) of the river, and then the pastor immersed the persons in the river three times. After that the pastor and the persons baptised went back to the river bank and were congratulated by the church members. Nearby, there was a group from another church having a prayer fellowship, yet the two groups did not disturb each other.

Baptism marks a person as the new member of the church; it is an important moment for both the pastor and the church members because it strengthens the bond among them. Baptism is not only about spirituality but is also a social activity for the members. Though their fellowship and eating together they become more closely bound. Through this ritual proceeding, all the aspects of fellowship are strengthened as the meaning of baptism is mediated back to the old members through both the ritual itself and through the feast before or after the baptism.

In both these baptism proceedings I have attended, the services were elaborately planned. Yet there are also spontaneous baptisms in which the person is visited by the Holy Spirit; these seem to only occur during revival services. The revival committee usually prepares a portable pool, which is built near the stage to accommodate those who want to be baptised during the service. Revival services start with a merry song which is repeated over and over. The song leader usually urges the congregation to sing the worship songs wholeheartedly in order to come closer to God, and asks those who are burdened to set their burdens aside. The sermon is the main point of the service. After the sermon is the altar call. The pastor keeps praying and exhorts the people to keep praying, while inviting people to raise their hands if they long for God's presence and want to repent. The assistants in charge of the service go to those with raised hands and lead them to the altar for immersion.

Immersion baptism is like a 'password' necessary before a person can be involved in church activities, and in some churches, the immersion must take place in the particular church. For example, in music ministry, the person not only needs to understand all the songs to be sung, but can join regular choir practice and participate as a choir member in weekly services only after receiving the immersion baptism. This baptism is required for everyone who wants to join church activities, sometimes even though they may have been already baptised in their previous church, or even already received immersion baptism in another Pentecostal church.

Strategies to Maintain the Church Members

Another type of adaptation aimed at making services ethnically attractive is to provide services in two languages, usually Indonesian and Mandarin or Indonesian and English, based on the need of the congregation, the church's resources, and the ethnic background of the majority of members. Some P/C churches also accommodate some aspects of ethnic tradition (with certain limitations) during services, for example Chinese New Year. For churches with many of Tionghoa ancestry, the churches allow Chinese decorations, songs in Mandarin and even Chinese fashion shows. Sometimes, if the majority in a P/C church is a specific ethnicity, the church also adopts cultural aspects and language. For example, among the Batak in North Sumatra, the church decor and the language of songs are Batak. However, this is more often the case among older, (Old) Pentecostal churches than in Neo-Pentecostal/Charismatic churches, and is a much less common phenomenon even among them than it is in mainstream Protestant or Catholic churches. The clear trend is away from ethnicity as identity. In the Charismatic churches, especially mega-churches, the identity on offer to members is that of a modern, well-educated, citizen of the world comfortable with the latest technology, protected and supported by the power of the Holy Spirit manifest in the global P/C community. Ethnicity is ancillary at most.

Membership in P/C churches is categorised into three general groups, based on their active participation in church and these groups are often considered to reflect spiritual levels. The first group is those who were active in the full range of church activities from the very beginning of their church attendance. The second is those who are registered in church but only come to Sunday services; they are rarely involved in other church activities. The last group is those who do become involved in church activities as well as Sunday services, but are not permanent (registered) members of the church. This third group tends to move between churches, both P/C and non-P/C.

This third group of church members who hold dual or even multiple casual church memberships came to be understood as a big problem. Some churches started to require registration and even to make permanent membership cards. Recorded membership became a pre-requisite for marriages and memorial services conducted in the church. Such measures were not only aimed at knowing who among attendees were members and who visitors, but were also aimed at preserving friendly relations with other churches. Churches consider this tendency of members to move from one church to another problematic, a sign of instability in the membership; out of this concern some P/C pastors created a network to share information about people who like to move from one P/C to another P/C church. However, although the pastors understand mobile worshippers as problematic, virtually all P/C services are open for visitors, including those moving from other P/C churches.

The mobility of P/C members is high, especially in the cities. It results in fierce competition among P/C churches to maintain the stability of their membership and to attract new members. In this competition, each church tries to present the most attractive façade, including the friendliness of ushers at Sunday services, the music, the use of technology, the style of praise and worship, the sermon, and the cell groups. Revival services are a key strategy for refreshing members' spirits and inviting newcomers. Revival services may be the initiative of one or a group of P/C churches. To attract non-members, the revival committee usually advertises, using banners, radio, pamphlets, and social networks, calling attention to the popular pastors who will speak. Famous figures who often appear on television, both Indonesian or from abroad, are invited to share their testimonies at the revival. One example of an international Charismatic figure who regularly appears in some Indonesian revival services is Pastor Benny Hinn from the U.S.

The Gift of Tongues

Speaking in tongues is one characteristic of P/C worship. However, not all P/C churches emphasise tongues; some do not even use it during services even though they believe in it. Based on the survey of 3748 members of P/C churches in five urban areas in Indonesia, 30.8% of members identified themselves as Pentecostal, 31.5% as Charismatic, 26.6 % as both Pentecostal & Charismatic, 4 % as Evangelical and 6.9% as Other. Among those who identified themselves as Charismatic, 69.90% claimed to have received the gift of tongues. Among the Pentecostal group, 51% mentioned receiving the gift of tongues, while 67.80% of the Pentecostal & Charismatic group claimed the gift of tongues. In the Evangelical group, 55% claimed the gift and of those who identified as Other 48.80% claimed this gift. While we might wonder that slightly over 11% of persons claiming membership in P/C churches do not claim the Pentecostal label for themselves (but rather Evangelical or Other), we should note that even in this group, about half do claim the gift of tongues, the most prominent traditional mark of Pentecostal and Charismatic identity.

Pentecost is one of the important days in church tradition, celebrated as the original emanation of the Holy Spirit which spread the seed of Christianity all over the world. For Pentecostal and Charismatic churches, Pentecost serves not merely as a historical remembrance, but is anxiously awaited as a recurring moment of spiritual experience in which the Holy Spirit descends upon contemporary people. Therefore, these churches organise ten days of

---

10. The survey data from Pentecostal and Charimatic churches in five large cities: Medan, Jakarta, Surabaya, Yogyakarta and Manado.

prayer before Pentecost, hoping God will send forth the Holy Spirit more forcefully.[10] I attended a service on the emanation of the Holy Spirit for children and teenagers. During the service, some of the children actively sang worship songs, some just sat quietly, and other children burst into tears. According to the pastor assisting at the service, these expressions were signs of the Holy Spirit descending upon the children: bursts of tears, speaking in tongues, standing up from their seats while praying aloud, or sitting in deep meditative prayer.

Anther service I attended was an adult service focused on the emanation of the Holy Spirit. The service was attended by both those who had spoken in tongues and those who hadn't. While the cantor and the musician sang *'roh kudus hadir di tempat ini (Holy Spirit is here)'* repeatedly, the pastor led prayer invoking the presence of the Holy Spirit and laying his hands on the people. Afterwards, waves of people started to speak in tongues. Spontaneously, I, too, stood up, sang the song, and started to pray in a language I have never learnt nor heard. I was aware of what I was doing but I could not resist the force in my mouth that pressed me to keep praying in that language.

The pastor approached me, laying his hands on my head, praying in an unknown tongue. I am not and have never been P/C; even during this research this was a rare personal experience. One of the respondents I interviewed described a similar experience:

> 'I brought my problem to prayer during the revival service. During the altar call, the pastor asked people with problems and the sick to come forward. Then, some people and I came forward near the altar and the pastor, laying his hands on each one of us, prayed. I saw some people in front of me fall after the pastor prayed. It was my turn, the pastor laid his hands on my head, praying, and I fell backward while praying in a language I have never known. The pastor's attendants came to me and prayed. I felt a surge of peace of heart at that moment.[11]

Regarding the gifts of the spirit, one pastor I interviewed mentioned that as with other gifts, tongues should be openly accepted; if not,

---

11. Sharing from one P/C church member to this observer.

tongues would remain a passive gift throughout the life of the recipient.[12] Tongues are only one of the signs that the person has received the Holy Spirit. Other gifts include interpreting the tongues, miracle healing, prophecy, preaching, evangelisation, and so on. Tongues is considered by many as the core of the gifts of the Spirit because it publicly marks the presence of the Holy Spirit in an individual's life. Even though this gift is experienced as a spontaneous individual spiritual experience, it can be contagious in large groups, where it is sometimes explained, almost always by non P/C persons, as mimicking. In one service in a P/C church, the pastor invited the congregation to pray in tongues, and then in a chorus, the whole congregation spoke in tongues.[13] This suggests that speaking in tongues is not only an individual experience but can be a collective experience when influenced by aspects such as the song leader, pastor, the choice of the songs, the music, the stage, lighting, and other service arrangements that facilitate collective spiritual experience in the congregation. Yet it is also true that tongues may emerge spontaneously from individual prayer. According to one pastor, the gift of tongues helps to both build an individual's spirituality and serve God.[14] Tongues, he says, is neither learnt, nor taught, nor memorised, but a secret divine language that links the human soul and God, and only the chosen can do it.

---

12. Interview with a pastor from a Charismatic Church in District Sumatera, Medan to whom I described my experience joining an altar call and speaking in tongues.
13. Observation in some P/C churches in Surabaya.
14. Interview with one pastor from a Charismatic Church in District Sumatera to whom I described my experience joining an altar call and speaking in tongues.

Chapter Four
Class, Status and the Theology of Success Among Indonesian Pentecostals/Charismatics

Ubed Abdilah Syarif

Thousands attend Sunday worship in Surabaya, Indonesia in a three story building with a towering dome, capable of holding twenty thousand people at the same time. Every Sunday, there are three worship services: in the mornings at 07:00 am and 09:00 am, and in the afternoon at 05:00 pm. Even the least well-attended service includes at least five thousand people, so every Sunday the church attracts fifteen thousand to fifty thousand people.

At every service, the parking area overflows, barely able to accommodate the various types of vehicles belonging to church members, which range from motorcycles to luxury cars. Often, there are several buses carrying church groups from outside Surabaya parked alongside the church parking area, on a side street in a residential area. Usually referred to as the Graha Bethany Nginden, the church is located in an elite residential area, the Nginden Intan Timur Housing in East Surabaya. The church's architecture is unusual for a church; rather than the imitation Gothic cathedral style of most Christian churches, this one has the size and style of a stadium. It occupies 6000 square meters. Its name (Graha Bethany) means Bethany *mansion,* an indication of the social class associations the planners intended. Yet despite the lack of typical church architecture, the surrounding communities understand well that the Graha is a Christian religious building.

A Mega-church Case Study

Graha Bethany Nginden is one of many mega-churches in Indonesia, in fact, one of many in the city of Surabaya. These mega-churches are usually identified with the Neo-Pentecostal, or Charismatic, movement within the larger phenomenon of Pentecostalism. In many ways, Graha Bethany Nginden is typical of other mega-churches. When entering the main building of Graha Bethany Nginden, one faces a spacious meeting room with a large altar/ stage with musical equipment that looks as if it has been set up for a rock concert. As in a music concert, all the performers enact their roles on stage without being disturbed by, or even noticing, the video cameras aimed at them—a mark of their professionalism. There are video cameras aimed not only at the stage but also at different parts of the room in order to broadcast and record congregational participation as well as altar activity. On the wall beside the stage there is an extra-large screen, and 40 inch LCD screens hang in some corners of the room, all of which broadcast the activity both on the stage, and in selected parts of the audience back to the congregation so that no matter where one is located in the room, one can see every other part of the room. Worship services are also aired live via internet streaming through the church website.

During the praise session of the service, the music, the voices of the worship leader and the singers as well as the sparkling stage, complete with spotlights, emotionally enchant and immerse the congregation in praise activity. Songs often begin with a slow and gentle rhythm which then slowly becomes faster and louder; sometimes later in the service the tempo reverses back to the slow and contemplative. The emotional atmosphere of the church seems to flow with the rhythm of the worship music. Worshipers feel free to express themselves through singing, clapping or praying loudly. Men and women dressed in black blazers greet and welcome the congregation with friendly smiles. Observers get the impression that the church does everything in an upscale, professional manner.

Bethany Church Nginden has a well-managed organisation that serves the church's needs both at Sunday services and outside the worship hour. The church office consists of a row of air-conditioned rooms as well as some space for exhibitions, a bookstore and a cafeteria. It even has a hall that can be rented by outsiders. This facility supports the activities of the church before and after worship.

The church also provides educational services, namely pre-school, kindergarten and a Theological High School (STT). As for healthcare facilities, there is Bethany Care, a clinic that charges minimal fees both for minor ailments as well as for serious treatments such as dialysis. Hundreds of people of all religions from the surrounding area come to this clinic for medical treatment every day. Bethany Care Subsidy funding comes from the congregation through a variety of fundraising programs. Bethany Care regularly works with the Indonesian Red Cross (PMI) to hold blood donation programs. Following the December 2004 tsunami in Aceh and the 2010 Mt. Merapi eruption in Central Java, Bethany churches, including this one, responded quickly to collect and distribute aid. While this kind of outreach beyond the church and neighborhood had been unusual for Pentecostal/Charismatic (P/C) churches until the 21st century, Bethany churches are not alone in being moved to establish outreach programs by Indonesia's recent experience of severe natural disasters.

On July 17–20, 2007 Bethany Church hosted the Twenty-First World Pentecostal Conference that brought delegations from thirty-four countries. All 20,000 seats in Graha Bethany Nginden were occupied. This triennial conference organised by the Pentecostal World Festival (PWF) is a network of world's pentecostal churches who share commitment to spread the gospel to the whole world. While the Bethany synod is among the leaders in global programs and networks in Indonesia, many other mega-churches are also involved. Their size and power push them to exert themselves in larger and larger forums.

One of the more distinctive activities of Graha Bethany Nginden is that every year since 2000, it, in the name of the Bethany churches as a whole, has hosted the Seminar on International Churches Multiplication (SPGI). This seminar discusses and delivers some of the materials and strategies useful in expanding the church's mission of evangelism nationally and internationally, and helps ministers of all kinds to comprehend new preaching materials. Also included in SPGI is the meeting of the Board and administrators of Bethany branch churches and affiliated churches to discuss agenda items within the organisation of the Bethany Church synod. Many pastoral speakers come from abroad to deliver SPGI material. Among the thousands of attendees, there are always both members of local congregations and branch church officials of the Bethany synod from all over Indonesia and overseas. Many churches even outside the Bethany synod send representatives to gain knowledge and build networks in SPGI.

Splits and Divisions in P/C Churches. Pentecostal churches around the world have a long history of internal splits and divisions forming new churches. While the Indonesian Ministry of Religion has prohibited the formation of new synods since 2005, before that time a number of synods had divided and subdivided since the 1920s. The Bethany churches were initially a part of the Bethel Church of Indonesia (GBI) synod, and were known as GBI Bethany. This GBI Bethany church group was well-established, having been founded by Rev. Abraham Alex Tanuseputra in 1978. Starting with a small fellowship led by Tanuseputra in his garage, Bethany Church developed both before and after the break with GBI until it now has tens of thousands of members and hundreds of branch churches/satellites in Indonesia and has spread into several other countries. When it was still affiliated with the Bethel/GBI synod, the GBI Bethany service area, consisting of many Bethany churches, was divided into three regions in Indonesia: Central, East and West. The Central region, the parent ministry of GBI Bethany, was based in Surabaya and led by Rev. Tanuseputra; the East area was centered in Denpasar, Bali, led by Rev. Timothy Arifin, while the West section was based in Jakarta and led by Rev Niko Notoraharjo. In the Bethany breakaway from the GBI synod, Tanuseputra created the new Bethany synod out of what had been the Central Bethany region of GBI, Arifin made the East region of GBI Bethany into a new synod, GBI ROCK (Representative of Christ

Kingdom), while Notoraharjo at that time chose to remain under the umbrella of the Bethel synod.

At the 2010 Seminar on International Churches Multiplication (SPGI) a special reconciliation meeting was scheduled for Bethany leaders who had earlier been GBI Bethany leaders but who later separated from GBI. They included Rev Tanuseputra, Rev Arifin, Rev Notorahardjo and Rev Dr Yusak Hadisismantoro. The meeting discussed a commitment to reconcile in the spirit of mutual cooperation and respect for each other's church, but the churches remained separate.

Mega-church Similarities. The activities of the major churches in the P/C mega-church category, such as Graha Bethany Nginden, Mawar Sharon Rose Church (Gereja Mawar Sharon) Surabaya, GBI ROCK, IFGF (International Full Gospel Fellowship) GISI as well as some other churches under the Bethel synod, have a number of similarities, despite some differences in their degree of mission emphasis, church management, church asset policy and organisational structure. For example, congregational management and development in these mega-churches usually rests on the cell system (cell group). Bethany Church has the most prominent cell group activities, particularly in East Java. Bethany claims to be the pioneer in introducing Neo-Pentecostalism/the Charismatic movement into Indonesian Pentecostalism, of which one important aspect is the cell system.[1] A cell group consists of several families within a particular area, such as a residential neighborhood or a regency.[2] In a large residential neighborhood there could be more than one cell group, depending on the number of the people or families who join. The cell meetings are usually a prayer meeting or fellowship outside the church worship schedule, held in members' homes. In this small community the church members can have a more intense interaction, sharing experiences and testimonies of God's love, and praying together. Typically, each group has a spiritual advisor, under the coordination of a pastoral assistant or a junior pastor. In the cell group everyone participates

---

1. This introduction involved a shift toward mega-churches, professional quality music and lighting, louder, rock-like music; the cell system, and management techniques adopted from late modern business methods.
2. A regency is a local governmental unit in Indonesia.

actively in worship either as the person in charge of prayer, or the one in charge of reflection, reading the Bible passage, or playing the music for the singing. Not everyone can be accommodated in these roles in Sunday worship, because of the size of attendance. But in the cell groups, everyone takes some responsibility for leadership. In short, the cell group aims to increase the congregation's spiritual growth and to build relationships between members. The spiritual advisor reports the development of his/her cell's worship activity and the spiritual growth of its members to a minister above; the reports are consolidated and move up the chain of command to the level of senior pastor.

In the cell groups I attended, meetings mostly took place at church members' homes in elite residential areas. Most of the members were young families with small children. Observation of their lifestyle and appearance led me to believe that they come from the upper middle class. Some drive luxury cars, while others come with a motorcycle or in groups by car. In the brief introductions at these meetings, a number of people described themselves as entrepreneurs or employees in mid-level to top management.[3]

In each mega-church, there are different types of worship devoted to specific groups or classes in the congregation. For example, there are services and activities for professionals and entrepreneurs (businessmen), for youth, and there are even 'Mandarin Services' that employ one of the Chinese languages. Most mega-churches are located in strategic areas. Graha Bethany Nginden is in an upscale residential area, the Nginden Intan Timur area in East Surabaya. Similarly, some satellites (branch churches) occupy one or two large lots in a residential area or in an office complex. Some other Bethany satellites rent space in supermalls or shophouses.

The Mawar Sharon Rose synod started from a small church building in a strategic location in the city of Surabaya, but its original

---

3. One demographic survey, although on a small scale due to methodological difficulties in collecting surveys, found that the proportion of entrepreneurs / businessmen in one Bethany Indonesia congregation reached 55%. (CRCS MA thesis by Cindy Quartyamina Koan: 'Theology of Success and Spiritual Capital: A study of the theology of success in Bethany Church Indonesia-Surabaya from the perspective of spiritual capital in the context of Indonesia, 2008)

congregation has become so large that its current complex also occupies land on both the front and one side of the original plot. One part of its current complex is a large multi-story building built as a K-12 school, which has a large dedicated parking lot.

The GBI ROCK (Rock Center) rents two floors of a hyper market for both office space and worship space. Malls and commercial buildings are very convenient for P/C churches, which in some places have trouble obtaining building permits, though this is not the case in Surabaya. Malls and commercial complexes offer good security, which is an important asset for Pentecostal churches, over a hundred of which have been burnt down in recent years.[4] Some satellite churches also locate in residential neighborhoods or rent office space. One GBI ROCK satellite is located side by side with an entertainment venue (a pub!), a swimming pool and commercial stores in a mall in the middle of an elite residential area of Surabaya. One pastor remarked that such locations were convenient for members, who could leave services and have close-by shopping and restaurants.

Similar locations for P/C churches can be found in other big cities in Indonesia such as Jakarta, Medan and Yogyakarta. P/C churches appear in prominent public spaces such as exclusive shopping centers or elite hotels. But there are also many small churches located in the slums, in middle class housing or in less strategic areas. Many of the initial church buildings were the houses of the pastor. Conflicts and some cases of intimidation (usually by extremist Muslim groups) or bans on church building do not discourage the development of P/C churches. Over the last decade, construction of new churches significantly larger than the worship spaces of other denominations and religions have been a principal indicator pointing to P/C church growth.

Global Influences on P/C Churches in Indonesia

In many ways the pattern of P/C growth and teaching in Indonesia are inseparable from global influences. Such influence is channeled directly through pastors who are part of global networks and indirectly through various mass media and electronic media. Many Indonesian

---

4. Allan Anderson, *An Introduction to Pentecostalism* (Cambridge University Press, 2004), 131.

P/C pastors learned evangelisation and media techniques directly from the movement in other countries such as the United States, South Korea, and Hong Kong. For example, Pastor Philip Mantofa, a young pastor at the Mawar Sharon Rose Church Surabaya (GMS), lived in Taiwan beginning in his teens. With his brother he later went to the U.S. to study, where he actively participated in church worship fellowships where Indonesian citizens converge. After some struggle and spiritual experience in which he received revelation from God, he promised to give his life to Jesus. He completed a theological program at the School of Theology at Columbia Bible College in British Columbia, Canada. On his return from North America, Mantofa served in some small churches until he became vice-pastor in the Mawar Sharon Rose Church that draws tens of thousands of young people.

Pastor Daniel Tanudjaya, an assistant pastor at GBI ROCK, also pursued graduate theological studies in America. Beginning as a teen, and during his study in Psychology at Surabaya University (Ubaya), Daniel served in youth ministry at Bethany Church, led by Rev Tanuseputra. He worked professionally in the field of banking while still active in the church, and also taught at Bethany Theology High School. He decided to deepen his theology and study in one of the schools of theology in America. When he completed his degree in America, he returned to serve as an active pastor in one church after another. He was later recruited by the senior pastor Ir Timothy Arifin, who recently separated from Bethany church and founded GBI ROCK.

The International Full Gospel Church Fellowship (IFGF) Gereja Injil Seutuh Internasional (GISI) is a church that was originally developed by an alliance of Indonesian students in America. After returning from America, they developed services in Indonesia to form a church with dozens of branches in various cities and thousands of members. IFGF has other national branches, in addition to those in Indonesia. IFGF GISI is called a globalising local church, a phenomenon often associated with P/C churches in the developing world.

In yet another example, Reverend Raymond Maxwell Njotorahardjo, chairman of Regional Council (DPW) of IFGF GISI in East Java, Bali and Nusa Tenggara, has served as vice chairman of IFGF Worldwide. While he studied in Seattle, Washington, in the US, he also served in churches in Seattle before returning to Indonesia and taking up full-time ministry here.

In addition to the globalising experiences of Indonesian P/C pastors, the existence of a global evangelical network has also had direct influence, not only through an exchange of pastors, but also through organised activities such as Worship Revivals, or Festivals of God's Power, which attract members of many churches to hear national and international preachers. Worshiping together on a regional scale such as in the 'Asia for Jesus' event which has been held in recent years in various cities in Asia, has also had an impact on the P/C movement and its growth in this country. Such exchanges and events raise the status of individual churches and assure members that they are part of a successful global movement.

In general, the development of P/C churches in Indonesia has brought many changes to the face of Christianity in Indonesia and elsewhere in recent decades. Georg Kirschberger and John Mansford Prior claim that the developmental paradigm in Christianity has now been changed structurally, socially, culturally and theologically. Christianity began to move from the West to the South 500 years ago, but now continues to move on to the East (Asia) in the last 50 years. This Asian (and many would say African as well) shift marks a change in mainstream Christianity: the center of spirituality, theology and ethical development is moving to what has in the past been the periphery. Kirschberger and Prior regard the Pentecostal community as one of the main factors in this paradigmatic shift.[5]

Class Indicators

Social scientists identify Karl Marx as the initiator of the idea and theory of classes. Indeed, the concept of class based in the mode of production is central to Marxist thought. In cultures of poverty, however, especially in village agricultural systems such as prevailed in Indonesia historically, Marxist distinctions between the working class, the *lumpen proletariat* and the bourgeoisie did not seem to apply well. Many rural farmers could own only tiny plots of land and had no employees, but their ownership of the means of production

---

5. Georg Kirchberger & John Mansford Prior, *Kekuatan Ketiga Kekristenan, Seabad Gerakan Pantekostal 1906-2006* (Penerbit Ledalero dan Candradita, 2007), 40.

nevertheless removed them from the working class in a Marxist system (and like the urban petite bourgeoisie in Marxist analysis, these poor farmers often identified with better-off farmers). Classes in Indonesia were traditionally variously defined along the lines of religion, economics, or community ties, rather than along Marxist lines.[6] Due to the confusions surrounding 'traditional' approaches to class in Indonesia, what has developed in the late modern period is a division of class based on consumption. The lower class is capable of only limited consumption, the middle class of more, and the upper class of still more. Consumption here refers not only to common consumer goods such as cars, refrigerators, computers or cell phones, but also to objective indicators of 'Socioeconomic status' (SES). SES refers to the material conditions of life enjoyed by someone. Examples of SES objectives are material wealth, the ability to access education, participation in social institutions,[7] access to quality healthcare, and secure housing. The SES approach is used in this context to understand the categorisation of class in society. While people's everyday appearance can give indications of socioeconomic status, appearances are not always correlative with the actual situation.

Ancestry. To better understand the composition of Pentecostal and charismatic congregations, we took a large sample and queried ethnicity, education level, household income level, and their relationships to the level of respondents' activity in the church and their belief in success. The survey findings on ancestral origins provide an overview of those groups of people who joined P/C churches. Among our 3748 respondents, 57.1 % of respondents claim to be native Indonesian, 34 % claim Chinese descent, 1.5 % European descent, 0.5 % American descent, 0.6 % Indian ancestry, 0.5% Middle Eastern descent and 5.8% mixed ancestry.

Education. In terms of highest education achieved, the vast majority of our P/C sample have a senior high school education or more: 42. 2% have senior high school diplomas, 10% have an associate's degree,

---

6. Stephen Rahoyo, 2010, 52
7. JM Oakes and RH Rossi, 2003. 'The Measurement of SES in Health Research: Current practices and steps toward a new approach.' *Social Science and Medicine* 56: 769-784.

25.2% have a BA/BS degree and 2.9% hold graduate degrees. Of those remaining, 14.1% have only junior high school education, and 5.4% have a primary school education or less. This is far above the general level of education in Indonesia: the national census in 2010 demonstrated that the average education level is comparatively very low: 16.89% had a junior high school education, 18.82 % a senior high education, 1.89 % an associate's degree, 3.1 % a batchelor's degree and 0.24% percent a graduate degree. Persons educated only at the elementary level were 30.55 %.[8] Thus while only about 5% of the general population in Indonesia has post-secondary degrees, almost 40% of our P/C sample had reached this level. At the other end of the scale, slightly over 30% of Indonesians have only an elementary education, but only 5.4% of our P/C respondants.

Household income. We asked our respondents to estimate their household income in terms of increments of the provincial minimum wage per month (UMP).[9] Though almost 18% did not know, or did not want to disclose their household income, the 82.1% who responded showed a diverse economic range. Among those whose ancestry is native Indonesian, the percentage who earn equal to or less than the UMP is 21.7 %. Those whose income is equal to or up to 1.5 times the UMP are 15.6 %, those earning one and a half to two times the UMP are 16.14%, those who earn twice to two and a half times the UMP are 7.4%, those who earn two and a half to three times the UMP are 8.6 %, those earning 3 to 5 times the UMP amounted to 7.6%, while the number claiming to earn five times the UMP or more was 6%. Comparisons are difficult, since each Indonesian province has a different UMP, reflecting the differing costs of living in that province. Among our five cities, the UMP ranges from 635,000 rupiah ($70/month) in Surabaya to 1,118,000 rupiah in Jakarta ($124.20).

Before examining the chart on the next page, we should understand that according to the 2010 census in Indonesia, 60% of households are low income, with monthly incomes at or below $190 in US dollars;

---

8. Statistics Indonesia 2010, http://www.bps.go.id/booklet/Booklet_Agustus_2011.pdf, accessed November 23, 2011.
9. The minimum wage (UMP) in Indonesia is a monthly wage, and it is different in each province, reflecting the cost of living in that locale. The differences can be extreme—for example, from $70 UMP in Surabaya to $124.20 UMP in Jakarta.

30% of households are middle income, with monthly incomes from $190 to $ 446 and 10% have high monthly incomes of between $447 and $1183. These ranges measure actual income in rupiah, converted into dollars, without taking into account the very different costs of living/minimum wage rates in the various cities. When we compare those ranges to the income data from our respondents, we see that the results are tremendously varied from city to city, but that overall, our P/C respondents are as a group better off than the general population. While Yogyakarta has 1% more, and Surabaya 8% more P/C members in the low income category than the Indonesian average, Jakarta P/C members are only 27% low income, compared to 60% for the nation as a whole, with Manado at 41% and Medan at 52%, all three considerably under the 60% national figure. While only 30% of the national population is middle income, 47% of Jakarta's P/C members, 38% of Manado's, and 31% of Medan's are middle income. Yogyakarta and Surabaya have slightly fewer middle income members (29% and 21% respectively) corresponding to their slightly higher numbers of low income households. At the high income level, Yogyakarta P/C members match the national proportion (10%), with Surabaya slightly above at 11%, but the other three cities have significantly higher proportions of high income households: 26% for Jakarta, 17% for Medan, and 21% for Manado. It is not completely clear why income levels for Yogyakarta and Surabaya are significantly lower than the other cities. But these two cities have much lower UMP($70/mo in Surabaya compared to $124 in Jakarta) based on much lower costs of living and since incomes were reported in terms of UMP, a family could have as much as 50% less income than middle income households in the other cities, and still live just as well. The national data for low, middle and high income do not take this into consideration. In the other three cities (Jakarta, Medan and Manado) whose UMP are considerably higher, there are significant low and middle income P/C households, and considerably more high income P/C households than the national average. If the census furnished low, middle and high income ranges for Yogyakarta and Surabaya, it is likely that our sample would also score well above the norms.

Household Income Levels for P/C Respondents by City

	Jakarta	Yogyakarta	Surabaya	Medan	Manado	Nat'l Average
Low Income	27%	61%	68%	52%	41%	60%
Middle Income	47%	29%	21%	31%	38%	30%
High Income	26%	10%	11%	17%	21%	10%
Total	100%	100%	100%	100	100%	100%

Ancestry and Income. Among the ancestry groups within our respondent sample, those of Chinese descent constituted the second largest group after those of native Indonesian ancestry, and indicated somewhat higher levels of income than other respondents, income levels significantly higher than the national distribution. Chinese ancestry respondents earning only the UMP or less were 11.1% compared to 17.1% of all respondents, those claiming 1 to 1.5 UMP were 9.4% compared to 13% of the whole, those earning one and one half to twice the UMP were 12.8% compared to 13.7% of the whole. The number of Chinese who earn twice to two and a half times UMP was 10% compared to 8.5% of the whole; two and a half to three times UMP, 11.2% compared to 9.7%; and three to five times the UMP, 12.9% compared to 9.6%. The percent of Chinese respondents who earn six times UMP or more is nearly 20 percent compared to 12% in the P/C group as a whole. Clearly, while these figures refute the popular opinion that all Chinese are wealthy (twenty percent are poor by Indonesian standards), they do reflect the large numbers of Chinese who are involved in large business entreprises at or near the top income levels.

P/C Churches and the Theology of Success

The Bethany Church Indonesia based in Surabaya is typical of many P/C synods in Indonesia in its approach to the theology of success. Bethany Church Indonesia clearly describes its congregations as made up of successful families. This claim is confirmed in the church's advertising, which frequently features a banner reading 'Successful Bethany Families.' The senior pastor at Bethany Indonesia clearly stated that one of the driving forces within this church is the theory and theology of prosperity. The slogan 'Successful Bethany Families' is included in the church vision in its constitution (AD/ART).

> The more we exalt God, the higher our potential for success, and the potential for it is greater. Therefore, Bethany boldly adopts the slogan 'Successful Bethany Families.' Indeed, the reality is that many people came, and those who were poor became so successful that even many people who were in a state of bankruptcy have become prosperous. Economic and social status increased for many; for example, there were even some so poor as garbage scavengers who joined us, and encountered wonderful blessing . . . It's also based on pastor Abraham Alex Tanusaputera's experience of many years that eventually one achieves a level of success. Because it's true: those who are guided will experience success. Success can also be be seen in the form of healing and miracles. These have also become a trademark of Bethany church and of all church branches under the Bethany Synod.[10]

The pastor above refers to the fact that before he was fully committed as a pastor, in his youth Abraham Alex had a construction business and sold used cars. He was born into an entrepreneurial family: his parents were both entrepreneurs in the pharmaceutical field as well as devout Christians. Tanuseputra correlates his successful business achievements with the development and growth of his faith and trust in the power of the Holy Spirit. When I talked with other pastors of Bethany Indonesia branches, they equated financial success with spiritual elevation, with proximity to God as representing potential to be tapped. One pastor at Bethany Sumur Welut, a branch of Bethany in the eastern suburb of Surabaya, expressed this equation:

---

10. Interviews with a vice pastor and secretary at Bethany Church Indonesia, November 2011.

> In our experience so far, success seems to depend on one's personal relationship with God. As long as the relationship with God is good, I am sure there will be growth. In connection with the power of the Holy Spirit, the individual's own spirit grows. With the Spirit, there will be hope in the future. The Bible says if we have hope in the future, then our spirit will be accelerated, and our activities will go well. The key is intimacy with God. Some people seem to have good spirit when worshiping at church but they become shriveled again back home. That's because there is no initimacy to God; that's the key.[11]

Spiritual asset development as a path to success is a suggestion that continues to be repeated in every sermon in worship, and in prayer and cell group meetings through the sharing of testimonies. Usually such testimony revolves around an account of healing, the solution of a vexing problem, or a release from debt and/or bankruptcy. This suggestion of a correlation between intimacy with God and material success is reinforced with Bible verses that remind everyone that through God they have the power to achieve what they want. Through sharing their testimonies, people feel they have support in finding a way out of the problems they face. They encourage each other by praying together. Some rituals give a feeling of emotional release: not only exuberant prayer, but also speaking in tongues. In these ritual expressions, members really feel the presence of God. At a more extreme level, they even can cry or laugh. In certain rituals, such as evening prayer, regular worship or feast worship, the emotion of prayer is further elevated by popular spiritual songs, especially when these are led by good musicians and singers. Music often plays an important role in regulating mood and triggering more 'extreme' expressions of prayer.

More intensive understandings and teachings about the theology of success are provided in the Serving Orientation Schools (SOM) to those people who are being trained to be church workers. Those who graduate from the SOM and become church workers can continue to advance in their ministry, perhaps becoming a pastor in the future.

---

11. Interview with a pastor at Bethany Sumur Welut, December 2010.

According to a former secretary of Rev Alex Abraham Tanuseputera, so many members of mainline churches moved to Bethany in its early years, that not only did mainline churches exhibit some jealous anger at Bethany's claim to model success, but other charismatic churches quickly modeled themselves on Bethany, including its promotion of the theology of success. Tanuseputra has repeatedly denied that success for Bethany is merely a material matter. Success, according to him, is having no problems, no anxiety. While it includes having the things one desires, it is rather more focused on having a happy life—one that includes spiritual happiness. Tanuseputra admits that the emergence of the Indonesian charismatic movement initiated by Bethany is in some ways socially and politically different from the American Pentecostal movement. Membership at Bethany offers success and happiness, but it is not a movement of the poor and marginalised, as was the early Pentecostal movement in the United States. Yet while the early US Pentecostal movement was largely a movement of poor blacks and whites, it developed, especially in the last four to five decades under the influence of the charismatic movement, into a more middle class movement, similar to Bethany and other P/C churches in Indonesia. Thus while the experience of so many P/C churches in Indonesia and much of the developing world does not parallel that of the original Pentecostal movement in the US, it is not very different from the US Pentecostal/Charismatic experience during the last few decades.

Tanuseputra's former secretary also refutes the common criticism that Bethany and other charismatic churches promise material success in return for piety; they are not a new version of the 'rice Christians' of the nineteenth and early 20th century:

> In Bethany's 'Successful Bethany Families,' the word success refers more to happiness than to material matters. So, this is the happy family of Bethany. People who have much money are not necessarily happy, and some are happy with simplicity. The perception that sees the theology of success as a deficiency in the Charismatic movement is unfounded and unwise. The Charismatic Movement has undergone numerous revisions and has

many variants. In our [Bethany] motto, success is being happy.[12]

At one level this refutation makes sense, in that at least among the youth attracted to the P/C churches, their significantly higher levels of education indicate not that they were poor and so were attracted to charismatic churches, but that they join P/C churches because they are on the path to material success already, and want a church that supports and respects that path to success, which is both material and personal.

Religious Identity

Readers may have noticed that Bethany pastors routinely refer to the movement in which Bethany is a leader as the Charismatic Movement. They are clear that in Indonesia the word Pentecostal refers to the older Pentecostal churches, and prefer the label Charismatic to the alternative label of Neo-Pentecostal. Pastors understand the Charismatic movement as giving more prominence to speaking in tongues and other gifts of the Spirit, more prominence to the theology of success, as well as having more contemporary, concert-like services, in what are often much larger and more elaborate mega-churches.

However clear these Bethany pastors, and many of those from other synods within the P/C camp, are about the distinctions between Pentecostals on the one hand and Charismatics/Neo-Pentecostals on the other, the people in the pews do not seem nearly so clear about this distinction. For example, our survey said members of the Bethany synod had many different ways to label the congregation in their church: 16.7% of respondents attending Bethany churches declared themselves to be Pentecostal; 29.3% claimed to be both Pentecostal and Charismatic. 44.3% claimed to be Charismatic, 2.3% identified as Evangelical, and the remaining members identified as Other, even though all of belong to, or at least worship at, a Bethany church.

There are some factors supporting this confusion. Using church appearance and the manner of worship as a whole, including sermons,

---

12. Interview with a pastor of Bethany Pitstop Center, Pakuwon Trade Center, Surabaya, November 2010.

it can be difficult to separate Charismatic from Pentecostal churches, even from those who were part of the old Pentecostal movement. The Neo-Pentecostal/Charismatic movement, with its more energetic and contemporary style, has been so successful at attracting members from the older Pentecostal churches, as well as from other non-Pentecostal Christian churches, that the old Pentecostal churches and mainstream Christian churches, even the Catholic church, have felt forced to adopt some parts of the Neo-Pentecostal/Charismatic style of worship, even some of their theological language.

Understandings of the theology of success in other Charismatic, and many Pentecostal, churches seem to be similar to those in Bethany. While believers are adamant that success does not only mean material success, their accounts make clear that whatever else success may include, it also includes material success—not necessarily great riches, but an elevation out of poverty and insecurity. Sometimes this theology is used as a tool for winning people to join a church congregation. The fact that members of this church are, by and large, more successful than average Indonesians means that many prospective members see what seems to be proof of the theology already present in the congregation. Testimonies from members virtually always corroborate this impression.

International Full Gospel Fellowship Indonesia IFGF GISI utilises this theology of success within the development of the congregation's evangelical program, which is called *iGrow*. The basis of success, the program claims, is salvific faith in the power of the Holy Spirit. The Full Gospel Fellowship's slogan for their church is 'The Holy Spirit Is Your Success Partner.' In this church, one is told, you are definitely safe, your efforts will be fruitful, and you will live a blessed life. Thus if you want to succeed in any way at all, seek God earnestly, and live holy. That is the concept basic to iGrow) in every Full Gospel Fellowship church.[13]

Charismatic churches in general have become very sensitive to criticisms of the theology of success, both local and global, and have tried to nuance their message in ways that are more conventional, and thus not so open to criticism. These churches, like Bethany, also deny that the application and implementation of the theology of success in

---

13. Interview with a pastor of IFGF GISI Surabaya, March 2011.

the church only use material standards. The standard of success, they say, is being blessed both physically and spiritually. According to a young pastor at Bethel HOME (House of Miracles) Surabaya, 'growth in spirit and faith will change someone's material growth as well; his life will be fulfilled. A person will be blessed if his life is attached to God.'[14] He went on to explain that there are three kinds of blessings; physical, spiritual and material, and the Spirit can grant all three.

Similarly, one Bethel ROCK assistant pastor insisted that a close relationship with God correlates with a good relationship to the environment and others. It will have an effect on all aspects of life. Divine (spiritual) values such as honesty, fairness, and respect can influence attitudes and bring people to success. He called the inclusion of God in one's life the key to real success.[15] When asked if those members who remained in poverty, in poor health and low spirits were then understood as not attached to God, pastors tended to insist that it was wrong to pass judgment, that the future was still open, that God works in mysterious ways that are not always ours to understand.

The correlation between respondents' education level with personal belief in the theology of success can give us an idea of how strongly the theology of success is understood and accepted by congregations. We asked the question: Does praying more, and believing in God and the power of the Holy Spirit, increase one's success? In the table below, we can see that 76.7% of respondents as a whole, including 71-86% of respondents at every level of education, believe that faith and prayer always bring success, and another 6-14% believe that faith and prayer bring success most of the time. Those with any doubts about the efficacy of faith and prayer in bringing success were only 10-12%.

---

14. Interview with a pastor of GBI Home (House of Miracles) Surabaya, March 2011.
15. Interview with a pastor of GBI ROCK, June 2012.

Does praying more, and believing in God and the power of the Holy Spirit, increase one's success?

Education	Yes, Always	Yes, Most of the time	Some-times	I'm Not Sure	Total
No certificate/ elementary only	159	23	11	9	202
	78.7%	11.4%	5.4%	4.5%	100%
Jr HS Certificate	377	83	42	24	526
	71.7%	15.8%	8.0%	4.6%	100%
Sr HS Certificate	1207	221	101	48	1577
	76.5%	14.0%	6.4%	3.0%	100%
AA Degree	282	54	22	14	372
	75.8%	14.5%	5.9%	3.8%	100%
BA/BS Degree	92	7	5	6	110
	83.6%	6.4%	4.5%	5.5%	100%
Total	2867	517	227	126	3736
	76.7%	13.8%	6.1%	3.4%	100%

However, this question is a tricky one for respondents, in that some who might have doubts might be reluctant to admit them, lest that indicate the very lack of faith that might deny them success. So attesting to belief in the theology of success can be a hedge against personal lack of success.

The bold application of the theology of success in P/C churches held great appeal to members of non-Pentecostal churches, encouraging them to convert to the P/C churches. Some charismatic church leaders, such as Rev Tanuseputra from Bethany and a number of others, readily admit that many in their new congregation came from other non-P/C churches. The theology of success, however, is not the only factor that attracts new members to move into P/C churches. When our respondents in the P/C churches were asked: What were things in your P/C church that first attracted you, or which keep you in this church? Many answers appeared. Some of them were: that this church offered new things in worship services; greater socialisation between congregations and between pastors and members, and a different, better way of treating church congregations.

It is not accurate to view P/C development in Indonesia as simply an example of the phenomenon of overall Christian growth here, because a great deal of the growth in P/C churches has been at the expense of other Christian Churches, sometimes through large defections. P/C circles managed to pull in both some mainstream Christian churches as well as a group of traditional Pentecostal churches, including, for example, the East Java Christian Church (GKJW), Indonesian Christian Church (GKI), as well as many individual members of the Roman Catholic Church. In the early growth and development of Bethany church, nearly half of the congregation of the Pentecostal Church Center Surabaya (GPPS), which was the largest Pentecostal church in Surabya at that time, left the church and turned to Bethany.[16] Overall, of the approximately half of our respondents who had converted to a P/C church from a non-P/C church or other religion, half came from other Christian churches, and half from other religions.

Possibly the most compelling reason for the migration to P/C churches is that it was sociologically fueled by the widespread desire to personally identify with the style of global late modernity, and the frenetic professionalism prevalent in the the P/C churches, particularly the Neo-Pentecostal or Charismatic churches. The icons of late modernity are prevalent in praise and worship sessions, as well as in the various other activities and communication methods of the churches. Ordinary citizens in poor developing nations tend to feel 'status-starved,' and have a hunger for recognition and respect. By joining these churches, many people come to feel that they have become a global citizen of late modernity—they are up to date, competitive, and worthy.

For example, many of the church workers were originally 'nobodies,' chosen out from among the regular congregation. But once chosen, they wear a suit and look sophisticated, both when

---

16. According to a pastor in Gereja Kristen Muria Indonesia (GKMI) , in an interview on June, 12, 2012.

performing or assisting in worship services and in their daily duties as a workers in the church office. Their 'selection' makes the workers feel as if their status has been lifted; it raises their self-image, increases their happiness and supports their family and spiritual life. It makes them feel blessed by God, and worthy of salvation. In addition to being well-dressed, many church workers are also well-equipped; sometimes they use church cars in doing their service activities such as visiting members and shuttling people to worship. Such activities make them feel a part of and comfortable with the flow of modernity. They feel improved and respected, personally, spiritually and socially raised by the way their P/C church treats them.

Sonny Saragih, a sociologist and former church activist in Surabaya, views this as one of the important identification factors that supported the early growth and development of Bethany Church Indonesia:

> People get into charismatic [churches] because they want to be modern, closer to the modernity identification. The icons of modernity are in them [the charismatic churches].[17]

The behavior and appearance of the members in the church also reflect the class to which they belong, or sometimes to which they are aspiring. During my observations, I saw many people carry a smartphone or blackberry in place of a printed Bible; they used them to bring up the Bible verses on which the pastor or other preacher is speaking. The pastors are often the most sophisticated; many pastors in charismatic churches not only have very stylish taste in suits, ties, and shoes but also demonstrate the very latest technology while delivering sermons, such as Ipads and other supported multimedia devices. All those technological accessories bring comfort to the church members during worship, making the congregation proud to be a part of such a church on the cutting edge of late modernity.

Cultural factors can also encourage people to move to a P/C church. Actually, according to Sonny Saragih, the style and pattern of P/C churches are congruent with many traditional beliefs, in that

---

17. Interview with Sonny Saragih, Pustaka Lewy activist, June 05, 2012.

the Javanese people and many other native groups have had strong belief in whispered revelation, supernatural insight, the importance of prophecy, and visions and mystical experience. Many P/C churches promote similar practices: they drain and then infuse the congregation with emotion during worship and preaching; preaching includes references to elements of the occult; and mysticism with a Christian flavor is common. For example, in order for members to solicit from the Spirit a prophecy, vision, inspiration, or success, P/C churches often invite the congregation to commit to fasting prayer: praying all night long, as the Javanese do in *tirakatan*.[18]

Some P/C churches also preserve elements of local culture, especially Javanese tradition, and adopt them into the worship. Dispensing anointing oil is common, and similar to what is found in Javanese practices, and among some Muslim groups. The oil is blessed by a minister and that blessing is repeated by the worshipping congregation, and then distributed. The blessing often fosters a belief or conviction that in the name of Jesus, the oil will help relieve pain and even heal. The pastor assures the congregation, that prayer and the medium of oil carry on the power of Jesus' miracles. This practice is reminiscent of some traditional Muslims who come to a *Kyai*, a respected religious teacher, asking for a healing miracle, or even success. The *Kyai* prays or recites Quranic verses over a vessel of water, and then gives the water to the requestor, asking him/her to consume the water at particular times in conjunction with specific prayers/action. In Javanese tradition, the sick used to come to the shaman, soothsayer or fortune teller for similar healing help through mediation with the Divine.

Chinese-Indonesian Identity

In the history of social classes in Indonesia, Chinese-Indonesian descent groups were given second-class status far behind Europeans during the colonial period. A discriminatory second class status was maintained in national New Order policy as part of the colonial legacy: Chinese continued to be excluded from the military, civil service, and politics, and to have only token access to public schools and universities. These exclusions pushed the Chinese into business in order to survive.

---

18. *Ibid.*

Some Chinese, through bribery of high level officials, were able to buy protection for themselves and their businesses. This patron/client relationship was known as KKN (Corruption, Collusion, and Nepotism); it enriched many an Indonesian politician. The resulting patron-client relationship between many Chinese businessmen and the government under Suharto's New Order had a negative impact on the economic system. In the social field this provoked jealousy among native Indonesians, who tended to mistakenly assume that all Chinese-Indonesians were illegitimately rich. Such assumptions deepened patterns of social segregation, worsening already poor social relations within Indonesian society.

During the New Order regime that lasted until 1998, systemic discrimination against Chinese was instituted in response to both popular resentment at the economic privileges of Chinese-Indonesians and fear of this group as agents of the powerful new China. A special stigma was assigned to Chinese descendants. They were labeled as 'the Other' and understood as *the* group of non-natives in this most ethnically diverse nation.[19] Thus the identity politics that occurred during the New Order era and earlier has created a unique position for Chinese ethnics: Chinese-Indonesians are not accepted either as fully Indonesian, or as fully Chinese. The New Order politicised this ethnicity, expecting them to become fully Indonesian through assimilation or indigenisation programs that would remove all the their 'Chineseness.'[20]

The systematic 'Othering' of the ethnic Chinese in the New Order period took on a meaning and life in itself: anti-Chinese rhetoric was expressed in many violent attacks on them. As a result, Chinese identities have been 'always under erasure' (Heryanto 1998: 104). The identity politics under the New Order, and even before,

---

19. At the time of independence following WW II, Indonesia included over 400 tribes with different languages and cultures, as well as persons of Indic, Chinese, European and African/Pacific descent.
20. Chang Yau Hoon, *Defining (Multiple) Selves: Reflections on Fieldwork in Jakarta, 2001*, http://bepress.com/changyao_hoon/5, accessed November 5, 2012. ; and Juliette Koning & Andreas Susanto, 2007, 'Proud to be Chinese? A Transforming Chine and Chinese in Indonesians,' paper presented in International Conference: 'Implications of a Transforming China: Domestic, Regional and Global Impacts,' Institute of China Studies, University of Malaya Kuala Lumpur, August 5-6, 2007.

created an either/or position for ethnic Chinese; they could either be Indonesian or Chinese, but not both. As argued by Chang-Yau Hoon: 'to be completely Indonesian, the Chinese had to give up all their 'Chineseness'.[21] The possibility of a hybrid identity, according to Ien Ang (2001), the more logical outcome of a Chinese migrant's daily life, and that of his/her descendants, in a non-Chinese environment, was never a real option.[22]

The history of social relations associated with Chinese ancestry since the New Order has been colored by violence and is full of discrimination. The summit of the violence occurred just prior to the *reformasi* era in Indonesia in 1998, when the military dictatorship was falling; thousands of Chinese were beaten or raped, some even killed, and their stores and homes burned in Jakarta and other cities. Only after the first few years of the *reformasi* era was Confucianism officially recognised as a protected religion by the government of Abdurrahman Wahid.

This history of 'Otherness' and discrimination connected with Chinese-Indonesians is likely one reason why this group became prominent in the new Pentecostal churches that were spreading in the 20th century. Pentecostals were a part of the Christian minority, but Pentecostalism was accepting of the Chinese-Indonesians, offering a new, less unpopular form of identity, and in some Chinese-dominated congregations, allowed some practice of Chinese customs within more tolerated Christian institutions.

However, the role of Chinese-Indonesians in the P/C churches of Indonesia is also a reflection of the rapid growth of Christianity, in particular Pentecostalism, in post-cultural revolution China. From the time when religious activities were repressed in China through 1995, Christianity in China grew from less than two million to 40-80 million people. In 2000 China had more P/C churches than any country in the world except Brazil and the US.[23] Chinese-Indonesians in post-reformation Indonesia were bolder and felt freer to speak out and express their political orientation, culture and religion.

---

21. Chang-Yau Hoon, 152.
22. Ien Ang, *On Not Speaking Chinese: Living Between Asia and the West* (London: Routledge, 2001).
23. Kirschberger and Prior *Kekuatan Ketiga Kekristenan Seabad Gerakan Pantekostal 1906-2006*, 41.

A number of large mega-churches, especially Charismatic, Neo-Pentecostal ones, are led by pastors of Chinese descent, including the well-known Rev Dr Stephen Tong, pastor of Indonesian Reformed Evangelical Church Kemayoran, the Rev Prof Dr Senduk Luke Ho (Ho Liong Seng), founder of the Indonesia Bethel Church (GBI), the Rev Dr Tanuseputera, the spiritual father of Bethany Church, and young Pastor Philip Mantofa, assistant pastor of Mawar Sharon Rose Church Surabaya, each of whom has been engaged in the service of the church since before the *reformasi*.

In *reformasi* politics, in advance of the 1999 general elections three political parties founded by prominent Chinese-Indonesians emerged: the Unity in Diversity Indonesia Party (PBI), Chinese Indonesian Reform Party (PARTI), and the Indonesia Reformation Party. But only one of these parties passed the verification by the General Election Commission (KPU) and participated in the 1999 elections: the Party of Unity in Diversity Indonesia (PBI). Many Chinese figures participated in the political elections and managed to become elected at the local, provincial and district/city level. Previously, politics seemed to be taboo for the Chinese, along with civil service and the military and police. Those of Chinese descent were too long ascribed simply as economic actors.

The Prosperous Peace Party (PDS) served as the political vehicle for Christians in the 2004 elections, scoring 2.1% of the popular vote and 12 seats in the legislature. But in the 2009 elections the PDS won only 1.5% of the popular vote, less than the threshold for seats in the legislature. Many Christians did not see the importance of a Christian political party, and instead supported parties understood as nationalist. Based on several interviews with P/C church leaders in Surabaya, Pentecostals have strongly participated in the political process. Some candidates of PDS, the Christian party, and even representatives in local bodies, were from P/C churches.

Within the Chinese-Indonesian community many have been closer to the established nationalist parties than to either Christian or Chinese-identified parties. Thus the Unity in Diversity Indonesia Party (PBI) lost in the 2004 election, and the Christian PDS did not even pass the verification for the 2014 election conducted by the General Election Commission. However, changes in the reform era have allowed radical social and political changes for both Christian communities and those of Chinese descent. One of the factors in the growth of Bethany Church under Rev Dr Tanuseputra is his ability to utilise his own sociological identity, especially in Surabaya, East Java, in appealing to Chinese Christian communities. As a descendant of China, he understands the condition of social, political and economic marginalisation of the Chinese-Indonesians. One of his close associates, former private secretary to Tanuseputra himself, told us that the phenomenon of Bethany is largely the phenomenon of Abraham Alex Tanuseputra:

> Abraham Alex came up with the appropriate changes in his day where he made a lot of difference. For example, once people felt ashamed, inferior, even worried to be Christians but Abraham Alex brought people to claim to be a Bethany Christian with pride. Speaking in a missionary sense, Abraham Alex brought the good news of Christianity in a proper context.[24]

Chinese-Indonesians involved in business activities, many of high social class, were treated by the Rev Tanuseputra in terms of Chinese cultural expectations. In some ways, similar customs in the native religions of China, Confucianism and Buddhism, also supported his efforts at conversion. There is a belief in Chinese culture, for example, that a contribution to a house of worship (temple, monastery) will bring rewards much larger than the donation. The sow-reap theology in P/C churches—one who sows will reap many rewards—parallels this customary belief in Chinese culture. Many new concepts and practices used by Tanuseputra in his ministry were also associated with the Chinese. He suggested themes for sermons that were more relevant and closer to the reality of the minority. For example, Tanuseputra's former secretary suggested that:

> The descendants of China in Indonesia emphasise material well-being more than any other kind. Success for the Chinese is being rich. While church movements before Bethany considered the rich to be sinful and going to hell, Alex Abraham (Tanuseputra), on the same

---

24. Interview with a former secretary of the Rev Tanuseputra, July 2011.

topic, preached that the rich man also goes to heaven. It was a new phenomenon that opened the Chinese to new Christianity. So there is a perception [that] a Christian is not forbidden to be rich. It was also Abraham Alex with his Bethany church who pioneered the use of good music and excellent sound systems. If the previous church's music equipment and sound system are just basic, Alex Abraham upgraded the music and sound system to accompany the prayer, praise and worship songs to make them more comfortable, more lively and more pleasant to hear. This upgrading is consistent with the development of a rise in members' welfare. People using the fine radio and audio system in their cars would come to church, and when they find simple music would get bored. When they came to Bethany, they were pleased that the music and the sound system are very good. Abraham Alex never, or rarely, prohibits or says 'do not.' We do not like negative language, but a lot of positive talk. [25]

The closeness between some cultural beliefs of China and the theology of success in the P/C churches was undoubtedly related to the numbers of Chinese-Indonesians who switched to P/C churches over the last decades. A pastor at Muria Christian Church of Indonesia (GKMI) insists that the closeness of the theology of success to more traditional Chinese prosperity theology made Chinese-Indonesians feel comfortable in the P/C churches. So successful have P/C churches been at attracting Indonesians of Chinese descent that at an interfaith meeting in East Java, I heard complaints from some Chinese-Indonesians, leaders of Confucianist and Buddhist groups, that many of their people had been converted to the P/C churches.[26]

The emergence of the charismatic movement with the doctrine of prosperity, success, riches, God's blessings both spiritual and material, was fully adopted by Bethany, enlarging its appeal and supporting its growth among Chinese-Indonesians and many hundreds of thousands of native Indonesians. The style and charismatic approach

---

25. *Ibid.*
26. Interview with a pastor of Gereja Kristen Muria Indonesia (GKMI), June 2012.

of Rev Dr Alex Abraham Tanuseputra affected all the branches of the Bethany Indonesia church, including many pastors who later split from Bethany and then built their own church.

While the example of Rev Tanuseputra and Bethany is one of extreme success, in many ways he is typical of other P/C pastors who have either modeled his approach, or discovered something similar on their own. They have changed the content of the Christian theology taught, as well as methods of church management. Before the P/C movement, mainstream Christian churches had taught more complex theology, scriptural exegesis and legal codes that made people bored and even 'dizzy,' as some explained to me. Tanuseputra teaches a simple message that touches and evokes feelings, more heuristic than systematic. Those ordinary people who follow his teachings through short programs of Bible study and attend the Serving School Orientation (SOM) were given the opportunity to work in the church and eventually become pastors. The congregation perceived such opportunities as a welcome change, an openness to laity, a signal of individual worth—and the number of Bethany congregations exploded.

Youth

Before concluding this chapter, we will take a look at the demographic most targeted by P/C churches: youth. So successful have the P/C churches been in attracting youth, that youth have become emblematic for the movement. Everywhere in Indonesia, but perhaps particularly in Surabaya, East Java, competition for young members among young church activists is very fierce. This is evident from the promotion of church events intended not only for internal distribution and consumption, but addressed to large groups outside the church. Promotion is done in public spaces, through multimedia advertising: billboards, newspapers and online media, including social media. Youth activists are expert in inviting other youth to 'try out' their churches' services.

P/C churches categorised as mega-churches have special multimedia divisions. These divisions work on publishing online media, and invitations on television, radio and in print, including newspapers. Such works are usually done by young people, who understand what will appeal to other youth. In addition to the church website, social media services are also used to convey the vision and mission of the church and everything related to the activities of the church, the preaching of the pastor, or the availability of counselling. Live streaming of worship services is delivered directly to members who cannot come to church.

The intended targets of these media campaigns are apparent: the young technology-literate who have access to the internet and mobile internet on smartphones or blackberries. Worship services are held specifically for young people, and are packed with uses of popular culture and media that appeal to young people. Places of Worship Revival (KKR) in prestigious places, such as the hall of a hypermarket, become automatic attractions. Youth can be entertained at worship, and then follow up with different kinds of entertainment, food or shopping at the mall.

The Army of God, the youth division of the Mawar Sharon Rose Church (GMS), is one example of Surabaya's P/C youth movement. Under the care of a young pastor graduated from a Biblical College in Canada, the Army of God (AOG) has been able to make this movement of young Christians in Surabaya quite prominent. The 'Before 30' movement initiated by this pastor instills in youth self-reflection along with a passion to serve. These young people then reach out to new members, often those who have been relatively successful before reaching the age of 30. The pastor motivates these new members to do the same, spreading the gospel, reaching new souls, as well achieving personal (material) success at a young age. In recent years, the 'Army of God' worship service routinely airs on private TV stations, serving a national audience.

At every revival (KKR), the Army Of God, with its slogan 'Highly Intellectual, Highly Spiritual, Highly Influential,' has been able to call together thousands of young people from various churches. KKR is held in strategic and quite prestigious places in the main hall of hypermarkets like Grand City or Tunjungan Plaza, exhibition hall Java (Java Expo) or in open spaces, such as football stadiums—the places where young people like to hang out. Similar meetings, in similar buildings, are also held in the satellites (branches) of Mawar Sharon Rose Church in cities all over Indonesia. At each KKR, several popular recording artists are brought in to perform songs and give testimonies about their successful lives, and the miracles they have experienced in their careers and spiritual lives.

The youth movement of P/C churches is emerging and affecting the youth scene in various major cities in Indonesia. One of the interesting factors that appeals to these young people in the P/C movement is a new social identification. Many young Christians who come from villages and towns to the city as students or workers discover P/C churches with practices that they had never encountered in their home churches in the countryside.[27] Intending to become part of the movement of modernity with a current lifestyle, many young people become actively involved. From demographic surveys done in the churches, the number of youth (20-40 years) who actively assist in services in P/C churches reaches nearly 50 percent.

---

27. Interview with Sonny Saragih, July 2012.

Chapter Five
Modifying Christian Sexism:
Gender and Modernity Among Indonesian Pentecostals and Charismatics

Christine E Gudorf

Gender in Indonesian Pentecostalism is complex, in that various synods as well as churches within synods are responding in different ways to the rapid changes in gender roles in the larger Indonesian society. As we will see, there is evidence of some gender experimentation going on; some churches are attempting to stay in step with the larger social changes around gender, without alienating their more traditional members. However, given the Indonesian demographic profile—many more millions of young people than there are old people—and the disproportionate ranks of the young in P/C churches there is significantly more pressure to keep up with the expanding public roles of women among the young than there is to maintain tradition.

The majority of Indonesian Pentecostals are female. Fieldworker observations repeatedly noted female majorities that ranged from five percent to occasionally as much as thirty percent. It was a relatively rare event to note a congregational service equally divided between men and women. Our survey respondents, too, were majority female: 53.6% female and 46.4% male.

Female majorities are more or less standard in Pentecostalism, as they are in most Christian denominations. A variety of reasons have been given in various cultural settings for this female predominance in modern Christianity, but as we will see in the next section, it is very difficult to see many of these as relevant in Indonesia. Yet while Pentecostal churches are certainly liberal in regard to gender compared to traditional Indonesian gender roles, which are heavily influenced by Indonesian Islam, women's leadership roles in the Indonesian Pentecostal/Charismatic movement are minimal compared to those in non-Pentecostal/Charismatic Christian churches in Indonesia, which have a much higher percentage of female pastors than do the Pentecostal churches.

Pentecostalism an Early Leader in Female Pastors

Female pastors have been present in Pentecostalism beginning with the Azusa Street Revival.[1] Far in advance of other Christian churches, Pentecostalism has had some women pastors and even women founders of churches, such as Aimee Semple McPherson. Traditional Pentecostal emphasis on the Holy Spirit choosing pastors by bestowing charisms that were then recognised by the community allowed some women with undeniable ministerial talents to become pastors, even to found Pentecostal churches, though there have always been some Pentecostal churches that denied women pastor opportunities. However, many of the latter churches, relying on New Testament texts, did have large numbers, even majorities, of women as missionaries and prophets. In fact, in countries such as Sweden it was the ridiculousness of denying pastorates to women who had returned to Sweden after decades of leadership in establishing Pentecostal missions abroad that finally caused policy change there.[2] Despite the head start that women pastors had in Pentecostalism, today mainstream Protestant churches have far outstripped Pentecostalism in proportions of women pastors, not only in Indonesia, but also in many other parts of the world.[3]

Within the Indonesian Pentecostal/Charismatic movement, the older Pentecostal churches are much more likely than the Charismatic/Neo-Pentecostal churches to have women pastors. One reason for this might be that many of the older churches are much smaller than the mega-churches that have come to dominate the Charismatic/Neo-Pentecostal movement. In smaller churches where people know one another, highly talented individual women are more likely to be recognised, given apprentice training or even sent for formal theological training. In a church of thousands where

---

1. Estrelda Alexander, *The Women of Azusa Street* (Cleveland: Pilgrim Press, 2006).
2. NO Nilsson, 'The Debate on Women's Ministry: Summary and Analysis,' *Cyberjournal for Pentecostal Charismatic Research* 5 (February 1999).
3. Eli Javier, 'The Pentecostal Legacy: A Personal Memoir,' *Asian Journal of Pentecostal Studies* 8.2 (2005): 304-305.

anonymity is the rule, there is more likely to be policy—written or simply assumed—based on general assumptions about men having more leadership characteristics than women, which thus bars women from the pastorate in general, or at least from senior pastor roles. JE Powers suggests that the Charismatic Renewal typically brought further pressure against women as pastors because although the Spirit renewed many churches it did so in the context of church structures that were traditionally patriarchal, and the Charismatic Renewal did not challenge those structures. Theologically, as other scholars of Pentecostalism have affirmed, Pentecostals have moved from an emphasis on calling, wherein women were able to follow the call they believed came from God and thus function charismatically, 'to a position where regimentation and structure dominated the processes of leadership, resulting in a decrease in women in leadership.'[4]

Christianity As Majority Female in Modernity

In much of the Christian West, religion has been understood as a female preoccupation for some centuries. In southern European cultures, both Catholic and Orthodox, an important aspect of women's role has been to be religious for the whole family—to pray into heaven the men in the family who were more lax about religious obligations. Also, until the last century in many parts of Europe, church was one of the few public places that women were allowed to attend unescorted by male relatives, and so churches often served as a social gathering place for women, young and old, as well as a place of worship.

Even as old rules around chaperonage of women died out and women had more freedom of movement, women continued to predominate in Christian ritual in the West, partly due to changes in mortality rates, and partly due to the construction of female social roles. Modern secularisation is more strongly represented among the young than the old, because religion has generally been of greater concern to the old than the young, and the combination of dropping

---

4. Keith Warrington, *Pentecostal Theology: A Theology of Encounter* (New York: Continuum/T and T Clark, 2008) 148, citing Charles H Barfoot and Gerald T Sheppard, ' Priestly vs Prophetic Religion: The Changing Roles of Women Clergy in Classical Pentecostal Churches,' *Review of Religious Resources* 2.1 (1980): 2-17.

maternal mortality rates over the last century, and the tendency for women to live longer than men has led to many wives outliving husbands by five to twenty years—much of that time often spent in church. Observers have long noted the predominance of grey-headed women in Christian services.

Another widely cited reason why women predominate in Christian religions is that religion—Christianity—in the West has been understood as feminine. This presumed cause for greater male absence is related to, but not limited to, Nietzsche's critique of the Christian ethic as one for slaves.[5] Nietzshe's perspective reflected an understanding of humanity (essentially men) that became dominant in the nineteenth century, and was a response to economic and political shifts in modernity. By mid-twentieth century feminist scholars began to point out, along similar lines, that the Christian ethic of neighbor love, self-sacrifice and turning the other cheek has seemed in conflict with western understandings of masculinity in the modern period, but served to make women accept subordination and even abuse as their lot in life.[6] The effects of modern capitalism on men were to reward ambition and daring, even cutthroat competition, at virtually all economic levels. Gradually the qualities thought appropriate for men came to be shaped by industrial and later forms of capitalism. But women continued to be understood as, and continued to be trained to be, submissive to men. Thus the Christian ethic of selflessness seemed to better fit their nature and situation than that of men, who were socially conditioned to be ambitious, to seek power, wealth and control. While it was acceptable for men to be religious leaders over subordinate (feminised) congregations, religious membership in those congregations—as opposed to leadership—was seen as more appropriate for women. Unless they were in leadership positions, devout men were often assumed to be thoroughly domesticated and were ridiculed as not truly masculine.

Christian churches attempted to counter this image in a variety of ways, principally by emphasising the (masculine) theological and legal aspects of church and by not only preserving church leadership

---

5. Frederick W Nietzsche, *On the Genealogy of Morality and Ecce Homo*, Ed and translated by Walter Kaufmann (New York: Vintage, 1989 [1887]).
6. Valerie Saiving's classic article,' The Human Situation: A Feminine View,' The Journal of Religion 40.2(1960):100

for men, but also by adopting what are sometimes termed 'Victorian' views of women: as more delicate, weak, compassionate and emotional creatures unfit for leadership. Church membership retained its feminine cast—and in some churches actually became more feminine as power was centralised in the clergy, which demanded submission from the pews. The Catholic Church is perhaps the most obvious remaining example of this model.

The last half century in the West—and to a lesser but steadily increasing extent in developing nations—has seen many changes in the prevailing understandings of gender roles. The global women's movement has generally shifted women's roles to include less self-effacement and less unnecessary sacrifice, but has had somewhat lesser effects on moving masculine socialisation in more compassionate, egalitarian directions. The changes made have not been sufficiently dramatic as to make mainstream Christianity seem more appropriate for men. It is still the case in most of the West that it is connections to women and children that most often place men in the pew; there are low percentages of single, divorced or widowed men active in churches. This is one of the reasons that the battle to preserve ministry, especially pastorates, as male preserves has been so fierce in so many Christian denominations. The pews are already largely female, and the fear is that if the altar and pulpit, too, become female, men will disappear altogether, leaving religion to the women. In churches that are the most heavily female, such as many African-American churches in the US, the felt need to preserve ministry as masculine is most acute. It is necessary, argue many of those who argue against women priests and ministers, to keep a balance in the church, and the only way to balance a majority female membership is with a masculine leadership corps.

Religion as More Masculine in Pentecostalism and in Indonesia

Pentecostalism has a somewhat more masculine image than mainstream Christianity, in part because of its stress on active evangelisation, but more because of the power associated with many charisms of the Spirit, especially the powers to heal, to preach, to exorcise demons and speak in tongues. These charisms are not only bestowed on Pentecostal ministers, but also on ordinary members, which in terms of traditional gender socialisation masculinises them.

The whole congregation has the potential to become a masculine nexus of power. This somewhat more masculine version of Christianity fits better in Indonesia, where 87% of the population is Muslim.

In Islam, religion has largely been the province of men, due to both the culture in which it developed and most of the cultures in which it has since taken root. While Indonesian women are not actively discouraged from attending the mosque for Friday prayer or other events, and more women, especially younger women, do attend mosque in the last decades under the influence of both the secular women's movement and the Islamic revival in Indonesia, the mosque is essentially masculine space. In Islam everywhere mosque attendance for Friday prayer is optional for women but normally required for men. Women are also excused from daily prayer during menstruation, and are taught not to touch the Qur'an during menstruation. The most rare and controversial mosque practice found in Indonesia today is mosque preaching by women to mixed crowds, though usually not at Friday prayer. (Traditionally, women have not been allowed to lead prayer in mixed sex groups, or to be visible to men at prayer in the mosque because it has been believed that the sight or sound of a woman are obstacles to men's praying.)

Therefore the dominant religious model in Indonesia is not religion as the province of women, but religion as the province of men. So if Pentecostal congregations are not so typically 'feminised' as most of mainstream Christianity, and in Indonesian majoritarian culture religion is the province of men, we must then ask: why is there nevertheless a female majority in Indonesian Pentecostalism?

The Pentecostal/Charismatic Message: Aimed at the Heart

Women seem especially attracted by the close social ties of the Pentecostal/Charismatic churches due to the strong emphasis on the heart, what Lengkong in chapter two calls romanticism. The preaching and music lyrics—the whole atmosphere of the liturgy—is emotional, evoking the fellowship that is so appreciated by members. Themes of love, mercy, forgiveness and community solidarity prevail. In some other Christian churches—and in traditional Pentecostalism as well—there has been more emphasis on doctrinal truths, legal codes, even sometimes on historical-critical study of scripture. In Pentecostal-Charismatic churches today, however, the primary emphasis is neither on knowing God intellectually nor obeying God's law, but on experiencing God in one's heart, and being transformed by the Holy Spirit. Such a message is tailor-made to appeal especially to women, who may not be confident in their ability to either know God intellectually or conform to God's will, but through their roles in the family feel that they understand the workings of the heart very well. Arousing highly emotional states is a central goal of both sermons and singing. As Warrington writes of Pentecostal music:

> Whereas their music was historically dominated by traditional hymns the last 30 years have seen an increase in the singing of many new choruses and hymns.[7] Increasingly, these are sung over extended periods in which the congregation often remains standing as opposed to a format in which hymns were mingled with other elements of the service, such as the reading of the bible or prayer. Music in Pentecostal worship is often very personal in terms of endearment and communication between the singer and God and songs are increasingly viewed as 'vehicles for people to communicate directly with God.' The songs have increasingly taken the form of more directional expressions to God than doctrinal reflections on His character. They function as modern day psalms expressing a wide range of emotions, requests, and statements of praise to God. The doctrinally-based hymns of past decades have been largely replaced by simpler songs that are easier to memorise and contain more emotionally charged lyrics of affection for God, readiness to serve Him, and prayer for his increasing involvement in the lives of the singers.[8]

Though this appeal to the heart is attractive to women, it is also attractive to many men in Indonesia, who do not identify so strongly with intellect and reason or feel so distant from emotion and feeling

---

7. D Lalford, 'Music, Pentecostal and Charismatic,' in Stanly M Burgess and Eduard M van der Maas, eds, *The New International Dictionary of Pentecostal and Charismatic Movements* (Zondervan, 2000), 911-20.
8. Warrington, 224.

as do men in the West. So we must ask: Is there something else that makes the Pentecostal/Charismatic movement more attractive to women than to men?

Looking to Other Regions for Clues: Latin America

In much of the research on Pentecostalism in Latin America in the 1990s, it was proposed that one attractor to Pentecostalism for women was healing. Pentecostalism tended to appeal to the poorest social groups in Latin America, those who had little access to modern medicine. Also, indigenous traditional medicine was holistic; many persons did not distinguish ailments of the body from those of the spirit, and thus understood religious healing as appropriate for both kinds of ailments. Women were commonly considered responsible for family health, and so were naturally attracted to healing services which offered to heal not only the physical diseases of the poor, but all the afflictions that accompany poverty itself, such as alcoholism, drug addiction, domestic abuse, gambling, and depression.

It was discovered that in many Latin American congregations there was a pattern of women joining the Pentecostal *templo* first, and then gradually convincing many of their husbands to first accompany them, and later to join themselves. The advent of husbands/fathers into the *templo* often initiated a huge improvement in family life. The men left behind the life of the 'the street' which included drinking, gambling, and often prostitutes, and instead spent time at home or in the temple. The proportion of income that supported the household increased because it was no longer spent in 'the street;' incidents of domestic abuse decreased along with consumption of alcohol, and the Pentecostal reputation for abjuring alcohol and thus becoming dependable workers often aided Pentecostal men in finding work and keeping steady employment.

Very little of this pattern fits Indonesia. Probably the overarching reason for the lack of fit is that Indonesian Pentecostals are not the poorest of the poor, as Pentecostals in Latin America were in the 1970s-2000, when much of the Latin American research on Pentecostals was done. On the contrary, as we saw in chapter four, Indonesian Pentecostals constitute one of the wealthier, better educated groups within Indonesia. This is almost certainly why healing is not a predominant attractor to Pentecostalism in Indonesia, either for men or for women. Only 36.1% of female respondents ranked healing as extremely important in attracting them to, or maintaining them in, Pentecostalism, compared to 34% of men, while over half of men and of women ranked both preaching and fellowship as extremely important. Pentecostals on the whole in Indonesia do not have a holistic understanding of healing; their high levels of modern education has taught them to understand physical disease as requiring scientific medicine, not religious ritual, and most can generally afford the required scientific medicine. The appeal of healing services in Indonesian Pentecostalism is chiefly for healing of the spirit, not so much healing of the body. This might explain why 2.5% more male than female members had attended healing rituals: though this pattern is changing, men are generally regarded in Indonesia as being more stressed than women, and having weightier responsibilities that make peace and internal harmony difficult.

The one part of the Latin American model that does seem to apply to Indonesia's female Pentecostal majority is that men may be pulled into the church by wives who joined earlier. Though we had 7.2% more women than men among our respondents, a significantly larger proportion of men among our respondents were married: 52.9% of men to 46% of women. Though the number of divorced persons was small (54) more than two-thirds of them were women. Furthermore, when asked if their spouse was a member, 75% of married men responded Yes, while only 63.9% of married women responded Yes. To another question which asked about how much of one's family also belonged to this church, 35.2% of men claimed that all of their family belonged to the church, while only 31.6% of women made that same claim. Female respondents had also belonged to their churches for a few years longer than male respondents. On the whole, then, the preponderance of evidence suggests that women join first, and later many of their husbands.

The one probable exception to this generalisation is men of Chinese descent, who slightly outnumbered women of Chinese descent (by 11) among our respondents. But for those with only Indonesian or mixed ancestry, who made up over 62% of our sample, a pattern was clear: fewer men, with more of them married and more claiming all their family in the same church than was true for women, as well as shorter periods of membership in the church than women.

One pastor proposed that the Chinese-Indonesian exception to the Pentecostal female majority pattern in Indonesia might be due to the fact that in some congregations in which Chinese-Indonesians are a large majority, there are valuable business connections to be made. Young men can meet and associate with older successful businessmen who can give their careers in business a push, and established businessmen can form useful relationships with one another that will benefit their businesses.

What Attracts More Women?

So again, what is it that attracts more women? One recent study of a Pentecostal church in Ghana and the Ivory Coast that was also majority female suggested that women's interest and activism in the church was in part a response to the extensive activism of government and NGOs on behalf of women in the previous decades.[9] Religion looks like a good fit for women emerging from domesticity and seeking a relatively uncontroversial, supportive public space in which to meet with other women and work on shared concerns.

There may well be something similar going on with Indonesian Pentecostal women, as there are many very active NGOs in Indonesia that have been devoted to various women's issues, from domestic abuse to micro-finance for women, for decades now. Work within religious organisations is generally considered more appropriate than, for example, working in secular NGOs as many women do, or working in various other types of work that involve work with strangers, especially strange men. With the single exception of Aceh, the area most devastated by the 2004 tsunami,[10] there are more and more service groups working on improving community welfare, and women are often the mainstay of such groups.

---

9. Inventing Indigenous Religious Belief and Practice with in the Spaces of Ghanaian Pentecostalism: The MameWata Healing Churches of Half Assini." Unpublished MA Thesis, Florida International University, 2008.

10. Such a large part of Aceh was destroyed, such a large part of the coastal population killed, with such delays in getting relief workers to even bury the hundreds of thousands dead, that the survivors were too traumatised to take charge, even take part, in most of the restoration works over the following years. The various world governments built new hospitals, schools, mosques, police stations, and port facilities for an area that lost most of its public officials, police and teachers,

In Indonesia as a whole, more women are educated than in the past, more women are employed, more women are driving motorbikes and cars, more women are seen in public unescorted, and more young women attend evening programs of various kinds. In the twelve years that I have been spending months in Yogyakarta, Indonesia, these changes are very apparent. In 2002, among university students, evening events, for example, a musical or dramatic performance on campus, were attended almost exclusively by single men or men and their wives. Single women were not often out at night, and few drove the ubiquitous motorcycles. Today, at any stoplight, even in the evening, anywhere from a 25-40% of the motorcycles in the street are driven by women. Each one of these changes supports and reinforces the others. About 51% of our Pentecostal female respondents are employed (compared to 71% of men), and though Pentecostal women respondents are slightly less educated than Pentecostal men, they still have a great deal more education than the average Indonesian, male or female.[11] As education levels rise for women all over the world, women want to use those educations; they want to find outlets that allow them to continue the personal development begun in educational institutions.[12] As women's education rises, so also do their age at marriage, their likelihood of careers, and their income contribution to the family, in turn lifting their influence in the family. Pentecostal churches in their religious education and service organisations offer to women yet another outlet for using

---

11. Among our Pentecostal respondents, 42.1% of men and 34.2% of women have post-secondary education, while 5.23% of all Indonesians have post-secondary education. At the other end of the spectrum, only 17.4% of male respondents and 21.4% of female respondents have less than a HS diploma, compared to 75.8% for Indonesia as a whole, according to the 2010 Indonesian census.

12. For example, see Anita Weiss, 'The Slow Yet Steady Path to Women's Empowerment in Pakistan' in Yvonne Yazbeck Haddad and John Esposito (Eds) *Islam, Gender and Social Change* (Oxford University Press, 1998), 124-143. Weiss points out that girls attending high school have broken out of the bonds of purdah to achieve tools for understanding and navigating the world, and that female university graduates want to employ their skills outside the home, but need help in matching them to real world careers, because they have no female exemplars. She also found that mothers often wanted more education for their daughters so that they would be able to support their families if husbands did not, for they no longer saw marriage as stable enough to support the futures of women and children.

their educations, the skills they have honed in employment, as well as their traditional concerns for family. While Pentecostal churches were often criticised in the past for being too focused inward, and not being involved in social justice outreach or community building, this has begun to change all over the world, seemingly in tandem with more educational and social service opportunities for women. Thus, in most Indonesian Pentecostal churches women's participation and activism, whether in evangelism or service programs, is not controversial, and raises no eyebrows. However, female leadership is another kettle of fish.

The sections that follow will elaborate the findings of our member survey, completed by 3748 members of P/C churches. While the differences between men and women in the findings are almost always very small (under 10%, and often under 5%), there is a consistent pattern to them. Special attention will be drawn to those very few responses, some sections on, which do not consistently conform to the explanation suggested for the differences.

Other Male/Female Differences

While about 51% of female and 50.4% of males in our survey had been Pentecostal or Charismatic all their lives, there were some slight gender differences in the churches and religions from which the converted half of our sample came. Although each of the individual differences are small—about two percent—slightly more male converts came from Catholic and other Pentecostal churches, while more female converts claim backgrounds with no religion, non-Pentecostal Christianity, Hinduism or Islam. Once in their Pentecostal or Charismatic church, women are 3% more likely than men to attend no other church, and men are 2% more likely to be registered in another church as well as this one. However, attendance rates are very similar, with 38% attending church three or more times a week, 64% more than once a week. It seems that for men and women members alike, the church is the center of social life.

Gender and Religious Self-Identification

In terms of religious self-identification there were also some gender differences. This issue of religious self-identification gets complex. Our interviews with pastors and discussions with the pastors who attended our conferences made evident that pastoral staffs are very clear about whether their church is Pentecostal, Charismatic, or Evangelical with some Pentecostal or Charismatic practices. Yet our member surveys made equally clear that these labels are not nearly so clear to the members in the pews. In the surveys from every single church, and thus in every synod, there were major differences in the labels claimed by members. Overall 30.8% of respondents claimed to be Pentecostal, with 31.6% Charismatic and 26.6% both Pentecostal and Charismatic, and 4% Evangelical, and many churches had similar proportions of members claiming these labels. But even in the churches where the majority agreed on a particular label, there were always more than 5% of members, and usually 20-30%, who differed from the rest in their designation. Overall, women were about 4% more likely to choose the Pentecostal label, while men were 2% more likely to choose Charismatic and 2.5% more likely to choose Both Pentecostal and Charismatic.

Our suggestion for understanding the male preference for the Charismatic label, and the female preference for Pentecostal alone is that the term Pentecostal generally refers to the long established Pentecostal churches, many of whom have been in Indonesia 50-90 years. Their worship tends to be more subdued, their music softer, their congregations smaller. Charismatic, on the contrary, generally refers to more recent churches that are often large, even megachurches, and which project an image of power in a number of ways. The style of music, the numbers of musicians, singers, and dancers on the altar/stage, the emphasis on miracles and the gifts of the spirit, as well as the style of preaching in the more charismatic megachurches, all convey more power and confidence. Many of them also demonstrate comfort with the late modern world, and seem to offer members confidence in their ability to succeed in that world.

We must be clear: it was not the case that more men belong to the more Charismatic churches and more women to the more Pentecostal churches. In fact, we would be hard pressed to reconcile such a finding with our interpretation that wives tend to join these churches first, and then draw in their husbands to the same church. But it may be the case that the elements which are more attractive to women—with which they identify—are those associated with the old Pentecostal churches, while more men find the image of the

Charismatic churches appealing. Thus in the same church, more men may gravitate to the more Charismatic aspects, and more women to the more Pentecostal aspects.

What Attracts Men and Women to Their Churches?

Though the differences between male and female respondents regarding how important various factors are in attracting them to their church are not large, women ranked all the listed factors as more important than men did: preaching, fellowship, music, support, healing and leadership opportunities. The women's slightly greater level of enthusiasm was evident in other ways, too. When asked how important it was that their church grow its membership, 83% of women, compared to 80% of men, answered that it was very important. This enthusiasm for evangelisation was not merely institutional; it was also personal. While 90% of men claimed to be active in spreading the gospel, 91% of women made this claim.

Almost 53% of female respondents indicated that fellowship in their church was Very Important, with another 19.4% indicating it was Somewhat Important in attracting them to and maintaining them in this church. This level of response, however, should not be interpreted strictly in terms of women finding church a safe and accepted social gathering place, for, again, the responses of men were only two percent lower. Rather this high score in fellowship, matched only by the attraction reported by both men and women for preaching, seems to reflect what our fieldworkers noted: that the church was the center of social life for most of its members, especially for those who either lived distant from extended family, or who were estranged from their family.

Leadership Roles and Gender

In terms of being active in service organisations within the church, 44% of respondents claimed to be active members, and 28% claimed to be active as leaders of service organisations in the church. But women surpassed men as members (46.2 to 41.4%) and men surpassed women as leaders (31.8% to 26.2%) within these organisations. One of the criticisms heard most often of Pentecostal and Charismatic Churches by the pastors and members of mainline churches refers to the low levels of female leadership compared to the mainline churches (except for the Catholic Church, which excludes women from all ordained ministry.) Our fieldworkers reported that the most common role for women on the altar was as singers. Though female ministers existed in many P/C synods at all levels (pastors, helping and junior pastors), they were few in the 170 churches we observed. Women were especially rare as senior pastors, and were present but rare as both preachers and masters of ceremony. However, our fieldworker observations uncovered less female leadership than the member surveys would seem to indicate.

	'In this church _____?'					
	Only men can be helping pastors, junior pastors or senior pastors	Only men can be junior pastors or senior pastors	Only men can become senior pastors	Both men and women can hold all positions, including senior pastor	Not sure	Total
Men	75 (4.3%)	55 (3.2%)	84 (4.9%)	1433 (82.8%)	84 (4.9%)	1731 100%
Women	53 (2.6%)	42 (2.1%)	72 (3.6%)	1742 (86.9%)	95 (4.7%)	2004 100%
Total	128 (3.4%)	97 (2.6%)	157 (4.2%)	3175 (85%)	179 (4.8%)	3736 100%

In the responses to the above question, over 80% of both men and women believe that there are no restrictions in their church on women becoming even senior pastors, despite the very small numbers of actual women pastors. They seem to think that the path is open, that there are simply not enough women who have both the desire and the charisms to be pastors. On the contrary, many of the pastor interviews acknowledged that at the present time women were restricted from being senior pastors in their synod, and other pastors admitted that while it was not formally forbidden for women to be senior pastors, there was an understanding to that effect, because women's gifts did not usually include the leadership qualities necessary for pastors. The gap between what pastors revealed of their synod's policies on women pastors and what members believed was the case seems very large. At the very least, it means that the churches' exclusion policies are not being emphasised to the membership. That 4% more women than men believe their church has no ban on women pastors at any level is also interesting, since this is a greater gap than we find in the proportion of the sexes in any synod.

This pattern seems opposed to what Keith Warrington reports as the current trend in global Pentecostalism:

> The situation in the early twenty-first century is that women are increasingly accepted in roles of leadership by Pentecostal denominations although they are not so easily welcomed by congregations, despite the increasing presence of women in the global marketplace, education and politics. Whereas denominational leaders and Pentecostal scholars and theologians are increasingly less comfortable with forbidding women from functioning in the church in leadership, individual churches are more resistant, though this seems to be changing slowly.[13]

Warrington goes on to suggest that one reason for the slow rate of change is that the impetus to change is restricted where there are very few role models in existence: the few women functioning in pastoral leadership are not visible to sufficient numbers of Pentecostals to allow for fast rates of change. However, the vast majority of Indonesian Pentecostals, both male and female, are sure that women can hold all leadership roles in their churches, even without having many role models available.

Gender and the Charisms of the Spirit

In the same vein, a slightly higher proportion of women than men have received baptism in the Holy Spirit: 70% of women respondents, compared to 67.7% of men. Since there are more women members, as well as a higher proportion of women with Holy Spirit baptism, we might expect women to be prominent in demonstrating the charisms of the Spirit. In perhaps the most visible of the gifts of the spirit, the gift of speaking in tongues, women do predominate. Reports from services where tongues were present repeatedly note the prevalence of women among members speaking in tongues. (In some churches,

---

13. Warrington, 146.

however, only pastors regularly spoke in tongues, and those pastors were usually men. In some others, no one spoke in tongues.) Slightly over 64% of women respondents claimed the gift of tongues, compared to 59% of men.

Thirteen percent of both men and women claimed the gift of interpreting tongues—the gift least often received. But in all the other gifts of the Holy Spirit that the survey queried, men prevailed. Men prevailed in the gift of preaching, 39.5% to 28.8%, in the gift of prophecy, 24.8% to 18.1%, in the gift of exorcism 40.8% to 32%, and even in the gift of healing, usually considered a female area, men prevailed, 40.7% to 39.2%. In the category of Other Gifts of the Spirit, 47.6% of men, compared to 41.5% of women, said Yes, they had been so gifted.

How do we make sense of this? The division between the gifts, with tongues on one side with its female majority, and preaching, exorcism, healing, and prophecy on the other side with a male majority, is not difficult to explain within a traditional Western Christian context. Tongues is expressive; it is emotional, and so it fits with many traditional understandings of femininity. The other gifts are not simply or even primarily expressive of emotion; they rather confer power on the recipient, the power to affect others. In traditional western gender terms, these gifts are masculine.

This of course brings up the question: To what extent are traditional western gender formulas relevant in Indonesia? Certainly they have some relevance, not only due to the history of Dutch colonialism in Indonesia but also due to the history of Indonesian Pentecostalism as beginning with European and American missionaries, and networked with contemporary global/western trends. In addition, western media—advertisements, movies, television and internet—which have conveyed western gender understandings and attitudes to the entire world-- predominate in Indonesia. Moreover, analysing gender associations in the underlying Indonesian culture which colonialism and post-modern media have affected is not by any means simple. Rather, the mix which we can call indigenous Indonesian culture is incredibly complex. Few generalisations can be made, for despite the political and to a lesser extent cultural domination of Java over the other islands before and after independence, there is a great deal of cultural variation within the many tribal traditions even of Java.

While most of the tribal cultures upon which foreign patterns—beginning with India in the 1st c CE, and followed by Islam in the 14th c—became imprinted were patriarchal, some were matrilineal, and, for example, were able to resist to the present day the imposition of Islamic law in the matter of inheritance, instead preserving equal inheritance for daughters.

Today one of the Indonesian gender features most striking to westerners is the intimate and emotional involvement of so many fathers with their very young children. In the mornings the streets are full of men on motorcycles carrying toddlers or elementary school children to their day care centers or schools, and the entries to these centers and schools, especially at the beginning of the school year, are filled with young men trying to comfort and reassure their children with hugs and kisses in the face of imminent separation. In many families fathers are the more playful parent, engaging children in games, and cuddling them on their laps, even in public.

But in the arena of male-female relationships in the family, the influence of both Islam and the Indic culture that preceded Islam has been patriarchal, with strong pressures for women to cede dominance to men and, especially in the case of Islam, public space to men as well. The effects of the women's movement, represented in large part by NGOs and educational institutions in Indonesia, have made significant inroads in these religiously rooted dominance patterns, but in most families these issues are still being negotiated both by husbands and wives, and by fathers and daughters. The men have tradition on their side, but the women have new tools of education, an increasing ability to support themselves, and more maturity than in the past when girls were married young, often to older men.

Pentecostal/Charismatic Synods and Gender

Pentecostal/Charismatic synods differ a great deal in the tightness of their organisation. Some exert fairly tight control over member churches, and some seem to have no control at all. The 2005 *Bimas Kristen* (government organisation under the Ministry of Religion) ban on new synods has kept some breakaways from occurring and increasing division within the synod. But the differences we are about to see in the way that our respondents characterise the teachings and practices of their churches on gender cannot be explained away by the range of diversity between churches in the same synod, for these differences are found in the responses that come from the same church within any given synod. Other explanations for these differences are called for.

On the issue of women holding positions as pastors, the majority response from all the synods from which we had sufficient respondents to analyse was that 'Both men and women can hold all pastor positions.' (See the chart below.) Fewer than ten percent of respondents from any of these synods—Pentecostal Church, Bethel Church, Bethany Church, GSJA, Isa Almasih, Pentecostal Tabernacle or International Full Gospel Fellowship[14]—cited restrictions on women becoming senior, junior or helping pastors.

In this church, _____(male/female responses in %)

GPdI	Bethel	Bethany	GSJA	GIA	GPT	IFGF	
85.3/89.7	78.3/79.5	74.8/81.7	84.1/89.2	83.7/81.0	75/89.7	86.7/90.3	Both men and women hold all pastor positions
2.8/2.2	4.3/3.9	6.1/2.0	2.3/3.1	0.0/1.3	2.3/0.0	8.3/1.6	Only men can be pastors: sr, jr or helping
3.7/3.2	3.4/3.2	3.4/4.6	2.3/3.5	5.4/5.1	2.3/0.0	1.7/1.6	Only men can be junior or senior pastors
5.5/5.3	7.1/5.5	6.8/3.3	4.5/1.5	6.5/5.1	0.0/0.0	1.7/3.2	Only men can be senior pastors

One interesting finding is that in very few of these responses are the male and female responses the same, and in many they are significantly different. The largest difference in the response that both men and women may hold all pastor positions is in the Gereja Pantecostal Tabernakel synod, where over 14% more women than men agreed that there are no bans on women pastors at any level, and the least difference was in the Bethel synod, where only 1.2% more women than men agreed that there are no bans on women as pastors. At the same time, in the group responding that in their church only

---

14. Gereja Pantekosta di Indonesia, Gereja Bethel Indonesia, Gerega Bethany Indonesia, Gereja Isa Almasih, Gereja Sidang Jemaat Allah, Gereja Pantekosta Tablernakel, International Full Gospel Fellowship.

men can be pastors at any level, there were more males than female in every synod except Gereja Isa Almasih—in this synod no males believed that only males could be pastors, while 1.3% of females so believed. Most surprising of all, is that there were neither any men nor any women in Gereja Pentecostal Tabernakel who thought only men could be senior pastors, but 4.6% of men who thought that women were barred from the *lower* levels of pastoring. One possible explanation is that all churches in each synod may not have the same policy on women pastors—though we heard nothing of this from pastors, and we are clear that at least in some synods, especially GPdI, the policy is consistent. More likely is that there is confusion in the minds of congregations about what the policy is, given that women are taking on new roles in many areas of life, including the church, and pastors do not want to deal with controversy from either formally excluding women or formally inviting them into the pastorate.

Interestingly, on the following question, which deals not with offices, but roles, the numbers that respond that in this church 'There are no limitations on women's service' drop significantly from those on the pastorate. (See chart below.) That is, significantly more persons believe that while women can hold all positions in the church, they cannot perform all the tasks involved in those positions.

In this church, _____ (male/female responses)

Pentecostal Church	Bethel Church	Bethany Church	Isa Almasis Church	Pentecostal Tabernacle Church	Internat'l Full Gospel Fellowship	Responses
41.7% M 38.3% W	53.9%M 52.9%W	32.0%M 41.8%W	73.9%M 78.5%W	63.6%M 55.2%W	71.7%M 69.4%W	No limitation on women's service
51.8%M 53.6%W	37.8%M 34.7%W	60.5%M 47.7%W	21.7%M 11.4%W	25%M 36.2%W	23.3%M 24.2%	Both men & women preach, but only men give communion
3.2%M 2.5%W	2.8%M 4.5%W	1.4%M 2.0%W	1.1%M 1.3%W	4.5%M 0.0%W	3.3%M 0.0%W	Women work under male supervision
0.0%M .6%W	2.2%M 1.6%W	4.1%M 5.9%W	1.1%M 2.5%W	0.0%M 0.0%W	1.7%M 6.5%W	Women's ministry is only to other women

Though in some synods there is more or less agreement (3% or less difference) between men and women on the roles closed or open to women, notably the Pentecostal Church of Indonesia Bethel Church, and the International Full Gospel Fellowship, there are some where the differences are wide, even 10-12%%. This latter group included Bethany Church, with over 12% difference between men and women over whether women can give communion, and almost 10% difference on whether women's service is unlimited or not, Isa Almasih with 10% difference over whether women can give communion, and Pentecostal Tabernacle with 10% difference over unlimited service for women, and 11% difference between men and women on women being barred from giving communion. It is unclear what to make of these differences.

Most significantly, however, though 75-90% of respondents had earlier replied that women could hold all pastoral offices, only 32-78% of the combined male and female responses claimed that 'There are no limitations on women's service.' Strikingly, percentages of between 21 and 60% identify the giving of communion as a practice from which women are banned. One must ask why there is such wide divergence among members within the same synod on whether or not women can distribute communion. At the very least, this must mean that women are not prominent among those who give out communion. It is also the case that there are differences in how often churches include communion in their worship; while the Tiberias synod offers communion in virtually all services and is known to limit administration of communion to men, *even when the pastor is a woman*, communion is infrequent in many others. None of these other synods formally exclude women from distributing communion, and yet anywhere from 11 to 60% of all our P/C worshippers believe that this is the practice in their church.

This issue of women distributing communion is difficult to understand. We can identify a number of practices from which individuals might have gotten the idea of communion distribution limited to men only. The Catholic Church allows women to distribute communion only in emergency situations, though in many parishes around the world, including Indonesia, women can be found distributing communion at major Sunday masses. Other possibilities are that respondents had some familiarity with the exclusion of women from giving communion in Tiberias Pentecostal church, or those churches in which pastors are only male, and only pastors distribute communion. Recognising that they see few women on the altars of their churches, perhaps P/C members are seeking some explanation for female absence, and a rule about not giving communion makes the most sense to them.

It is commonly recognised that those Christian denominations which are the most sacramental are those which are most resistant to women's ordination and priestly ministry. Catholics do not ordain women; American Lutherans split over this issue and Missouri Synod Lutherans do not ordain women; and the Episcopal/Anglican church has gone into a schism, begun by the ordination of women, and finalised by the consecration of female and homosexual bishops. The most common explanation for this is that Baptism and Eucharist, the two Catholic practices accepted by Protestants (even if not as sacraments), are spiritual versions of the *quotidien* activities of women: birthing new life into the world and maintaining it through feeding families meals. The associations with women in these two rituals are so close to the surface that allowing women to administer them, it is argued, could obscure the religious claim of male ministers that they, too, have the power to bring new life into the world and to maintain that life.[15] (We did not ask questions about who baptises, but all the baptisms our fieldworkers witnessed were by pastors.) This of course, is only another version of the religious believer as feminine, requiring male leadership to achieve balance in the religion.

In a third question, 'This church teaches that in the home _____,' majorities of 66.7-86.4% chose the response that 'Men are heads of households who care for women and children.' At least some respondents undoubtedly found this answer acceptable not only because it is traditional, but also because while it mentions male headship along with men's responsibilities to care for women and children, it does not spell out headship in terms of female submission to men. The second most chosen response—but one chosen by only 9-28%—was ' Men and women are equal partners in parenting and decisionmaking,' and on this response there were some

---

15. Christine Gudorf, 'The Power to Create: Sacraments and Men's Need to Birth,' *Horizons* 14.2 (1987).

interesting differences both between male and female responses, and between synods. (See chart below.)

This church teaches that_____. (male/female responses)

Pentecostal Church	Bethel Church	Bethany Church	Isa Almasis Church	Pentecostal Tabernacle Church	Internat'l Full Gospel Fellowship	Responses
79.8%M 73.8%W	84.2%M 73.7%W	83.7%M 76.5%W	84.8%M 84.6%W	86.4%M 69%W	66.7%M 79%W	Men are heads of households who care for women and children
13.8%M 18.1%W	10.5%M 15.3%W	10.9%M 17.6%W	12%M 10.1%W	9.1%M 24.1%W	28.3%M 19.4%W	Men and women are equal partners in parenting and decisionmaking
2.8%M 2.8%W	1.5%M 4.2%W	1.4%M 1.3%W	0.0%M 0.0%W	0.0%M 3.4%W	0.0%M 0.0%W	Mothers have principal care for children
1.8%M 3.7%W	1.5%M 1.9%W	2.7%M 2.0%W	1.1%M 0.0%W	4.5%M 3.4%W	1.6%M 0.8%W	My church has no clear teaching on this

While only very small percentages (0.0-4.5%) say that their church has no clear teaching on this, those who believe that they know what the church teaches sometimes vary a great deal by sex. It is, however, striking that fewer than 5% of men or women in any synod claim that the church teaches that women are the principal caretakers for children. This reflects not only the 51% of female respondents who work outside the home, but also traditional Indonesian culture in which men have important roles in childrearing.

The egalitarian response was claimed by 9-30%, with the highest percentage the 28.3% of men in the International Full Gospel Fellowship who make this claim, compared to 19.4% of IFGF women. One pastor interpreted this result by saying that this church, that began in the U.S., more closely follows the western pattern than other P/C churches, but this does not answer the question as to why men and women in the IFGF differ so widely. One female pastor whom we asked about this responded that the church members were simply reflecting the confused message that the church leadership in all these churches was providing on gender issues. The patriarchal pattern of male headship still was still alive in church teachings on the responsibilities of men to lovingly care for women and children, though the churches tend to downplay other traditional teachings on male authority and headship. And though the churches were generally not stressing either female subordination or inferiority, and defended female dignity, they did not press the equality issue too forcefully for fear of blowback. Female pastors, whether senior pastors or not, she said, are loath to take up the banner of sexual egalitarianism lest member resistance to that message affect acceptance of their own office. That leaves championing sexual equality to men, many of whom either are not totally convinced of sexual equality, or even see it as threatening their present status. Thus it is no wonder that responses from members often reflected that part of the church's mixed message that the member was most comfortable with. The shift from patriarchy to sexual egalitarianism in Christian churches is generally drawn out over more than a single generation, and, not surprisingly, seems to be increasingly complicated in some parts of Indonesian Pentecostalism/Charismaticism by a growing biblicism.

Pentecostal and Charismatic churches have not been historically biblicist, though like most Protestant churches, the bible has had special status, venerated as holy revelation. Pentecostals have historically relied more on guidance from the Spirit than from the bible—often supporting the voice or action of the Spirit with verses plucked from the bible. That is, as Warrington explains:

> Where Pentecostals have encountered God in a given setting, that often subsequently determines how they respond to a particular issue as referred to in the bible. Thus they are prepared to draw their conclusions with reference to empirical as well as textual evidence; personal experience has, at times, preceded their hermeneutics. [16]

But recent global shifts have begun to change that. As membership in Pentecostal and Charismatic churches in Indonesia and elsewhere

---

16. Warrington, 192.

becomes ever more middle class and educated, pastors are increasingly pressured to obtain formal training. Educated professional members of the church want their pastors to have formal theological training, regardless of more historical views that understood possession of the charisms of the Spirit as evidence of having been chosen to lead. Much of the education and training that pastors obtain is in the bible—sometimes in seminaries that teach modern historical-critical method, but often in Bible colleges teaching biblical theology, whose method has more often involved memorisation and word association. More biblicist pastors or synods will inevitably point to the Pauline verses on women keeping silent in church and being to man as man is to God, and will thus understand the bible as requiring resistance to sexually egalitarian social trends. One Pentecostal Tabernacle Church senior male pastor in Manado, for instance, decreed that women must be garbed in white from head to toe while in church, including veiled heads, and are forbidden to speak in church. Such stances, however, are very rare now, and are even less likely to be accepted by future congregations because women are becoming increasingly educated, and increasingly employed in professional work that makes them more socially and economically independent. It is also possible that the moves on the part of both the P/C churches and the Ministry of Religion to raise educational standards in theological schools through the accreditation process (see chapter 6) may positively impact the use of the bible in the defense of patriarchal exclusion of women from sharing authority in the P/C churches.

The present degree of congregational confusion as to the teachings and practices of Pentecostal and Charismatic churches in Indonesia on sex/gender roles and offices in the church is not likely to be resolved in the immediate future. But in some ways this is an encouraging fact. For if the teachings of the P/C churches were strongly and clearly patriarchal, the members would have some clarity about the stance of their church. The fact that they don't indicates some openness on the issue on the part of the churches, an awareness that sexual mores are changing in Indonesia as elsewhere, and an unwillingness to come down on the losing side of the issue.

Chapter Six
Autonomy, Splintering and Growing Ecumenism: Governance and Organisation in Pentecostal and Charismatic Synods in Indonesia

Angie Olivia Wuysang & Marthen Tahun

This chapter explores the ongoing development of the form of Pentecostal church organisation in Indonesia, most often named synod. From among the many churches in the five large metropolitan areas studied in this project, this chapter will focus principally on four major churches: the Pentecostal Church in Indonesia, *Gereja Pantecosta di Indonesia* [GPdI]; Indonesia Bethel Church, *Gereja Bethel Indonesia* [GBI]; Indonesia Bethany Church, *Gereja Bethany Indonesia*; and International Full Gospel Fellowship-*Gereja Injili Seutuh Internasional* (IFGF GISI). Using different terms to refer to their church organisation, including synod, assembly, and apostolics, these four churches largely represent the range of diversity within the Pentecostal churches in Indonesia, in that they each include megachurches as well as smaller congregations, and are found in metropolitan areas, urban areas, and in the country-side. These churches also began (in Indonesia) in different periods and developed different forms.

In Indonesia, most of the Protestant synods joined one or more of the three big ecumenical organisations, usually but not always based on a match between their tradition and theological orientation and that of the ecumenical organisation.[1] Although there are a number

---

1. The Indonesian Communion of Churches is the example of how tradition and the church theological orientation does not always serve as the core principal to establish ecumenical organisations; in this case the Communion consists of mainstream churches in Indonesia (mostly Calvinist churches) and some first wave Pentecostal churches.

of P/C synods, especially newer ones, which do not yet belong to an ecumenical association, the common Christian stereotype of Pentecostal churches as being non-ecumenical is not supported in the case of Indonesia. The purpose of joining an ecumenical organisation is to unite Christian (Protestant) churches as well as to politically protect the churches, especially in obtaining government building permits and legal protection. The three ecumenical organisations in Indonesia are the Indonesian Communion of Churches, *Persekutuan Gereja-gereja di Indonesia* (PGI), the Pentecostal Church Fellowship, *Persekutuan Gereja Pantecosta Indonesia*(PGPI), and the Fellowship of Indonesian Evangelical Churches and Institutions, *Persekutuan Gereja dan Lembaga Injili Indonesia*(PGLII). Some of the P/C churches joined both PGPI and PGLII (the specifically Pentecostal and Evangelical associations) while some first wave Pentecostal churches, including: Bethel Full Gospel Church *Sepenuh Injil Bethel Church*; Pentecostal Movement Church, *Gereja Gerakan Pantecosta* [GGP]; the Pentecostal Movement Church in Surabaya, *Gereja Pantecosta Pusat Surabaya* [GPPS]; and Isa Almasih Church, *Gereja Isa Almasih* [GIA], joined the Indonesian Communion of Churches (the largely mainstream Protestant association). Interestingly, the Indonesia Bethel Church, *Gereja Bethel Indonesia* [GBI], one of the largest P/C churches, slightly later became a member of all three ecumenical organisations.

There are three systems of governance practiced in Indonesian churches, namely Episcopalian-Roman Catholic, Congregational, and Presbyterian-synodal. Most of the the traditional mainstream churches in Indonesia commonly adopted the Presbyterian-synodal system rooted in Calvinism, which emphasises the role of the pastor, presbyters (members of a council of elders), and deacons. In this system, pastors, presbyters, and deacons constitute the general assembly/synod whose responsibilities include monitoring theological teaching and church assets in all congregations. Also, the general assembly/synod has the right to formulate the church's terms and references which are enacted during its assembly attended by all the members of the synod. The relationship between churches and synods has undoubtedly and importantly nurtured the churches; though each synod is divided into many different local churches, they share the same doctrine and mission. Among many others, some of the

Calvinist type Presbyterian-synodal churches in Indonesia include: the Christian Evangelical Church (*Gereja Masehi Injili*) in Minahasa (North Sulawesi), the Protestant Church in the Moluccas (*Gereja Protestan Maluku*) in Moluccas, and the Christian Church of Sumba (*Gereja Kristen Sumba*) in East Nusa Tenggara. These mainstream churches adopted Calvinism, yet they are territorial churches that are clearly rooted in the ethnic (tribal) culture dominant where they are located.

The second church organisational system is the Episcopalian-Roman Catholic, which is mainly adopted by Catholic churches in Indonesia. In this system, authority runs from the top down: the Pope appoints and supervises the bishops, who ordain, appoint and supervise the pastors, who administer the local parishes. In this system, the church members do not participate in church governance either at the local or the national level. At the national level, the bishops' organisation is called The Indonesian Bishops Conference (KWI); this organisation is only for bishops.[2]

Unlike Catholic or mainstream Protestant churches in Indonesia, most P/C churches in Indonesia adopted the Congregational system, though a few try to combine the congregational with elements of the Catholic/Episcopalian form. The congregational system allows the local churches sovereignty and autonomy to draft work programs, doctrine, finance, and mission. This model best fits most P/C churches whose pastors would find it difficult to accept much external control or supervision. Instead, each church independently develops its own theology even though they are all under the same synod.

The autonomous characteristic of the congregational model provides charismatic individuals—both pastors and church members—freedom to participate in church as long as their general theology can be accommodated within the church's/synod's vision. In traditional churches, on the contrary, strongly charismatic individuals can become suspect, because both members and pastors are expected to conform more rigidly to the synodal tradition. In other words, in this congregational model the individual's relationship to Pentecostal doctrine is spontaneous and guided by the Holy Spirit while in

---

2. Indonesian Conference of Catholic Bishops (*Kantor Waligereja Indonesia*) www.kawali.org (retrieved on February 12, 2013).

traditional Calvinism it is more rigidly regulated by the general assembly.

In this chapter the further elaboration of synods, the main organisation of Pentecostal and Charismatic (P/C) churches, is divided into four parts: (1) brief history of the synod institutionalisation; (2) comparison of the organisation system and church' ministries of Pentecostal and Neo-Pentecostal concerning on how the synodal system contributes to the growth of the church; (3) the church members self-identification; and (4) conclusion.

Brief History of Synodal Institutionalisation

Pentecostal Church in Indonesia (GPdI). The Pentecostal Church in Indonesia was a *Vereeniging* (club/association) named *Der Pinkster Gemeente in Netherlandsche Indie* when first recognised by the Dutch East Indies in 1924. It was renamed the Pentecostal Church in Indonesia in 1942.[3] The history of Pentecostalism in Indonesia had begun in 1921 when two Dutch descendants, missionaries from the Bethel Pentecostal Temple Inc. in Seattle, WA, United States, Cornelius Groesbeek and Richard Van Klaveren, came to Indonesia with their families. Between 1921 and 1923 they successfully introduced the Pentecostal faith to local communities in Bali, Surabaya, and Cepu. Yet, interestingly, most histories of Pentecostalism in Indonesia record that the first Pentecostals to spread the faith, who became the pioneers of the movement, were a group of Minahasan descendants: R Mangindaan, SIP Lumoindong, HN Runkat, A Tambuwun, J Lumenta, AE Siwi, J Repi, and GA Yokom. In 1937, the Dutch East Indies provided a concession to the *Vereeniging* by recognising it as a *Kerkgenootschap,* or church. Henceforth, '*Pinkster Gemente*' was changed into '*Pinksterkerk in Nederlansch Indie,*' based on Government Beslit No. 33 dated 4 June 1937, Staadblad No. 768. In 1942, under Japanese occupation, that name was changed into 'Gereja Pantekosta di Indonesia' (Pentecostal Church in Indonesia) and the Board of the General Assembly at the headquarters was led by HN Runkat.

---

3. Pentecostal Church in Indonesia website: http://www.gpdi.or.id/index.php/profil/sejarah-gpdi (retrieved on December 5, 2012).

As it grew, internal conflict within the Pentecostal Church in Indonesia was unavoidable, generating disunity among church members. Some vital figures even left and established new churches. The disunity in fact had already started when Pentecostalism was still under the name *Pinksteer Gemeente* and led by FG van Gessel, an Evangelical Christian who worked for *Bataafsche Petroleum Maatschappij* (Dutch East Indies Oil Company) in Cepu, Central Java.[4] In 1946, Tan Hok Tjwan was ordained a pastor by van Gessel. Soon afterward, Pastor Tan Hok Tjwan left the Pentecostal Church of Indonesia and established the *Sing Ling Kauw Hwee Church*; this name was later changed to the Isa Almasih Church after independence.[5]

While Runkat was the chairperson, twenty-two pastors left the Pentecostal Church inIndonesia because his leadership was said to contribute to the lessening of church members' spirituality; it was also said that the people who worked at church headquarters were authoritarian.[6] Then, in 1952, *Sepenuh Injil Bethel Church* (Bethel Full Gospel Church) was established in Surabaya, instituting a major split. The conflict continued and was followed by the establishment of other new P/C churches.

Indonesia Bethel Church (GBI). The history of the Indonesia Bethel Church, a major P/C synod today, is related to the emergence of the Bethel Full Gospel Church from the Pentecostal Church in Indonesia (GPdI), founded by the two missionaries. Among the twenty two pastors who left the Pentecostal Church in Indonesia was Pastor H.L. Senduk.[7] Working with Pastor FG van Gessel, he established a new church named the Bethel Full Gospel Church (GBIS) on 21 January 1952 in Surabaya. Van Gessel served as the 'spiritual leader' for church members in Surabaya, and also worked in Jakarta while Senduk functioned as the leader of the church in Jakarta.

As the church developed, issues arose between Bethel Full Gospel Church and the Church of God (COG) in the United States,

---

4. February 20, 2013).
5. *Ibid.*
6. HL Senduk, as cited by Rijnardus Van Kooij & Yam'ah Tsalatsa, Bermain dengan Api: Relasi antara Gereja-gereja Mainstream dan Kalangan Karismatik Pentakosta (Jakarta: BPK Gunung Mulia, 2007), 28.
7. *Ibid.*

eventually leading to a signed agreement. The agreement outlined the amalgamation of Bethel Full Gospel and the Church of God in many fields, including finance and sending American missionaries to Indonesia. This agreement was signed by the leaders of the two church synods in Cleveland, TN and Jakarta in 1967.[8] The provisions of this agreement stimulated many debates among pastors and members of Bethel Full Gospel. As a consequence, many congresses were conducted in 1968 and 1969. The congress in Parapat, North Sumatera in 1969 decided to dismiss Pastor HL Senduk from his position.[9] The conflict was getting worse, with significant support for and against Senduk, until finally the Indonesian Minister of Religious Affairs released decree No. 68/1970 on May 16, 1970 that put Senduk on leave and replaced him with Pastor J Setiawan as head of Bethel Full Gospel. While a governmental intervention in a church would be extraordinary in many nations, especially to the extent of replacing the leader (for example, one cannot imagine Italy deciding to put the sitting pope on leave and appointing another), in Indonesia it is generally accepted that the task of the Ministry of Religion is to promote and preserve religious harmony, so that stepping into a divisive dispute within a church seems to many an exercise of legitimate authority.

A few months later, on October 6, 1970 in Sukabumi, West Java, Pastor Senduk and some of his friends established a new church named *Gereja Bethel Indonesia* (Bethel Church of Indonesia, often simply GBI). After the government recognised and legalised Bethel Church in 1972, it grew rapidly in terms of church members and adopted a more systematic synodal model. For example, the synod's general assembly in 1999 decided to eliminate all names and titles following the Bethel name (or more often, the initials of the church, GBI) and replace them with the name of the location/neighborhood where the church had been built.[10] This decision affected the name of most of the congregations in the synod, even where the majority of members of a specific congregation self-identified with the earlier

---

8. *Ibid.*
9. *Ibid.*
10. *Ibid* 37
11. Churches named *Gereja Tiberias Indonesia* (Indonesia Tiberias Church) and *Gereja Bethany Indonesia* (Indonesia Bethany Church).

name. The decision was therefore negatively received in many places, causing some churches to leave the synod.[11] The synod has since 1999 been insisting on the name change, and most congregations have complied, but some, especially larger, older congregations, continue to insist on using their own names based on their vision and mission, for example GBI Rock (Denpasar, Bali), GBI Shower of Blessings (Manado), and GBI Aletheia (Yogyakarta).

Bethany Church of Indonesia. Bethany Church of Indonesia is a Charismatic church with headquarters located in Surabaya, East Java. This was the first church established in the era of post-colonial Indonesia. The central figure in this church is Abraham Alex Tanuseputra, a dynamic pastor who first served Bethany when it was part of the Bethel Church of Indonesia, and known as GBI Bethany. Tanuseputra became a charismatic Christian in the 1960s and claimed many encounters with the Holy Spirit.[12] He moulded his extended family into a prayer fellowship named 'Bethany' which means 'shelter home' (*rumah persinggahan*). Later, supported by his wife, Yenni, he sold all his belongings in order to build a house of worship in Surabaya.

His prayer fellowship was so well received, and grew so much, that in 1978 he decided to change 'Bethany' into a legal church and joined the Indonesia Bethel Church (GBI) synod. His church was then called GBI Bethany; it was located at Manyar Rejo, Surabaya. His enthralling charisma spread across Indonesia; his appeal caused many people to join his church. In 1998, he launched new branches which were named after the area, namely GBI Bethany West Indonesia, GBI Bethany Central Indonesia, and GBI Bethany East Indonesia.[13] Tanuseputra also appointed pastors to lead each area; 'Successful Bethany Families' was the vision originated by Tanuseputra and is continued until today.

When the general assembly decided in 1999 that all Bethel churches should substitute the location for individual church names, it presented Tanuseputra with a dilemma.[14] The word 'Bethany' had

---

12. GP Harianto and Bambang Yudo, *Abraham Alex Tanuseputra: Sang Visioner* (Yogyakarta: Penerbit Andi, 2012), 38-40.
13. Ibid, 90-91.
14. Ibid.

been emblematic of Tanuseputra's vision and mission to lead the church, and 'his' churches were identified with the Bethany name. Finally, two of his churches, GBI Bethany West Indonesia and GBI Bethany East Indonesia, decided to submit to the synod regulation and eliminated the word 'Bethany' from their names, while GBI Bethany Central Indonesia refused the name change and decided to leave the Bethel synod. Upon the departure of GBI Bethany Central Indonesia, Pastors Leonard Limato, Hana Asti Hanuseputra, Pohan Efendi Harliman, and Gunawan Sutjiotomo initiated the Indonesia Bethany Church on December 11, 2002.[15] Indonesia Bethany Church Synod received legal recognition on January 17, 2003 and Pastor Leonard Limato acted as the chairperson.

However, Tanuseputra and his GBI East and West Indonesia churches (now no longer named Bethany) remained within the Bethel synod yet nevertheless supported the Bethany Church Synod. This led to internal conflict within the Bethel synod body. Finally the Bethel synod issued a letter of dismissal for Tanuseputra and he eventually joined Indonesia Bethany Church. In September 2003, at the first Indonesia Bethany Church general assembly, he was appointed the chairperson of the synod.

International Full Gospel Fellowship-Gereja Injili Seutuh International (IFGF GISI).

The International Full Gospel Fellowship-*Gereja Injili Seutuh Indonesia* (IFGF GISI) was another of the Pentecostal-Charismatic churches that originated in post-colonial Indonesia. The Indonesian synod of this international church(International Full Gospel Fellowship) was based in an Indonesian students' fellowship in the United States in 1980. Jimmy Oentoro initiated IFGF GISI; he was a young entrepreneur actively involved in many fellowships and charismatic movements both in Indonesia and abroad. The seed of IFGF GISI as an apostolic church was started in 1980-1985 when Oentoro introduced a US revival service, called the Full Gospel Fellowship, to Indonesian students in the United States.[16] In 1989, when their studies in the US were completed, Oentoro and his friends brought this fellowship to Indonesia as a new church. They moved the

---

15. *Ibid*, 114.
16. An interview with one of the senior pastors of IFGF GISI Keluarga Allah, Jakarta.

headquarters of their fellowship to Jakarta, Indonesia. In 2004, the name IFGF—*Gereja Injili Seutuh Indonesia* was changed into IFGF—*Gereja Injili Seutuh International*, to not only accord with the name used in the US and elsewhere, but to make clear that its activities were not limited to Indonesia.

The International Full Gospel Fellowship (the Indonesian-based synod)now exists in 13 countries with 200 churches. In the beginning, the members of IFGF GISI consisted of Indonesians living abroad, but now many non-Indoneisans have joined. Indonesian-initiated churches in IFGF GISI now exist for example, in The Netherlands, Nepal, and Singapore, with local citizens as church members.[17] This spread was what initiated changing the word 'Indonesia' in IFGF to 'International'.[18] Jimmy Oentoro became the central figure and general secretary of IFGF GISI and was titled 'Apostolic Chairperson'. The spread of IFGF GISI worldwide attracted Oentoro to establish an international social mission, World Harvest, which operates through divisions in communication, education, and media. IFGF GISI is an example of a para-church that grew into an established church. The factors supporting the development were financial support from the pioneers and first activists, and a post-colonial Indonesia relatively tolerant towards new ideas.

Pentecostal/Charismatic Synods Today

The four P/C synods discussed above are only examples of the many synods/church organisations registered with the government that multiply their numbers every year. In 2002, 270 different Christian synods were registered with the Ministry of Religious Affairs. In 2005 the Ministry banned any new synod registration for a few years. However, by 2013, 323 synods were registered and 50-60% were Pentecostal-Charismatic. Many of these new churches were not yet members of any national ecumenical organisations, neither the Communion of Churches, nor the Pentecostal or Evangelical associations. Following a government evaluation of all the registered synods, it turned out that 30-40% of the still registered synods no longer existed. Cross-checking the synods' statutes, annual reports,

---

17. An interview with one of the senior pastors of IFGF GISI Centre, Surabaya.
18. *Ibid.*

registration documents, and churches' addresses helped the government learn that many of the synods no longer existed. For example, letters sent by the Ministry of Religious Affairs to a synod were often returned with an 'unknown address' note. Whole synods had dissolved and its churches morphed into one or more new synods. Most of the morphing seems to have occurred within the P/C churches. According to Ministry data, some synods rapidly grew and some suffered severe decreases of church members. As mentioned, internal conflicts within the Pentecostal body caused disunity. The roots of conflict varied, but prominent were differences over leadership, church assets, and even church doctrine. One example of a synod's internal conflict was in Manado where some churches and members insisted that the deity should be called 'Yahweh' and other churches and members insisted on 'Allah.'[19]

Comparing Organisational Systems and Church Ministries in P/C Churches

Not only do the history and organisational structures of our four P/C synods differ, but the ministerial methods of these four synods also differ. This section will not only compare the ministerial methods of the four synods, but will also evaluate how these either support or hinder the development of the churches.

Congregational style P/C churches tend to be functional/pragmatic in their church ministry while the traditional Presbyteran-synodal churches are more territorial, with deep historical roots in each location. A principal difference is that Presbyterian-synodal churches focus on contextualisation into local culture; each congregation is a local community that brings its ethnic identity into worship. (Ethnic identity among native Indonesians is extremely complex, as there are more than four hundred different tribal ethnicities, complete with their own languages and customs.) The traditional-territorial churches, introduced by the European Zendeling, encourage indigenisation, the implementation of local culture into theology and practice, not only to facilitate evangelisation, but also to allow the natives to 'own' their Christian faith. One main theme in their theology is enculturation,

---

19. Presented by Edison Pasaribu, chief of *Bimas Kristen*, of the Religious Affairs Ministry of the Republic of Indonesia. May 8, 2012 at CRCS, UGM, Yogyakarta.

which manifests in liturgy by inserting local tradition or local values into the theological teaching and practice.

Different from mainstream traditional churches with a context of enculturation,[20] the congregational style P/C churches in Indonesia are neither territorial nor culturally based. The cultural context is not a focus of their theological teaching. The congregational churches try to bypass or ignore tribal identity in order to embrace a wider audience from different cultural backgrounds, a wider audience that is more modern, and oriented not to traditional local culture, but to more national and international mass culture. Based on our observations, P/C churches are hardly involved at all in an enculturation process—the single exception would be some accommodation for Chinese New Year and some use of Mandarin in some, not nearly all, of those congregations in which the majority of the membership and pastorate are of Chinese descent. Even within this exception, many informers see this as a decreasing phenomenon, as younger Chinese now have more opportunities to participate in the wider Indonesian/international culture (in part, within the P/C churches themselves) and are thus not so self-identified with their Chinese ancestry.

The following part will discuss and evaluate how the congregational-functional system affects the churches' sustainability.

Church Governing System

Pentecostal Church in Indonesia: The Majelis Pusat and Majelis Daerah. The Pentecostal Church in Indonesia is the biggest and the oldest P/C church. It utilises congregational style. In its hierarchy, the *Majelis Pusat*, the general assembly, is the highest authority. Every five years, Pentecostal Church in Indonesia holds a *Majeilis Pusat*, at which it appoints its executive and determines the outline of the Working Program for the next five years.[21] Under the *Majelis Pusat*, there is in every area a *Majelis Daerah*, a provincial assembly. Through 2012, the Pentecostal Church in Indonesia is recorded to

---

20. From our research in five large cities in Indonesia, there are at least three traditional churches with local oriented context, namely Huria Kristen Batak Protestan (HKBP) in Medan, Gereja Kristen Jawa (GKJ) in Yogyakarta, and Gereja Masehi Injili Minahasa (GMIM) in Manado.
21. Pentecostal Church in Indonesia website, http://www.gpdi.or.id/index.php/profil/organisasi (retrieved on December 4, 2012).

have 32 *Majelis Daerahs* in Indonesia and abroad (the United States and Australia). Each *Majelis Daerah* is responsible for appointing persons and delegating duties to the *Majelis Wilayah*, the regional assemblies held in districts or municipal areas. Based on the statutes and church guidelines (*Juklak*), each of these assemblies chooses senior pastors and church members to work on steering committees, ministries, special bodies and commissions. This hierarchy and layers of delegation in the Pentecostal Church in Indonesia project an image of a well-organised and well-managed church.

The selection processes of both *Majelis Pusat* and *Majelis Daerah* are democratic processes in which all the candidates are selected in a series of steps prepared by a special commission, which consists of senior pastors or chosen delegates in a forum. All of the regulations about the rights and responsibilities involved in both national and regional deliberation, including voting, are regulated in the statutes of the church.

The principal positions in both *Majelis Pusat* and *Majelis Daerah* are independent of church congregations; they are never derived from roles in particular church congregations. Therefore, pastors who serve in either level of the *Majelis* have only their pastoral authority in their own church, not any authority derived from their *Majelis* role, though, of course, there is some degree of prestige associated with higher postions in the *Majelis*.

Synods of Indonesia Bethel Church and Indonesia Bethany Church. The two Neo-Pentecostal churches, Indonesia Bethel Church and Indonesia Bethany Church both utilise the synod structure. The structure of the Bethel synod is similar to that of the Pentecostal Church of Indonesia in its principal officers, ministry and commission bodies. There are seven ministries in Bethel: the Ministry of Theology and Education, the Ministry for Women, the Ministry of Evangelism, Ministry of Social Mission, Ministry for Law and Organisation, and the Ministry of Foreign Affairs. Bethel also established special bureaus and commissions, such as those for Bethel Seminary, Bethel World Mission, Bethel Empowering Centre, Bethel Crisis Centre, the Bureau for Media, Research and Development, and the Maintenance and Building Management Bureau. All the ministries, bureaus and

---

22. Synod of Bethel Church Indonesia website, http://www.sinodegbi.org/home/ (retrieved February 20, 2013).

commissions are controlled by the Synod Executive Committee, the *Badan Pekerja Harian*.[22]

The highest level in the Bethel organisation is the Synod General Assembly that meets every four years in order to, among other things, approve the main programs of Bethel Church, approve amendments to church regulations, appoint members of the Full Working Council (*Majelis Pekerja Lengkap*), and elect the chairperson of the Executive Board, the *Badan Pejerka Harian*. The Full Working Council, the *Majelis Pekerja Lengkap*, meets annually, and its members are a combination of Executive Board committee members and representatives of the regional operations management teams, *Badan Pengurus Daerah*. The duty of the Executive Board, *Badan Pejerka Harian*, is to manage operations, including the implementation of all synod decisions. The *Badan Pengurus Daerah* organises the district fellowship (*Perwil*) that consists of local Bethel congregations.[23]

From the very beginning, Bethel has routinely held general assemblies every four years attended by all members of the *Majelis Pekerja Lengkap* and the chairpersons of the *Badan Pengurus Daerah* committeees, pastors, assistant pastors invited guests and observers.[24] As of 2012, Bethel had 38 *Badan Pengurus Daerah*s in Indonesia and one in Canada.[25]

In 2012, Bethel changed the name of its general assembly to the Pastoral Assembly. The change had a major impact on the assembly, which previously had been attended by members of all structural committees; attendance has now been limited to pastors only. The change is in fact in line with Bethel's vision of pastoral leadership of the church; henceforth the assembly is a forum of pastors.[26] The pastors who are eligible to join the assembly are limited to the senior pastors, junior pastors, and curates/vicars, as long as they have church members and represent their congregation. However, only senior pastors have the right to select the general secretary of the synod.

Bethany Church of Indonesia. This church was established during the reformation era in Indonesia with its headquarters located in

---

23. An interview with a Bethel pastor who also acted as the Bethel synod's official in Jakarta, November 10, 2011.
24. *Ibid.*
25. *Ibid.*
26. *Ibid.*

Surabaya. Bethany sets out the general principles and regulations governing all the local congregations under its synod. Its organisation consists of decrees about church organisation and authority, principles, visions, disciplinary acts and all commissions established by the church. While many issues related to the local congregation and the detailed ministerial works incumbent on it are regulated in the church's precepts, yet Bethany Church Regulation article 3(1) states that each local church within Bethany is autonomous.

Based on its statutes, Bethany Church's organisational structure consists of *Majelis Pekerja Lengkap*, the general assembly; the *Majelis Pekerja Sinode*, the synod assembly, a standing group that plans and holds the *Majelis Pekerja Lengkap*; *Majelis Pekerja Daerah*, the regional assembly, and pastors, elders, and Council Defenders, all of which have complete job descriptions in the precepts. Based on the statutes, the general assembly is the highest court and is held every four years and is attended by all representatives of the regional assemblies as well as representatives of the local congregations. The general assembly, among other tasks, ratifies performance and accountability reports of previous general assemblies and synod assemblies, ratifies changes in the synod's statutes, and inaugurates pastors who have passed the test to join Bethany Church. After the general assembly, the regional assemblies must hold meetings in which they submit to and implement all decisions made in the general assembly.[27] Even though each local congregation is understood as autonomous in general, each should work together to implement the decisions of the regional and national assemblies.[28]

The chairperson of the synodal assembly is the person responsible for the general assembly of Bethany Church every four years. The synodal assembly has the right to establish ministries, commissions, committees, and an advisory board (*Dewan Kerasulan*).[29] Composition of the synodal assembly in Bethany is simple, with one chairperson, five heads of ministries, one general secretary, one

---

27. *Ibid.*
28. Indonesia Bethany Church Statutes.
29. The statutes of Indonesia Bethany Church article 9. *Dewan Rasuli* could be literally translated as the apostolic team. To distinguish the Apostolic Team in Bethany church and the Apostolic Team in IFGF-GISI, we use *Dewan Rasuli* for Bethany Church.

secretary, one general treasurer, and one treasurer. The five ministries are: (1) Theology and Teaching, (2) Indonesia Bethany Women - adult, youth, teenager, and children, (3) Media, Social service, and Church networking, (4) Evangelism, Mission, and Pastoral Care, and (5) Research and Development, and Internal and External Organisation.[30] All the job descriptions for each member of the synodal assembly are clearly outlined. Besides the synodal assembly, Bethany Church also has an Apostolic Board of Trustees (*Lembaga Dewan Rasuli*), which operates under the leadership of Alex Tanuseputra, the founder of Bethany Church, also known as 'Bethany's father.'

International Full Gospel Fellowship IFGF GISI: Apostolic Team. Indonesia's International Full Gospel Fellowship is affiliated with the Full Gospel Fellowship of Churches and Ministers, International, and like it is governed by an Apostolic Team, led by a chairperson and consisting of seven regional chairpersons from the seven apostolic districts. The seven apostolic regions of IFGF GISI are spread across the world, namely: Apostolic Region 1 in Indonesia and Middle East, Apostolic Region 2 in Africa, Apostolic Region 3 in North America and Europe, Aposolic Region 4 in South and Central America, Apostolic Region 5 in the ASEAN countries, Apostolic Region 6 in Asia Pacific and Oceania, and Apostolic Region 7 in India, Pakistan, and Nepal. Apart from the aforementioned Apostolic Team, in each Apostolic Region there are national synods, and in each synod there are three personnel managing daily operations, namely a President, Secretary, and Treasurer. The President in charge of operations also serves as the synod's chairperson.[31]

Local congregations that have spread across Indonesian cities and even into other countries are called satellites.[32] Although each satellite is autonomous in terms of being self-operating, it participates in all programs defined by synod headquarters and sends regular tithes to the synod headquarters in Jakarta.[33] The synod's general assembly is

---

30. Synod of Bethel Church Indonesia website, www.sinodegbi.org/home (retrieved on February 20, 2013).
31. An interview with the senior pastor of IFGF GISI Jakarta.
32. International Full Gospel Fellowship website, www.ifgf.org. (retrieved on March 1, 2013). Some countries that have IFGF GISI satellites are Dusseldorf (Germany), Paris (France), and London (UK).
33. *Ibid.*

held every four years and is attended by all pastors in the church. The agenda of this assembly includes appointing a new synod chairperson and the members of synod committees.[34]

Unlike the elected leadership of the national synods, the Apostolic Team does not have term limits. Therefore, it can be said that IFGF GISI applies two different systems of governing: the congregational system in the national synods and Episcopalian-Catholic (within the non-periodical Apostolic system).

Pioneering Pastors

There are some charismatic persons who figure prominently as pioneers and activists in the establishment of these four and other churches. One example would be Pastor HL Senduk who, with some other pastors, established Bethel Church after leaving the Pentecostal Church of Indonesia. The initiation of Bethel Church also marks a transitional era in which megachurches emerged, many made possible by the charisms of their own central figures. In 2000 the Indonesia Bethel Church Tiberias separated from Bethel and became Indonesia Tiberias Church, led by Pastor Yesaya Pariadji, who has made Tiberias one of the largest and most distinct of the P/C churches. Another example is Bethel Bethany that became Bethany Church in 2003 with Pastor Alex Tanuseputra as its inspiration and eventual leader. Similarly in IFGF GISI, Jimmy Oentoro brought this prayer fellowship from the United States to Indonesia and founded a strong Indonesian P/C church. In these two cases, the birth of these huge churches was so recent that the initiating pastors are still leading the church. Each church reveres and honors its founder by elevating them above ordinary office: Indonesia Bethany Church makes Alex Tanuseputra the chairperson of *Bethany Dewan Rasuli* and Jimmy Oentoro became the chairperson of the Apostolic Team in IFGF GISI.

Types of Ministerial Service

As autonomous congregational churches, P/C churches depend largely on the local pastor's creativity in developing ministerial service. However, in some church organisations, the synods provide structural guidelines for each local congregation in developing their

---

34. *Ibid.*

ministry. This section will elaborate types of ministries or services specifically developed by the Pentecostal Church of Indonesia, Bethel, Bethany, and the Full Gospel Fellowship International (IFGF GISI).

Pentecostal Church in Indonesia. The Pentecostal Church in Indonesia has a structure consisting of a number of commissions and departments involved in ministerial work. The commissions and departments include: the Commission for Ministry to Children, Commission for Ministry to Teenagers, Commission for Youth Ministry, Commission for Women's Ministry, Commission for Men's Ministry, Commission for Ministry to Professionals and Entrepreneurs Ministry, Commission for Children of God's Servant, Commission for Student Ministry, Commission for Evangelical Ministry, Department of Pastoral Care, Intercultural Ministry, Department of Foreign Affairs, Multimedia Ministry, Research and Development Ministry, Publishing Ministry, Department of Social Care, Department of Church Development, Department of Education and Training, and the Supreme Auditing Body, which supervises the rest. All of these structures are the responsibility of the *Majelis Daerahs*; all local congregations institute local commissions corresponding to those for children, teens, youth, women, men, professionals and students.

Apart from these ministries, the Pentecostal Church sets up external social ministries. Local congregations with many members over age 15 tend to develop and organise their own social ministries in order to help the church members and their neighborhood; the most common social ministries are founding and operating orphanages and nursing homes.[35] The Pentecostal Church in Indonesia also owns many seminaries and bible institutes. [36]

Bethel Church. The internal ministerial divisions in Bethel Church are similar to those of both the Pentecostal Church and Protestant mainstream churches, but are named bureaux. Bethel synod

---

35. For example, two out of three Pentecostal Churches in Tondano-Manado have established orphanages and nursing homes which are managed and owned by the local congregation.
36. See Pentecostal Church in Indonesia website: http://gpdi.or.id/index.php/gpdi-network/sekolah-alkitab and http://gpdi.or.id/index.php/gpdi-network/sekolah-tinggi_(retrieved on December 4, 2012)

established two bureaux, namely the Central Bureau and the Supporting Bureau. The Central Bureau includes the Children's Bureau, the Teenagers' Bureau, the Youth Bureau, and the Mature Youth Bureau. Interestingly, Bethel does not have either a Women's Bureau or a Men's Bureau. In Bethel, women have a special division called the Women's Division; it is one of seven divisions under the supervision of the synod chairperson. Men have neither a division nor a special bureau. However, most local congregations have an active men's group.

As for the Supporting Bureaux, they are: the Information Media Bureau, the Networking Bureau, the Bureau for Public Relations and Research and Development, the PI-Mission Bureau, the Social Community Bureau, the Certification and Teaching Bureau, the Empowerment of Young Entrepreneurs Bureau, the Maintenance and General Bureau, and the Regional Empowerment Bureau.[37] The ministerial work of these bureaux is obviously both internal and also aimed at the external larger public. For example, the Information Media Bureau and Department of Evangelism manage and supervise radio broadcasting activities run by local congregations.[38] The Bethel synod feels that media is the most effective strategy to contact wider audiences, hence some local congregations run their own radio broadcasts (GBI REM, radio SSK). Local congregations are largely independent and given opportunities to develop ideas for using media in ministerial work, such as broadcasting specific programs on both radio and television (an example is Pastor Niko Njotorahardjo's *Healing Movement* program).

Bethany Church. Bethany Church in Nginden, Surabaya has been the trend setter for ministries developed by other Bethany churches; its overall ministerial model has become virtually universal within the synod. One example is that Bethany Church Nginden established a kind of school of ministry, called Serving Orientation School (SOM), an informal school to instruct church members in studying the bible; instruction focuses on the Holy Spirit, church leadership and the

---

37. Synod of Bethel Church Indonesia website, www.sinodegbi.org/home (retrieved on February 20, 2013).
38. An Interview with one of Bethel pastor in Bethel synod office Jakarta, November 30, 2011.

Second Coming. After attending this school, it is hoped that church members will grow spiritually; the SOM is in many congregations regarded as a path to ministerial posts in the church. At the academic level, Bethany Church also established the theology school *Sekolah Tinggi Teologia* (STT) Bethany, whose students come not only from Bethany Church but also some other P/C Churches.

Ministries in Bethany Church are hierarchically regulated, with the senior pastor supervising all local ministries. To simplify the chain of responsibility, Bethany Church distributes ministerial responsibilities and duties based on ministerial districts; each is led by a District Pastor assisted by a district committee. Each district has a number of sectors led by a Sector Pastor assisted by a sector committee. Each sector has one or more Family Altar Group, helped by the Family Altar Committee.

Family Altar is the smallest unit in the Bethany Church ministerial work; in effect, it is a cell group composed of a group of families who live near each other. FA groups are led by a pastor and assisted by the church's Family Altar Committee. The FA's activities (usually praying or bible study) are conducted in different homes depending on geographical location and members' preferences. FA members share their lives and support each other in order to keep the group sustainable, fulfilling their commitment to the group through prayer, bible study, and sharing. FA members also receive counseling and special pastoral care from the pastor based on their need, for example, pastoral care when they are sick. This ministerial hierarchy allows information on both family need and individual and group spiritual progress to travel upward from the family level to the senior ministry staff. Bethany's cell group system has been adopted by other Pentecostal churches and modified, based on their own preferences and experience.

International Full Gospel Fellowship-Gereja Injili Seutuh Indonesia (IFGF GISI).
Pastor Jimmy Oentoro of IFGF GISI pioneered World Harvest, an international social service organisation that works across denominations. Jimmy Oentoro also initiated a Christian television channel called 'U Channel,' which is transmitted to some Asian countries and the Middle East. Seventy-five percent of programming is in the Indonesian language; the channel airs Christian spiritual

movies and songs, Christian documentary movies, sermons, and some church discussions.

As mentioned in the previous section, this church utilises the synodal structure. The synod's chairperson (also called the president) is in Jakarta and is responsible for all leadership duties and supervising operations of all local congregations (satellites) and all churches across the world. Yet, this entire structure is under the Apostolic Team with Jimmy Oentoro as its president.

IFGF GISI has various categories of ministry. Their ministerial groups include: ministry to children (GolKids), ministry to teens (Golteens), youth ministry (Gol), Women of Virtue, and Living to Lead for men.[39] In addition, there are also small groups that focus on specific issues/subjects, such as *iGrow* for Christian education and *iCare* for health and social service aimed at both members and non-members. For outreach or external service, IFGF GISI implemented a creative body named *iShare*, in addition to the existing World Harvest. These groups are involved in social services such as collecting and giving humanitarian aid to the victims of natural disaster, or helping underprivileged people. Recently, World Harvest and IFGF GISI *Peduli* launched the 3R program, Rescue, Restore, Rebuild, which focuses on helping flood victims in Jakarta.[40]

Theological Education

In the past, Pentecostal churches did not put much emphasis on theological education. After the Ministry of Religious Affairs invited the formation of institutions for theological training, many P/C theological schools bloomed. Almost all P/C synods have or are attempting to establish their own theological school. Though there are about 250 P/C theological schools in Indonesia, many do not have any form of accreditation, have more or less informal and volatile curricula, short terms, and no trained faculty. Only a very few of the doctoral programs offered require persons to already have masters

---

39. Interestingly enough, despite the very traditional gendered labels for women's and men's ministries, both the sermons and other teachings of the church seem to assume equality, and women are included in leadership, though their rates are below those of men.
40. International Full Gospel Fellowship website: www.ifgf.org (retrieved on March 1, 2013)

degrees or even bachelors degrees. The Ministry of Religious Affairs is beginning to demand accreditation reviews of theological schools, causing problems for many programs which have grown very rapidly without much quality assurance.[41]

At the same time, many Pentecostal churches have begun to realise the importance of theological education to manage their churches' development and existence. In part this is because the educational level of their membership is, for Indonesia, extremely high, and thus the expectation of many members of pastors and of the organisations themselves are very high. Their pastors, for example, must be able to answer the questions of the increasingly literate, connected church membership. Prosperous middle class members want to know that their financial contributions are being used effectively. Theological schools function not only to teach church doctrine, but are also the 'laboratory' for testing and training new church leaders in ever- wider perspectives. The schools have important roles to play in developing and strengthening the church and its position *vis a vis* other churches and religions. Therefore, some P/C synods establish, own, and manage theological schools in many different places. This is not a new Christian phenomenon in Indonesia. Some evangelical theological schools had been established at the same time that the church was established, as was the case for the first evangelical church and school established by missionaries in the Dutch East Indies. The first evangelical school established in Indonesia was *Nederlandsche Indie Bybel Institut* (NIBI) in Malang, East Java in 1935 by William West Patterson, an American missionary. Van Gessel had first instituted the idea of evangelical schools, and was helped by HN Runkat, a Pentecostal activist, in supporting the founding of the *Institute* by Patterson, but the school did not survive; it was closed during WW II. Then, in 1948, RE Edmondson from Bethel Temple, Seattle came to Indonesia and opened the STT Lawang Theological School; this school was then moved to Beji, Batu (East Java) in 1959, beginning a trend: many bible schools started to emerge in all areas of Indonesia.

---

41. Presented by Edison Pasaribu, chief of Christian Protestant Mass Guidance Body of Religious Affairs Ministry of Republic of Indonesia. May 8, 2012.

Pentecostal Church in Indonesia Seminaries. Due in part to its age, the Pentecostal Church of Indonesia is reported to have many bible schools in Indonesia compared to other P/C churches. As of 2011, the Pentecostal Church owned seminaries or bible schools in almost every province in Indonesia. The schools are usually established and managed by the local *Majelis Daerah*, as regulated in the Pentecostal Church statutes, Part II articles 5 and 6 about education. Article 5 explains the dependence of spiritual growth on the education possible from building and operating bible and theological schools. Article 6 explains the church's responsibilities to share responsibility for developing national education by active participation in both formal and informal education, starting from kindergarten and extending through higher education. The Pentecostal Church has about 30 bible or other religious schools , including the Bible Academy /ATHAS of Central Java, Batu Bible Institute of East Java, Cianjur Bible School and Cianjur Bible Institute of West Java, Agape Theological School of Bandar Lampung , El Shaddai Theological School ISTTI of Manado in North Sulawesi, Purbasari Bible School in North Sumatera, Nias Bible School, Kupang Bible School, Anjungan Bible School in West Kalimantan, Tana Toraja Bible School in South Sulawesi, Ambon Bible School in Moluccas, Manokwari Bible School, and Biak Bible School of Papua/Irian Jawa, as well as others.[42]

Bethel Seminaries. The Bethel synod runs a theological school that was established in 1954 by the earlier incarnation of Bethel. In the beginning, it offered evangelical courses in Petamburan, Jakarta based on a Bethel High Court II decree. Pastor HL Senduk was one of the supervisors. In 1980, the director of *Bimas Kristen* of the Ministry of Religious Affairs appointed Bethel Seminary to establish and operate a pilot program in Christian Education (PAK), using a curriculum designed by the Ministry of Religious Affairs. In the same year, the Bethel Foundation handed over seminary management to the Bethel Church Operational Management Body.[43]

Between 1968 and 1994 the seminary established by the earlier

---

42. Pentecostal Church in Indonesia website: www.gpdi/or.id/index.php/gpdi-network/sekolah-alkitab (retrieved on December 4, 2012).
43. Synod of Bethel Church Indonesia website, www.sinodegbi.org (retrieved on February 20, 2013).

Bethel Full Gospel Church underwent many changes. For one, the government, through *Bimas Kristen*, intruded again in 1983 'suggesting' a new name for the school: the Bethel Theological Education Institute of Jakarta.[44] In 2003, the name was changed again, this time to Jakarta Bethel Seminary, supposedly in line with the Bethel Congress' decree regarding naming, though that reasoning is not apparent, especially given the names of some of the other Bethel seminaries below.

In addition to this seminary in Jakarta, local Bethel congregations also established and manage some seminaries on their own; the Bethel synod provides permits for local congregations to establish their own seminaries.[45] Some of those seminaries are: Bethel School of Theology 'The Way' run by Bethel Gatot Subroto in Jakarta, the Karisma School of Theology run by Bethel Church Bandung, and the leadership program run by Bethel REM.

Bethany Church Seminaries. Thus far, Bethany Church of Indonesia has only one theology school, offering programs for both bachelors and masters degrees.

International Full Gospel Fellowship IFGF GISI Seminaries. IFGF GISI established and runs a theology school in Tangerang called *Sekolah Tinggi Teologi* International Harvest Theological School. It was established in 1993 by Dr Jimmy Oentoro, the president of the IFGF GISI Apostolic Team; he has served as the chairperson of this theological school since then. The school offers not only bachelors programs but also masters and doctoral programs.

As we have seen here, P/C churches have begun to realise the importance of theological education for pastors and pastor candidates. However, thus far they have lacked consistent and serious efforts to provide quality education. Many churches race to establish their own schools, often ignoring essential 'equipment' such as buildings, trained faculty, and adequate curricula. They offer academic degrees —masters and doctorates—whose content is extremely questionable, as when doctorates are conferred on persons without prior graduate

---

44. *Ibid.*
45. Interview with a Bethel Church pastor.

degrees, or when masters degrees are earned in a matter of weeks. Quality control has thus far been a major weakness of P/C seminaries and theological schools. However, recently both the Ministry of Religious Affairs and the leaders of the many of the P/C churches have become increasingly attentive to the needs in this area.

A number of critics, both internal and external, explain the underlying problems with theological education in the P/C churches to be that many lack a well-developed theology or a consistent scriptural method that could be the foundation of seminary study. Charisma, and communication with the Holy Spirit are difficult to teach. The one aspect of pastoring skills that P/C churches tend to teach consistently well is church management. For the rest, there is division over whether a consistent theology will simply take more time to develop, or if being open to the pushes and pulls of the Holy Spirit in the contemporary world makes a consistent theology even possible, much less necessary.

Self-Identitification of P/C Church Members

This section examines the self-identification of the church members of the four churches selected above.

Age Range. In our survey of 3748 respondents from all the churches we observed, the church members' average age was 32.71 year-old, with 52% of respondents between 20-39. This average age is considered young, compared to the average age in P/C churches in other countries as observed by PEW Forum.[46] The average P/C member age in the USA was 46, in Chile 41, South Africa 40, the Philippines 40 and South Korea 41. This accords with the popular perception in Indonesia that the Pentecostal churches are filled with young people. Since we did not ask persons under 15 to take surveys (though we had a handful of teens under 15 who did), the true average age in P/C churches is actually much younger, since many persons in their 20s, 30s and 40s have children under 15.

---

46. *Spirit and Power—A 10 Country Survey of Pentecostals* (Washington: PEW Forum on Religion and Public Life, 2006), 40.

The table below shows age data of our four selected P/C churches.

Church / Synod	N	Average Age of Respondants	Mean Standard Error
Pentecostal Church of Indo	471	33.08	0.702
Bethel Church	542	34.65	0.539
Bethany Church	301	37.38	0.756
IFGF GISI International Full Gospel Fellowship	116	29.56	0.973

IFGF GISI has the youngest average age compared to other Pentecostal churches, 29.56 years old, with 58.65 % of respondents ranging between 20 and 34 years old. Next youngest is the Pentecostal Church with a 33.8 year average age of respondents, and 65.5% of respondents between 15 and 39 years old. The average age of respondents in Bethel Church is 34.65 years old, with 68.5% of respondents between 20 and 39 years old. The oldest average is in Bethany Church, 37.38 years old, with 54.6 % of respondents between 25 and 44 years old. The 14-25 year age range for teens and young adults has the largest number of respondents in all four of these churches.

Church Affiliation. How do church members identify themselves within the larger Pentecostal/Charismatic movement? Respondents from every church surveyed were asked their affiliation, with the following choices: Pentecostal, Charismatic, Pentecostal-Charismatic, Evangelical, and Other. Each category provided refers to the historical background of Pentecostal church development in Indonesia. In our minds, and in the minds of many pastors and Christian scholars, the first category, Pentecostal, refers to the early growth of the Pentecostal movement (first wave Pentecostal); one of the first wave Pentecostal groups is the Pentecostal Church of Indonesia. Charismatic refers to groups that emerged in a later era, originally both in Christian Catholic and mainstream Protestant Christian churches. In many charismatic groups, early fellowship groups within mainstream churches were transformed into independent charismatic churches, although this transformation was not the original goal of the charismatic movement in Indonesia. Neo-Pentecostal is the term used to denote the continuation of the previous process into generating megachurches in Indonesia; the terms Neo-Pentecostal and Pentecostal-Charismatic are often used interchangeably. The next group is Evangelical, with its emphasis on reformation and renewal, and its spotlight on holiness. The last option is 'Other' which is meant for non-Pentecostal movements/groups not included in the other four categories provided.

Synod / Church	N	Church Members Self-identification (%)				
		Pentecostal	Charismatic	Pentecostal-Charismatic	Evangelical	Others
Pentecostal Church of Indonesia	471	66.5	5.1	20.8	3.6	4
Bethel Church	542	15.5	41.0	31.7	3.7	8.1
Bethany Church	301	16.6	44.7	29.1	2.3	7.3
IFGF GISI International Full Gospel Fellowship	116	11.2	28.8	25	15.5	9.5

The table above shows how members in the Pentecostal and Charismatic churches which we observed identify themselves.

Respondents from the Pentecostal Church of Indonesia are the clearest about their identity as Pentecostal, yet even there, in the oldest Pentecostal church in Indonesia, 34% of members either see themselves as both Pentecostal and Charismatic, or non-Pentecostal. In Bethel, Bethany and the International Full Gospel Fellowship the single largest group (41%, 44% and 38.8% respectively) identify as Charismatic, but between a quarter and a third of the members of these churches identify as both Pentecostal and Charismatic, and between a quarter and third do not identify as Charismatic at all. We can either conclude, as did many of the pastors we consulted—who are for the most part very clear about in which column *their* church belongs—that these members are ignorant or confused about the meanings behind these labels, or we can question to what extent the teachings and practices of these churches are distinct. Our suspicion is that the pastors are influenced by their knowledge of the history and affiliations of the church, but that the imitation of the worship style of Charismatic/Neo-Pentecostal churches by other churches has blurred the lines between them for congregants.

On the other hand, the blurred lines between categories of church may also help explain the ecumenical affiliations of many P/C churches in Indonesia. A number have joined the national evangelical ecumenical association, and even the Indonesian Communion of Churches (mainstream Protestant) instead of only the Pentecostal association. These different affiliations of the churches may contribute to the member responses concerning their religious identity. But there are also very diverse characteristics among churches in the same synod. For example, the Pentecostal Church of Indonesia is the oldest and best recognised Pentecostal institution in Indonesia. However, field observation revealed that this synod contains many different worship characteristics; some Pentecostal Church congregations do not emphasise speaking in tongues during service, while others strongly urge the use of tongues, like the Charismatic churches. Also, temporal mobility from one church to another church is a common phenomenon for members, especially in big cities. Thus church members' self-identification may be formed not only by their home church's character but by a combination of different P/C churches they have attended. Some are clearly still periodically attending previous mainstream churches where they used to be members, which may also affect their identification.

Conclusion

The history of institutionalisation of the four churches discussed in this chapter began with the first wave Pentecostal churches that were brought by American and European missionaries during Dutch East Indies and Japanese occupation in Indonesia. The Pentecostal Church of Indonesia, as the first Pentecostal church acknowledged by the Dutch East Indies government, encountered internal conflicts leading to the emergence of new Pentecostal churches like Isa Almasih Church (GIA) and Indonesia Bethel Church (GBI), which developed as part of the second wave of Neo-Pentecostal or Charismatic churches. Bethany represents the post-*reformasi* wave of church development.

Different from most of the mainstream churches in Indonesia with their presbyterian-synodal system, Pentecostal churches organise their churches based on a congregational system, sometimes combining the congregational with the Episcopalian system or some other model. Some P/C churches, such as the Pentecostal Church of Indonesia and Bethel Church, attempt to improve the synod organisation by rotating leadership to prevent prolonged terms by individual persons. However, in the local church, leadership is usually inherited and handed over to figures close to the church pioneers—often to sons or wives, or long-serving associate pastors. This pattern in local churches developed because originally the church was often a kind of family patrimony: it began in the home of the pastor, who might not have been full time in the beginning. When the church expanded, it sometimes took over the pastor's home, or was built on the land of the pastor, and the original funds for expansion often came from the extended family of the pastor, as in the case of Bethany.

Unlike the first wave Pentecostal movement, whose centralised synodal system has been passed through generations, most of the Charismatic/Neo-Pentecostal churches are still under the same leadership that established them: the pioneers of the church. The role of these leaders in Charismatic/Neo-Pentecostal churches is central and they are internally accepted as charismatic figures. Some churches adopt a strategic system to place these figures in a central post but still give opportunities for others to become involved in church leadership. With this system, some of these figures appoint or give opportunity to members of their family to join in managing the church. In Bethany Church, for example, despite adopting the synodal system that invites potential candidates into church leadership, the *Dewan Rasuli* is headed by the pioneer of the church and is structurally above the synod. Meanwhile, IFGF GISI, which has also developed synods, has an Apostolic Team led by the pioneer of the church; the Team is also above the synod. In these two examples, leaders at the synod level are chosen in the congress/general assembly, while the *Dewan Rasuli* and Apostolic Team reign supreme for an unspecified length of time—but seemingly by consensus. Many local churches tend to follow this example, positioning the pioneer pastors as the central figure in church, calling on the same charisma that began the church to continue to manage the church. However, internal conflicts in Pentecostal churches have taught them the need to adopt a good organisational structure that can sustain the churches' existence by preventing internal conflict either from leadership changes or disputes over church assets.

A Forum for Theology in the World Vol 1 No 1/2014

Chapter Seven
Fractured Ecumenism and Attempts at Fence-Mending: Relations Between Pentecostals and Non-Pentecostals in Indonesia

Marthen Tahun

Pentecostalism has been globally perceived as one of the orthodox Christian communities since being recognised by the World Council of Churches (WCC) in 1950. The Pentecostal/Charismatic (P/C) movement serves as a fourth form of orthodoxy along with eastern Orthodoxy, Catholicsm and more mainstream Protestantism.[1] The *Iglesia Pentecostal de Chile* and the *Misión Iglesia Pentecostal* were the first of the Pentecostal/Charismatic churches that joined the WCC; they joined in 1961 at the WCC congress in New Delhi.[2] In Roman Catholicism, Pope Paul VI recognised Pentecostalism in 1973; the first Catholic Charismatic mass (with Pentecostal elements, but Catholic theology and liturgy) was conducted in 1975 at St. Peter's Cathedral, Rome.[3] Other P/C churches then followed the lead of these Latin American P/C churches.[4] WCC membership hence indicates that the P/C movement, which had previously been viewed as a fringe phenomenon, has developed into a principal stream of Christian orthodoxy and is acknowledged as an established Christian voice. In fact, charismatic movements can now be found in many different Christian traditions, including Roman Catholic, Anglican, Orthodox, and many more.

---

1. Tim Dowley (Ed) *A Lion Handbook: The History of Christianity.* (Oxford: Lion, 1977), 647, 649, 650.
2. 'The Significance of the Chilean Pentecostals' Admission to the World Council of Churches,' *International Review of Mission* 51(1962), 480-482; Manuel de Mello, 'Participation is Everything,' *International Review of Mission* 60 (1971), 245-248.
3. Dowley, *A Lion handbook,* 647.
4. David Bundy. 'The Ecumenical Quest of Pentecostalism.' http://www.pctii.org/cyberj/cyberj5/bundy.html. (Retrieved on February 28, 2013).

The entrance of many P/C churches into the WCC organisation demonstrates that P/C churches and WCC ecumenical organisations can work together.[5] The *Joint Consultative Group*, a regular meeting including both parties, has confirmed how seriously P/C churches and the WCC are building their relationship. P/C membership became even more prominent when the ecumenical dialogue, the WCC Canberra Assembly of 2001, was conducted in Australia with the theme 'Come Holy Spirit: Renew the Whole Creation.' Within this meeting there was a special work group on 'Pentecostal and Charismatic Movements.'[6] P/C participation in some dialogues conducted by the WCC has emphasised the unity of Christians in attempting to establish justice and peace in the world. It also represents an understanding shared by many P/C churches that Christian churches are called to collectively respond to problems threatening human sustainability.

Some P/C churches have not only joined international ecumenical organisations, but also national ecumenical organisations, such as those in Korea, Indonesia, Brazil, and other nations. However, Pentecostal churches have not historically been ecumenical, and though this is changing, especially in the charismatic part of the Pentecostal/Charismatic (P/C) movement, the majority of P/C churches have not wanted to affiliate with inclusively Christian ecumenical organisations; when they have joined, most have tended to limit their ecumenism to P/C organisations.

In Indonesia, some P/C churches joined the Indonesian Communion of Churches, *Persekutuan Gereja di Indonesia* (PGI), in which most member churches are mainstream Christian, but most P/C churches have preferred to locate their ecumenism within the Indonesian Pentecostal Church Fellowship, *Persekutuan Gereja Pantecosta Indonesia* (PGPI) or, less often, the Fellowship of Indonesian Evangelical Churches and Institutions, *Persekutuan Gereja dan Lembaga Injili Indonesia* (PGLII). The Indonesian Communion of Churches, as a national ecumenical organisation in Indonesia, tried to build relations with Pentecostal churches from the very beginnings

---

5. Alan Anderson. *An Introduction to Pentecostalism: Global Charismatic Christianity*. (Cambridge, UK: Cambridge University Press, 2004), 254.
6. Anderson, *An Introduction to Pentecostalism*, 254.

of its establishment, but with the vast majority of its members being mainstream churches, it was difficult to attract P/C churches. The Isa Almasih Church, *Gereja Isa Almasih* (GIA), is recorded as the first P/C church to join the Communion, in 1956. It was then followed by other P/C churches, such as the Full Gospel Bethel Church, *Gereja Bethel Sepenuh Injil* (GBIS); the Indonesia Bethel Church, *Gereja Bethel Indonesia*(GBI); the Pentecostal Movement Church, *Gereja Gerekan Pentacosta* (GGP); God's Church in Indonesia, *Gereja Tuhan di Indonesia*; Central Pentecostal Church of Surabaya, *Gereja Pentacosta Pusat Surabaya* (GTdI), the Pentecostal Movement Church in Surabaya (GPPS); the Assembly of God, *Gereja Sidang Jemaat Allah* (GSJA) and some other P/C churches.[7] Not only do these churches routinely pay the membership fee of the Indonesian Communion of Churches, but they have also actively participated in their activities.[8]

As mentioned earlier, some mainstream and P/C churches have for some time initiated ecumenical partnerships at both the international and national levels. This chapter will probe the pattern of relations between the mainstream and P/C churches historically, both relations between P/C churches and other churches and the relationships of P/C churches with national Christian ecumenical organisations.

The Response from Churches and Government: Historical Overview

Generally, the P/C movement in Indonesia is categorised into three waves. The first wave marks the beginnings of Pentecostalism in Indonesia, first in 1921-1923. The second wave is often called the Charismatic movement. It was a wave not of new churches, but of

---

7. Indonesians are even more prone to using initials for organisations than most English speaking cultures, and this is at least as true of Indonesian Christians as of the rest of the population. Hence these churches and synods are usually, but not always, known by their initials, but there are so many, that for purposes of clarity for an audience not previously acquainted with any of these churches, we will continue to use the full English names, listing the Indonesian names and initials only in the first mention of the church.
8. Andreas A Yewangoe, 'Gereja Kristen Pasundan dan Gerakan Pentakosta.' In Onesimus Supriatno and Daryatno Dani, *Merentang Sejarah, Memaknai Kemandirian : Menjadi Gereja bagi Sesama* (Bandung: Majelis Sinode Gereja Kristen Pasundan; Jakarta: BPK Gunung Mulia, 2009), 42.

the Pentecostal spirit within the Catholic and mainstream Protestant churches. It grew in Indonesia in the late 1960s and became well and widely established in the 1970s. The third wave is called Neo-Charismatic or Neo-Pentecostal; it emerged in the 1980s, and is often collapsed into the Charismatic movement, with whom it shares a number of characteristics. (Many of the charismatic movements within the mainstream and Catholic churches had either been forced out, or left out of disappointment at the failure of the churches to fully embrace them, and founded new churches.)

The post-*reformasi* democratic era in Indonesia, marked by Suharto's fall in 1998 after 32 years of rule, opened up opportunities for diverse religious institutions, among many others, to openly and clearly express their beliefs. Pentecostal and Charismatic churches were among those seizing the moment for self-expression; not only did some new P/C churches arise with more varied practices and expressions, but other P/C churches already established became much less covert, building more visible, even attention-grabbing, complexes, advertising more publicly, and becoming more present in the media.

For many of the early years, having different doctrine and liturgy from the Christian mainstream restrained the growth of the P/C movement in Indonesia. Its growth was opposed by both the mainstream Christian churches and the Indonesian government, which desired neither further differentiation within the Christian minority, nor disharmony within that minority.[9] Though a new movement, and despite such opposition, Pentecostalism seems to have grown and spread rapidly after the 1920s; the East Indies government (part of the Dutch colonisation of Indonesia until 1945) saw the P/C movement as a threat, contributing to both disunity and conflict. In Bali, for example, the East Indies government had ordered the Cornelius Groesbeek and Richard (Dirk) van Klaveren families, the

---

9. Under the Dutch, the government clearly favored the Dutch Reformed Church, and thus discouraged competing Christian churches, more of which might also arouse Muslim anger. Since independence, Indonesia has had a Ministry of Religion, whose function is to monitor and protect all religions, maintaining religious harmony in the nation. Multiplying divisions within the Christian minority made monitoring more difficult; this constant splitting and formation of new churches and synods continues to be a prominent complaint of officials in the Ministry of Religion about the P/C movement.

first Pentecostal missionaries in Indonesia, to move to Java because the government was afraid of disturbance if the Hindus in Bali resisted the spread of Pentecostalism. These two families had been sent by Bethel Temple Church in Seattle, Washington, USA in 1921.[10] The government refused to give permission for the two families to remain after they had been working in Bali for 2 years (1921-1922), they were then moved to Surabaya on Java. Richard (Dirk) van Klaveren then extended evangelisation efforts to Batavia (now Jakarta) while Groesbeek pioneered evangelisation in Surabaya, and then Cepu. In Cepu, Groesbeek met Pastors JG Thiessen and FG van Gessel, who also became actively involved in spreading Pentecostalism.[11] From this point in 1923, it was clear that Pentecostalism had taken form and shape.

Theodore van den End recorded that Indo-European (mixed-race Indonesian and European) and Tionghoa (those of Chinese descent) were the first groups interested in Pentecostalism; these two groups had often been forgotten by the mainstream churches.[12] As Pentecostal evangelisation spread, other non-Javanese Christians started to convert and follow Pentecostalism. Afterwards, a number of other Indonesian figures made significant contributions to the rapid growth of Pentecostalism in other parts of Indonesia.[13]

Unlike missionaries from the mainstream churches who introduced Christianity to different areas in Indonesia, Pentecostals preferred to set their sights on areas already Christian; hence most early Pentecostals were Christians coming from either Protestant or Roman Catholic churches. Unavoidable conflicts emerged as Pentecostal evangelism reached into areas already affiliated to a

---

10. Nicky Sumual, *60 tahun Pantekosta Indonesia: Suatu Sejarah*. (Manado:no publisher, 1981), 51.
11. Steven H Talumewo, *Sejarah Gerakan Pentakosta*. (Yogyakarta: Penerbit ANDI, 2008), 55-58; Theodore van den End, & J Wetjens *Ragi Carita 2: Sejarah Gereja di Indonesia 1860-an – Sekarang*, 8th edition (Jakarta: BPK Gunung Mulia, 2008), 271-272.
12. van den End & Weitjens, *Ragi Carita 2* p 272; Bnd M Tapilatu, *Gereja-gereja Pentakosta di Indonesia* (tesis MTh.; Jakarta: STT Jakarta, 1982), 16-32; and Th Karunia Djaja, *Sejarah Gereja Pantekosta di Indonesia*. (Semarang: GPdI, 1993), 13-44.
13. Talumewo, *Sejarah Gerakan Pentakosta*,57; van den End & Wetjens, *Ragi Carita 2*, 271.

particular mainstream church. A common accusation addressed to Pentecostals by the mainstream churches was 'internal proselytising' (converting those who were already Christian) by targeting teenagers, youth, students, professionals, entrepreneurs, and important figures in the church as potential Pentecostal members.[14]

Pentecostals and mainstream churches have different understandings of Christian evangelisation. The mainstream churches viewed, and many still view, P/C churches as violating tolerance and disrespecting other churches by 'converting' their already baptised Christians to Pentecostalism. On the other hand, Pentecostals believe that true Christian conversion goes beyond baptism by water; for them full conversion involves other aspects of doctrine and experience, including being born again, holiness, Spirit baptism, and divine healing. They see themselves as completing the conversion experience begun by other Christian churches.

Mainstream churches have also been affronted over the practice of re-baptism in Pentecostal churches.[15] This conflict typically occurs in areas where Christians are the majority. Some Pentecostal churches are so non-ecumenical that they rebaptise not only Catholics and mainstream Protestants, but also those already baptised in other Pentecostal churches. One part of this conflict is based in different understandings of baptism. For mainstream churches, baptism is a once-only experience which marks one's permanent status as Christian. For many Pentecostals, the focus is instead on the divine encounter that occurs in baptism—an encounter so foundational that it is better to repeat than to risk deficiency in the first ritual. Baptismal repetition in the P/C churches is, then, not so problematic, for even a second or third baptism is seen as being efficacious in supporting Christian life.

The Pattern in Current Relations

Our interviews with the leaders of both mainstream and P/C churches in five large urban areas in Indonesia indicated some assumptions underlying the tensions between mainstream and P/C churches. On

---

14. Eka Darmaputera, 'Menuju Teologia Kontekstual di Indonesia,' Eka Darmaputera (Ed), *Konteks Berteologia di Indonesia*. (Jakarta: BPK Gunung Mulia, 2004), 3-4.
15. A Heuken, *Ensiklopedia Populer tentang Gereja Katolik di Indonesia* Vol.I. (Jakarta: Yayasan Cipta Loka, 1989), 88.

one hand, the mainstream churches have developed negative attitudes towards Pentecostal churches who: 'entice' the young generation to their church (causing low numbers of youth in mainstream churches), rebaptise Christians who join the Pentecostals, and target 'the best and the brightest' members of other Christian denominations for conversion. On the other hand, P/C churches perceive the mainstream churches as lacking the Holy Spirit in their services and as needing to be born again; inheriting Christianity, they say, is not enough.

Some pastors in mainstream churches view the shifting of young people to Pentecostal identities as just temporary, meaning that these young people are only seeking something new and different not found in their home churches. Afterwards, they think, when these 'new' things are no longer new, these young people may return to their home churches. But this interpretation suggests that the problem for the mainstream churches may not merely be the 'moving out' trend among the young, but also the 'moving in' trend, because those who return to their home churches will almost certainly bring with them some P/C elements. Therefore, many have suggested that mainstream churches should critically evaluate their liturgies to ensure that they are offering attractive, quality services for the young generation. In practice, this has meant that many mainstream churches are attempting to imitate the bands and lights, rock music and enthusiasm of P/C worship, at least in services for the young.

Though the dispute between the mainstream churches and P/C churches that began in the past continues today, it is somewhat reduced in scope. National Christian organisations have initiated reconciliation between the two parties. For example, the Indonesian Communion of Churches, whose majority membership is mainstream Christian, has openly embraced Pentecostals; twenty Evangelical and/or Pentecostal synods have joined the Communion. Years of this process have positively influenced how mainstream churches perceive Pentecostals/Charismatics: assumptions of heretical or fallacious teaching in the P/C movement have slowly ebbed away. As an ecumenical organisation, the Indonesian Communion of Churches strives to articulate possibilities for mainstream and P/C churches cooperating and working together both within itself and in other Evangelical/Pentecostal organisations. At the synodal level, key figures within the mainstream churches have determined their own models for, and opinions on, working with Pentecostals. In general, how mainstream churches in PGI perceive networking with Pentecostals can be divided into three categories: repugnant/negative relations, accommodative/ adaptive, and cooperative.

Repugnant or Negative Relations. Churches that find working with Pentecostals repugnant include the Protestant Christian Batak Church, *Huria Kristen Protestan Batak* (HKPB); the Kalimantan Evangelical Church, *Gereja Kalimantan Evangelis* (GKE); the Christian Church of Sumba, *Gereja Kristen Sumba* (GKS), and the Protestant Church in Moluccas, *Gereja Protestan Molu*cu (GPM). These churches are classified as traditional or ethnic churches because from their origin they incorporated one of Indonesia's particular ethnic traditions. The Protestant Christian Batak Church is rooted in North Sumatra with the Batak ethnicity as the majority. This denomination is one of the churches which has never had any association with Pentecostals. Its main objection to working with Pentecostal is mainly that many of its registered church members attend Pentecostal services.[16]

There are also other mainstream traditional churches in North Sumatra whose members are also mostly from the Batak ethnicity. One of them is the *Batak Karo* Protestant Church, *Gereja Batak Karo Protesta*n (GBKP). The relationship between the *Batak Karo* Protestant Church and the P/C churches seems very negative; the church has even organised special pastoral care for members who have joined Charismatic 'prayer groups.'[17]

Unlike these two North Sumatran mainstream churches, the Kalimantan Evangelical Church, *Gereja Kalimantan Evangelis* (GKE), is a mainstream church born in Kalimantan (Borneo). Nowadays, the dominant church in Kalimantan is no longer the Kalimantan Evangelical Church, but rather churches with Evangelical or Pentecostal backgrounds, which together claim more or less seventy denominations. As a synodal organisation, the Kalimantan Evangelical Church has established good relationships with Catholic and other denominations, including the Indonesia Bethel Church, Bethany Church, Seventh Day Adventists, and David's Tent. However, at the

---

16. Research Team of Biro Litkom PGI, *Perbandingan Potret Diri Antar-Gereja, Tantangan dan Tanggapan.* Zacharia J Ngelow, Ed (Jakarta: Biro Penelitian dan Komunikasi PGI, 2010), 55.
17. Research Team of Biro Litkom PGI, 57.

congregational level, problems regularly occur between Kalimantan Evangelical Church congregations and Pentecostals/Charismatics in terms of 'sheep stealing' (referring to accusations that Pentecostals are stealing the church's members).[18]

The Christian Church of Sumba, *Gereja Kristen Sumba* [GKS], is a mainstream traditional church on Sumba Island. Similar to the Kalimantan Evangelical Church, the Christian Church of Sumba has established good organisational relations with other churches in Sumba but encountered conflict with the Bethel Church when it began spreading its evangelism in Sumba. This conflict between them raised not only theological issues but also issues of identity. The Christian Church of Sumba is identified as a local and traditional Sumba church, while Bethel Church is characterised as an outsider (P/C) church so affiliated with the Tionghoa (persons of Chinese descent) that the local Bethel church is also called 'the Tionghoa Church.' The Tionghoa are mostly traders and relative newcomers.[19] In recent years Bethel has not been the only Pentecostal church pioneering in Sumba; there are other Pentecostal denominations as well.

In Ambon and some other islands in the Moluccas, the Protestant Church in Moluccas, *Gereja Protestan Moluccu* [GPM] has been renowned for its efforts in planting Christianity in the Moluccas for hundreds of years. The Protestant Church in Moluccas and other Christian organisations, such as the Salvation Army and the (Pentecostal) Assembly of God, have long-established partnerships that are in the main very positive. However, small conflicts began to grow between the Protestant Church in Moluccas and the Salvation Army because the latter is accused of stealing the former's church members; the Salvation Army is assumed to be looking down on the Protestant Church in Moluccas as the 'low people's church.'[20] Recently, various other P/C denominations have begun establishing their churches in Ambon, too.

Accommodative or Adaptive Approaches. Some mainstream churches at the local level have initiated diverse responses to Pentecostal development, instead of simply opposing it.

---

18. Research Team of Biro Litkom PGI, 50-51.
19. Research Team of Biro Litkom PGI, 52.
20. Research Team of Biro Litkom PGI, 60.

Implementation of a self critical attitude has led some churches to an internal evaluation that showed they had offered minimal services aimed at youth, and so should not be surprised that their youth were attracted elsewhere.

In response to the loss of their youth in the rapid development of P/C churches, some mainstream churches have now opened multiple opportunities for youth to participate in church services and service ministries based on their area of interest. For example, the Protestant Church in Western Indonesia, *Gereja Protestan di Indonesia bagian Barat* (GPIB), the Indonesia Christian Church, *Gereja Kristen Indonesia*(GKI) and the Javanese Christian Church, *Gereja Kristen Jawa* (GKJ) at the regional level have added more worship services to accommodate the creativity of their youth. While this adaptation has not been formally established as the synodal consensus, it allows regional churches to monitor and accommodate P/C trends found in their youth. The format of the new worship services tends to involve youth in prominent roles and is designed with different names, such as youth service, creative service, inclusive service, and so on. In general, those services, begun as experimental, have been creatively formatted. Their innovative liturgies have either combined traditional hymns and contemporary/pop Christian songs or rearranged traditional hymns for various musical instruments (full band or musical ensemble). These types of services accommodate elements attractive to youth such as dance, alternative lighting, rock music, and decorative elements, including costumes, multimedia, and more.

Christian popular songs are one way of accommodating youth; these songs are commonly characterised as Pentecostal songs because, in contrast, most of the mainstream churches' songs have been traditional hymns taken from the *Kidung Jemaat* (*Indonesia Church Hymns*), the *Nyanyian Kidung Baru* (*The New Song Book*), the *Pelengkap Kidung Jemaat* (*Supplement Song Book*), or the *Kidung Persekutuan Reformed Injili* (Evangelical Reform Song Book). The content of the song books is mainly hymns for organ by long dead foreign composers with lyrics translated from European languages, with some spiritual songs composed by Indonesian composers. The longstanding tradition in mainstream Christian churches has been to use these hymns, many dating to 17th and 18th century Europe and 19th and 20th century North America, in their services. The new Christian music—popular rock-type songs—is largely associated with P/C churches. However, the fact that the mainstream churches have lately introduced these popular songs into their youth services is changing the perception that these popular Christian songs are only associated with P/C churches. Increasingly these popular songs are understood as popular across Christian denominations, so that singing popular Christian songs can no longer be used as an indicator that a person is P/C, especially for youth.

The tendency to use popular song does not completely eliminate hymns from mainstream church liturgy. Part of the adaption process has been an attempt to attract and to interest people in singing traditional hymns, which are in large part carriers of Reformation theology. For example, some traditional churches allow their musicians to arrange a hymn in the *Kidung Jemaat* according to different genres of music such as jazz, pop, country music, and *keroncong* (a genre of Indonesian traditional music).

Another adaptive method on the part of mainstream churches is Serving Orientation Schools [SOM], which correspond in some ways to schools for lay ministers found in Catholic areas experiencing chronic shortages of priests. Some traditional churches have also adopted SOM to answer the needs of their churches. In P/C churches, laypersons, especially those who are being drawn into ministry, attend in order to upgrade their biblical knowledge and pastoral skills for ongoing ministry. SOM offer Bible study, basic practical theology, and discipleship training. In some traditional churches, the curriculum of SOM are adjusted to prepare laypersons with skills and knowledge in such areas as counselling, prayer, basic Christian faith, church teaching and more advanced practical theology.

Cooperative Approaches. One of the mainstream traditional churches that has built a substantial networking relationship with a Pentecostal church is the Protestant Christian Church in Bali, *Gereja Kristne Protestan Bali* (GKPB). This Protestant Christian Church in Bali synod and the International Full Gospel Fellowship-*Gereja Injili Sepenuh Indonesia* (IFGF GISI) signed a Memorandum of Understanding in 2010 to jointly develop both churches. The Protestant Christian Church in Bali is a mainstream church in the Balinese ethnic tradition, an offspring of the Christian Missionary

Alliance. The baptism of twelve Balinese on November 11, 1931 by a Christian Missionary Alliance leader is marked as the birth of the Protestant Christian Church in Bali.[21] At the national level, it is registered in the membership of the Indonesian Communion of Churches, and is also a part of the *Protestantse Kerk in Nederlands* (PKN), the Protestant Church in The Netherlands, along with more or less thirty other churches and ecumenical organisations. The International Full Gospel Fellowship of Indonesia is a P/C church begun by Indonesian students in the USA as a prayer group, and later established as an Indonesian church in 1980.[22] Among the national ecumenical organisations, the Indonesian International Full Gospel Fellowship is registered as a member of PGLII, the evangelical ecumenical association.

While the partnership between the Protestant Christian Church in Bali and the International Full Gospel Fellowship is only bilateral, it has also come to involve the Protestant Church in the Netherlands, with which the Protestant Christian Church in Bali is also associated. After seeing the importance of cooperation between mainstream churches and P/C churches in the Protestant Christian Church/ International Full Gospel Fellowship partnership, the Protestant Church in the Netherlands churches in Indonesia initiated discussions on 'sharing best practices' for youth in both P/C and mainstream churches. As reported in the *Karismatik-Indonesia* blog,[23] a live-in program was held in International Full Gospel headquarters in Lippo Karawaci, Tangerang on November 1-5, 2012, attended by twenty leaders of Protestant Church in the Netherlands congregations in Indonesia. The program aimed to build goodwill among churches so they know and understand each other well in order to build future partnerships. A steering committee was established and led by Pastor I Made Priana, secretary of the Protestant Christian Church in Bali. Even though Protestant Church in The Netherlands associate churches have not all built as strong a relationship with P/C groups as

---

21. Indonesian Communion of Churches archive - *Gereja-gereja di Indonesia 2010*. (Jakarta: PGI, 2010), 28; Karel Steenbrink, 'A Small Christian Flock in Bali,' Jan S Aritonang and Karel Steenbringk (Eds), *A History of Christianity in Indonesia*. (Leiden/Boston: Brill, 2008), 731-741.
22. Extracted from interview with pastor IFGF GISI Keluarga Allah, Jakarta. http://www.ifgf.org/index.php/content/journey (Retrieved October 2012).
23. http://kharismatik-indonesia.blogspot.com/ (Retrieved in February 2013).

has the Protestant Church in Bali, the initiative to conduct a dialogue for leaders and youth in mainstream churches with the full range of P/C churches (old Pentecostal, Charismatic, and Neo-Pentecostal) clearly signals a breakthrough. It is hoped that the initiative will build a solid foundation for future partnerships between mainstream churches and P/C churches.

An alternative approach can be seen in the partnership between Isa Almasih Church and mainstream churches. If the previous example demonstrated one way influence from the P/C movement towards mainstream churches, the Isa Almasih represents a different, almost reverse pattern. The Isa Almasih Church originated in a Pentecostal fellowship called *Sing Ling Kauw Hwee* (Holy Spirit Fellowship) which was started as prayer group in Pastor Tan Hok Tjwan's house. It then grew into a church organisation established legally on July 21, 1946.[24] The GIA's founding father, Tan Hok Tjwan, was from the Pentecostal Church in Indonesia, so Isa Almasih's theological identity is Pentecostal. After Tan Hok Tjwan passed away, however, following generations tended to implement the the typical Calvinist system of governance of the Indonesian Christian Church—the Presbyterian-Synodal system—although Isa Almasih has never formally adopted this system.[25] This development is largely due to Isa Almasih's geographical location in central Java, where the influence of the Indonesian Christian Church of Central Java is strong.[26]

The Isa Almasih Church was the first Pentecostal church to join the Indonesian Council of Churches, which it did in 1956 when it celebrated its sixth anniversary. (Now the Indonesian Council of Churches is called the Indonesian Communion of Churches.) Isa

---

24. Rijnardus A van Koij & Yam'ah A Tsalatsa, *Bermain dengan Api: Relasi antara Gereja-gereja Mainstream dan kalangan Karismatik Pentakosta*. (Jakarta: BPK Gunung Mulia, 2007), 26-28; Direktori PGI - Gereja-gereja di Indonesia 2010. (Jakarta: PGI, 2010), 33.
25. Indrawan Eleeas, *Gerakan Pentakosta Berkaitan dengan Sejarah dan Teologia Gereja Isa Almasih* (Semarang: GIA Pringgading, 2008), 172.
26. Research Team of Biro Litkom PGI, 39-40. Also see Jakub Santoja, *Memahami Perkembangan Teologia Pentakosta di Indonesia,* a paper presented at the conference 'Memahami Fenomena Kebangkitan Agama: Perkembangan Pentakosta di Indonesia', conducted by Graduate School of Center for Religious and Cross-Cultural Studies, Gadjah Mada Universitas, Yogyakarta, January 17, 2010.

Almasih nurtures good relations with the Indonesian Communion of Churches as seen from its active participation in all of the Communion's national and regional congresses. Some Isa Almasih pastors have even been appointed to strategic positions in the regional organisations of the Communion. In addition, Isa Almasih has also built good partnerships with non-P/C organisations abroad, such as the Christian Conference of Asia and the Presbyterian Church of Korea. In order to improve her human resource capacity, Isa Almasih Church sends pastors and lecturers at her theological school to study in Presbyterian Calvinist accredited institutions, such as Duta Wacana Christian University in Yogyakarta.[27] Additionally, Isa Almasih has built goodwill with other religious institutions, for example at the Peace Concert for Indonesia, *Kidung Damai untuk Indonesia* on July 13, 2010. This event was held in the parking lot of Isa Almasih Pringgading, Semarang and was attended by thousands of people from different religious backgrounds. This event was initiated by Junior Pastor Rony C Kristanto, a graduate of Duta Wacana Christian University, where he was educated in ecumenism and social responsibility as aspects of ministry.

National Christian Organisations and Government Supervision

The Indonesian government, through its Ministry of Religious Affairs, has established some General Directorates that work with specific religious institutions. The General Directorates that specifically work with Christian institutions are the *Bimas Katolik* (Catholic Guidance Body) and the *Bimas Kristen* (Christian Guidance Body). These government bodies work with national Christian organisations, namely: The Indonesian Bishops Conference, The Indonesian Communion of Churches, Indonesian Pentecostal Church Fellowship (PGPI), the Fellowship of Indonesian Evangelical Churches and Institutions (PGLII), the Indonesian Baptist Fellowship, the Salvation Army, the Seventh Day Adventist Church, and the Indonesian Orthodox Church.[28]

Christian organisations in Indonesia are identified and monitored

---

27. Research Team of Biro Litkom PGI, 39-40.
28. Indonesian Communion of Churches archive - *Gereja-gereja di Indonesia 2010*. (Jakarta: PGI, 2010), 349.

by the government with an eye toward protection and harmonisation among religions. Each national Christian organisation/synod/ecumenical body mentioned above has a different theological orientation, yet they are expected by the government—and generally do—work together toward these general goals. The Indonesian Christian Communication Forum is one such example. As the 1998 fall of the Suharto New Order government approached, religion became increasingly politicised—which in Indonesia meant that the rights and even existence of non-Muslim religions became questioned by some Muslim extremists—and many churches were vandalised and burnt. To respond to such situations, in 1997 the Indonesia Christian Communication Forum, *Forum Comunikasi Kristen Indonesia*(FKKI), was established. This forum extended across denominations and attempted to rebuild destroyed churches; it also provided assistance to victims as well as sent letters of complaint to the Indonesian President, the House of Representatives, and the United Nations, expressing abhorrence at these attempts to suppress Christianity.[29] The weakened state of the democratic governments since 1998 have necessitated the continuation of the defensive efforts of the Indonesian Christian Communication Forum and similar groups.

Almost all of the church synods in Indonesia affiliate themselves to the major ecumenical organisations, the Indonesian Communion of churches, or to the Pentecostal or evangelical associations , though a small percentage have joined Baptist, Adventist, Salvation Army, and Orthodox organisations. The following section will discuss briefly the three major ecumenican organisations.

Indonesian Communion of Churches. As mentioned above, the first name of the Indonesian Communion of Churches was the Indonesian Council of Churches, established on May 25, 1950 as an ecumenical organisation; at its 10th congress in Ambon (1984) the name was changed to the Indonesian Communion of Churches. Church fellowship in unity and catholicity became an imperative

---

29. Bambang Budijanto, 'Evangelicals and Politics in Indonesia: The Case of Surakarta,' David Halloran Lumsdaine (Ed), *Evangelical Christianity and Democracy in Asia* (New York: Oxford University Press, 2009), 163-164.

and the principal motto for the organisation. Eighty-eight synods/ denominations, chiefly mainstream, but also including twenty Evangelical and/or P/C denominations, joined the Communion.[30] As the largest ecumenical organisation in Indonesia, the Indonesian Communion of Churches is estimated to represent more or less 80% of Christians from all denominations in Indonesia.[31] Since its establishment in 1950 the Communion has become the oldest ecumenical national Christian organisation; not only does the Communion serve as the ambassador for Christians to respond to church issues in Indonesia, but it also represents Indonesian Christians to the world.

All churches in the Communion are bound to an agreement called the Five Documents of Church Unity, whose content includes a charter of trust and respect for each other (*Piagam Saling Mengakui dan Menerima*), binding on all its member churches.[32] All Pentecostal churches in the Communion are also bound to follow these regulations, including those concerning church membership transfer and baptism.[33]

The Communion is also involved in the Indonesia Religions Council, *Majelis Agama Indonesia* (MAI), whose membership consists of, in addition to the Communion of Churches, the Indonesian Bishops Conference, *Komisi Wali Gereja Indonesia*, (KWI); Indonesia Ulema Council, *Majelis Ulama Indonesia* (MUI);the Council of Hinduism Society in Indonesia, *Sekretaris Parisada Hindu Dharma Indonesia*, (PHDI); Buddhist Council of Indonesia, *Perwakilan Umat Buddha Indonesia* (WALUBI); and Confucius Supreme Council of Indonesia, *Majelis Tinggi Agama Konghucu Indonesia* (MATAKIN).

Indonesian Pentecostal Church Fellowship. The history of the Pentecostal Church Fellowship dates back to 1955 when pastors from Pentecostal churches established a forum called the Indonesian Pastors Assembly (*Persatuan Antar Pendeta-Pendeta Seluruh Indonesia*). It was the first Pentecostal organisation in Indonesia,

---

30. A list of the Indonesian Communion of Churches membership is found in *Buku Almanak Kristen Indonesia* 2010 (Jakarta: Bidang Koinonia, 2009), 20-57.
31. Indonesian Communion of Churches archive—Gereja-gereja, 2.
32. *Dokumen Keesaan Gereja, DGD-PGI, 2009-2014.* (Jakarta: PGI, 2010), 7.
33. *Dokumen Keesaan Gereja*, 122, 125.

which was then followed by other Pentecostal organisations, such as the Indonesian Pentecostal Christ Churches Partnership (*Dewan Kerjasama Gereja-Gereja Kristus Pantekosta Seluruh Indonesia*), and the Indonesian Pentecostal Fellowship (*Persekutuan Pantekosta Indonesia*). On September 14, 1979, the Pastors Assembly and the Pentecostal Fellowship held a big meeting in Surabaya where they agreed to merge the two organisations into one, named the Indonesian Pentecostal Council. After a convocation in Bogor in October 2008, the Pentecostal Council changed its name to the Indonesian Pentecostal Church Fellowship(*Persekutuan Gereja-Gereja Pantekosta Indonesia*). As of 2012, the Fellowship was comprised of 81 Pentecostal and Charismatic synods/churches. As mentioned earlier, even though the Pentecostal Fellowship invites all Pentecostal and Charismatic churches to join, it does not prevent the double membership of some P/C churches who also belong to either the Communion of Churches or the Fellowship of Indonesian Evangelical Churches and Institutions, or both.

Fellowship of Indonesian Evangelical Churches and Institutions. The original name of this fellowship was the Indonesian Evangelical Fellowship, an evangelical organisation established on July 17, 1971 in Malang, East Java. The name change was the result of a congress in 2006 which determined that the present name bestowed a clearer identity to and equality between Evangelical churches and other Evangelical organisations in Indonesia. Unlike the Communion of Churches and the Pentecostal Fellowship, whose membership is limited to church synods, this evangelical fellowship consists not only of church synods but also various other Christian organisations in Indonesia. Membership is divided into full and associate membership. Full membership is bestowed on churches and organisations that have been recognised at national congresses of the Fellowship of Evangelical Churches and Insitutions, while associate membership is for those awaiting such recognition.

In 2012, the Fellowship of Evangelical Churches and Institutions had 99 synods as members, of which 20 were P/C, and 106 evangelical organisations working in different fields. Approximately 20% of the synodal membership in PGLII is not active, and almost half of the registered Christian organisations are also inactive. In some areas, some organisations having membership in the Fellowship of

Evangelical churches and Institutions initiate prayer groups which later may develop into new churches.

Because in the last decade so many new Christian synods registered with the government, the *Bimas Kristen* (Directorate for [Protestant] Christians), the Ministry of Religious Affairs stopped the process in 2005, announcing that no new synods could form. This decision attempted to prevent the establishment of new churches resulting from internal conflict within an existing church body. Based on the data gathered by the *Bimas Kristen* in 2012, of the 323 church synods in Indonesia, an estimated 50-60% are Pentecostal-Charismatic groups. Many, especially newer, churches registered with *Bimas Kristen* have not joined any national ecumenical church organisation. After evaluating all the names recorded in the data, Bimas Kristen discovered that 30-40% of the registered synods no longer exist, most of them P/C synods. The indicators of their 'extinction' are the absence of a registration letter, annual report, and synodal statutes, as well as difficulties in finding the physical address of the churches/ organisations. For example, more often than not letters sent by the Ministry of Religious Affairs return marked 'unknown addressee.' From this data about Pentecostal-Charismatic synods, the Ministry concludes that some synods have grown rapidly while some have lost members all together. This is evidence of a great churning in the membership of P/C churches. It seems to us that the churning occurs at a number of levels: individuals leave one P/C church for another, individual churches leave one synod for another, and synods split to form new synods.

The reasons why synods prefer joining one particular ecumenical organisation instead of another are based in their historical background, similarities in theological doctrine, and practical reasons (for example, affiliation with certain organisations gives easy access to and from government). Most of the P/C churches in Indonesia affiliate themselves to the Fellowship of Pentecostal Churches or are registered in both the Pentecostal and Evangelical Fellowships. From a theological perspective, P/C theology is closer to Evangelical theology than to mainstream Protestant theology because P/C and Evangelical groups approach the bible similarly, as well as basic traditional principles of holy living. However, Evangelical groups refuse to be called Pentecostal because they say they do not emphasise

Holy Spirit Baptism or the charisms of the Holy Spirit as Pentecostals and Charismatics do.[34]

Critical Issues

As mentioned earlier, despite the clear rapprochement between many P/C churches and mainstream Christian churches in Indonesia, there are still some unsettled issues. This section discusses the issues of membership transfer and rebaptism, based on thousands of P/C member responses to a survey conducted in five big cities in Indonesia in 2010-2012 by the Center for Religious and Cross-cultural Studies at Gadjah Mada University, Yogyakarta, in conjunction with the Pentecostal and Charismatic Research Initiative at the University of Southern California University.

Membership Transfer. As is generally assumed, the significant decrease of youth attending regular church services in mainstream Christian churches is caused by their transfer to P/C churches. In the mainstream view, P/C churches are accused of 'stealing sheep' from other churches. P/C churches answer this accusation by saying that 'the sheep' come by themselves, of their own free will; they are not herded to the P/C churches.[35] There is so much movement between churches, that disputes about whose members are whose seem inevitable.

Apart from this church, are you also registered at any other churches?

Response	Number	Percent	Cumulative %
No, only this one	2944	78.5	78.5
Yes, one other church	635	16.9	95.6
More than one other church	165	4.4	100
(Missing)	4	100	
Total	3748	100	100

---

34. Talumewo, *Sejarah Gerakan Pentakosta*, (revised edition), 3. See also Jan S. Aritonang, *Berbagai Aliran di Dalam dan di Sekitar Gereja*. (Jakarta: BPK Gunung Mulya, 2003), 84.
35. Extracted from interviews with pastors from mainstream Christian and Pentecostals churches (September – November 2011).

As is clear in the above chart, responding to the question 'Apart from this church, are you also registered at any other churches?' in the survey, the majority of the 3744 respondents answered that they only belong to the current church, but 21.2% claimed to belong to two or more churches. However, when asked how many churches they had attended in the last year, the results were rather different, as can be seen in the chart below. This chart makes it clear that though almost 80% claim to only belong to one church, many worshippers (62%) in P/C churches do attend other churches—which may be either other P/C churches, or mainstream Protestant or Catholic churches—and raises the question as to what exactly church registration means, and how uniformly it is implemented at Christian churches across the board.

How many churches have you attended in the past year?

Response	Number	Percent	Cumulative %
Only this one	1438	38.4	38.4
Two	1480	39.5	78.0
Three	529	14.1	92.1
Four	117	3.1	95.2
Five or more	178	4.7	100
(Missing)	6	.2	
Total	3748	100	100

The questionnaire also asks the respondents their previous church identification. Because we had done calculations from crossing respondent age with numbers of years in this church, we were not surprised that of 3696 respondents to this question of previous religious affiliation, 43.8% had always been P/C.

Have you previously been a member of another church or religion?

Response	Number	Percent	Cumulative %
This or other Pentecostal church	1643	43.8	43.8
Catholic church	325	8.7	52.5
Non-Pentecostal Christian	1071	28.6	81.1
Muslim	147	3.9	85
Hindu	27	.7	85.7
Buddhist or Confucian	244	6.5	92.2
No other church or religion	239	6.4[36]	98.6
(Missing)	52	1.4	100
Total	3748	100	100

But what was new information was that 37% of our respondents originally came from non-Pentecostal Christian or Catholic churches—the source of the accusations of sheep stealing. Using cross tabs we determined that while at least twelve percent of the all respondents who originally belonged to a non-P/C church or religion admit to still belonging to another church or religion, the proportion is significantly higher for those coming from Catholic or non-P/C Protestant backgrounds:

---

36. In Indonesia, tribal religions are not recognised as religions, but as cultures. In order to have proper citizenship/identity papers, one must be registered as a member of one of the six recognised religions. These persons without a prior religion seem to be tribal persons, who have acquired, along with Pentecostal membership, full citizenship and identity papers.

In addition to this church, do you belong to any other church (religion)?

Previous Church or Religion	No, only this one	Yes, one other	More than one other
Pentecostal/Charismatic	81.2%	15.1%	3.7%
Non- P/C Protestant	73.4%	20.3%	4.6%
Catholic	74.2%	22%	5.2%
Muslim	87.8%	8.8%	3.4%
Buddhist	85.2%	11.6%	3.2%
Hindu	77.8%	22.2%	0.0%
Confucian	87.3%	10.9%	1.8%
Other	85.8%	13.4%	.8%

What is most interesting about the above chart is the uneven distribution of the significant number of persons who claim to belong to more than one church (religion). Given the many shifts that occur within P/C churches, it is to be expected that some persons will come to belong to one P/C church without completely severing previous membership at another, where they may still have friends and other connections. As we have seen, P/C churches and synods rise and fall; people commit to pastors who move to other churches or synods or die, prompting new church allegiances in their followers. Also, while membership in mainstream Christian and Catholic churches—as well as to a certain extent membership in other religions in Indonesia—is strongly linked to either ethnic identity or geographical location, this is not generally true of P/C churches, who claim a kind of global identity and community which can support movement between churches.

At the same time, there are about 10% *more* respondents from non-P/C Protestant Christian or Catholic backgrounds who are attending another church in addition to the one in which they were surveyed, than there are from Muslim, Buddhist, Confucian or Other backgrounds. The only background religion whose P/C members attend another church at near the rates of previously Catholic or non-P/C Protestant members is Hindu. Our speculation is that this finding may result from the very small number of former Hindus in our sample (27). It may also be the case that some of this small number of Hindu converts to P/C churches continue to attend village temples with family when they return to their home villages, especially in Bali, where Hinduism is as much or more collective cultural practice as religious practice.

This brings up one of the more interesting characteristics of P/C churches in Indonesia: their relative comfort with some of what Pentecostals in North America, Europe and Africa would term 'pagan practices'. Just as the Indonesian government has defined what are clearly tribal religions as not religions, but 'cultures', so many P/C pastors label some aspects of Confucian, Hindu, and even Muslim holiday celebrations as cultural and not religious adaptations. In this way, they resemble Indonesian Islam, which over the centuries adopted many traditional tribal customs which the major Muslim association in Indonesia defends today as Indonesian Islam, though this characterisation is challenged by the smaller modernist association, Mohammadiyah. While both Islam and P/C Christianity are exclusivist historically, in Indonesia both traditions are undoubtedly affected by the attitude of Asian religions, which do not demand the religious exclusivity typical of the Abrahamic religions.

Rebaptism. As mentioned above, P/C and mainstream churches have different theological understandings of baptism. In general, Pentecostal churches only consider immersion baptism as the legitimate baptism. In other words, any of their church members who have not received immersion baptism, even though already baptised in their previous church, need to be baptised again. In general, P/C churches also disapprove of infant baptism, and insist that the individual be able to choose baptism for him/herself, though they differ greatly as to what age they regard children as competent to make such a choice.

For the mainstream churches, baptism for both children and adults is done by sprinkling water on the baptised. Yet these churches also accept immersion baptism as legitimate. Legitimate baptism, for the mainstream churches, does not depend on how it is done, how much water is used, where it is done, or who performs it, but rather to whom the baptised are committed. As long as the baptism is done in the name of God the Father, the Son, and the Holy Spirit and witnessed by other church members, that baptism is legitimate.

Because of the Communion of Churches' agreement on respect, if any member of a P/C church registered in the Communion moves to a mainstream church in the Communion, they do not need a new baptism; their new membership is announced to other church members during a service.[37] While the reverse should also be true, the practice of re-baptism continues even within P/C churches of the Communion, and suspicion about 'sheep stealing' endures, though much more strongly concerning P/C churches outside the Communion.[38] The Communion of Churches has not conducted a thorough study evaluating how well its members adhere to the agreement on respecting other members' baptism.

When we asked our respondents about baptism, 40.5% had been baptised in their present church, 40.9% were baptised in another church, and 11.8% had been baptised in another church but rebaptised in this church, confirming accusations of rebaptism. (Almost 7% had not yet been baptised.) Though the results show that some Pentecostal churches do have re-baptism, the number rebaptised is small compared to those who came from other churches but were not rebaptised. Of the 11.8% who were baptised in other churches but rebaptised in this P/C church, it turns out that 191 (43%) came from mainstream Protestant churches, 143 (32.8%) from other P/C churches, and 57 (13.1%) from Catholic churches. Thus concerns about infant baptism or lack of immersion do not account for all the rebaptisms, since the 32.8% from other P/C churches would have all been baptised by immersion, and not as infants. Clearly, there are sometimes other concerns regulating rebaptism as well, which may be the reason that the Pentecostal Fellowship does not have an agreement among the members of its ecumenical organisation to recognise the baptism of all its member churches.

---

37. *Dokumen Keesaan Gereja*, 125.
38. Yewangoe, 'Gereja Kristen Pasundan, 42.

The absence of a baptismal consensus among P/C churches in the Fellowship of Pentecostal Churches gives each church autonomy on baptism. A P/C church—more exactly the pastor—has the right to determine whether baptism in his/her church is more legitimate than baptism conducted in other churches, including those who receive immersion baptism in other churches. Those who receive re-baptism are told the baptism they have received in their previous churches is incomplete; it requires completion with another baptismal ritual from the new church they attend. In other words, they are taught that re-baptism functions to strengthen and complete their spiritual lives. This is in addition to the standard understanding of baptism as a sign of and pre-condition for entering a new spirituality as a child of God, marking a clear division between one's old life and the new life of holiness. In many Pentecostal churches, immersion baptism is an absolute requirement for involvement in the ministries of that particular church.

Survey data from P/C churches can also be used to see how the Communion of Churches agreement of respect is implemented concerning re-baptism in P/C members of the Communion. We use Bethel Church as representative of other Pentecostal members in the Communion of Churches because it is the largest of the P/C churches in the Communion, and has the most ecumenical experience and status, as it is registered in all three national ecumental organisations –the Fellowship of Pentecostal Churches and the Evangelical Fellowship of Churches and Institutions as well as the Communion of Churches.

Five hundred forty two Bethel church members were survey respondents; 16.5% answered that they had 'received baptism from another church and were rebaptised in this current church.' In this group of rebaptised, 51.2% were from Protestant non-Pentecostal churches, 33% were from Pentecostal churches, and 15% were from Roman Catholic churches. Thus rebaptism is clearly not a synod-wide practice in the Bethel churches (since only 16.5% of members were rebaptised, while about half of members came from non-P/C churches), nor does it seem to be aimed, by the individual churches that do rebaptise, at any particular group of previous churches or baptismal practices.

Initiatives for Dialogue

Assumptions by non-Pentecostals/Charismatics that P/C churches and members are not aware of contextualised theology, interfaith dialogue, or Christian social networking—that they focus only on internal spirituality development instead of social issues—challenge relations between P/C and non-P/C Christian churches. What P/C involvement there is in social issues and politics is often viewed in terms of individual charity or a church's political agenda.[39] However, Miller and Yamamori, in writing of global Pentecostalism, state that among the diverse P/C groups, there are Progressive Pentecostals who are highly responsive to social issues round them, such as HIV/AIDS prevention programs.[40] This has also been the case in Indonesia, especially around relief efforts following the many natural disasters that regularly befall Indonesia. Some P/C churches and synods have distinguished themselves regionally for their commitment to relief work.

Apart from the challenges hampering both sides, P/C and non-P/C churches have made efforts to understand each other at the regional, national, and international level. The next part will discuss shared efforts and/or dialogues between P/C and non-Pentecostals in all levels.

Local Level. Many initiatives have been made to settle issues between Pentecostals and mainstream churches. At the local level, for example, some churches work hand in hand maintaining houses of worship. Various forums for Christians from diverse churches have been initiated by both private groups and government (eg, *Bimas Kristen*, Directorate for Christian Affairs); these forums involve various activities and goals and are attended by local P/C and mainstream churches.

The national *Bimas Kristen,* together with city councils or regency governments, established the Church Partnership Body,

---

39. Junifrius Gultom, 'Doing Theology in Context of Religious Resurgence: An Indonesian Pentecostal-Charismatic Perspective,' in *CTC Bulletin* (Chiang Mai) Vol 24, No 3 (December, 2008), 36, 41.
40. Donald E Miller and Tetsunao Yamamori, *Global Pentecostalism: The New Face of Christian Social Engagement.* (Berkeley/Los Angeles/London: University of California Press, 2007), 1-5.

Badan Kerjasama Antar Gereja (BKAG), an interdenominational organisation for churches registered in national Christian organisations. The Church Partnership Body embraces all Christian denominations but does not deal with internal church matters.[41] As a local organisation, the Church Partnership Body's main activities are coordinating Christmas and/or Easter celebrations, joint training for Sunday school teachers, offering seminars on peaceful living in diversity, and coordinating social response to natural disasters. Although the Church Partnership Body was initiated by the central government, this body also receives financial support from local governments. The church representatives in the Partnership Body are chosen from both P/C and non-P/C churches. While each locality should have its own Church Partnership Body, not all localities do as yet.

There are also efforts limited to single areas or regions. The Organisation for Interchurch Consultation, *Badan Musyawarah Antar Agama* (BAMAG) is a Christian interdenominational organisation established in Surabaya in 1975, and registered with the local government as as *ormas* (mass organisation) whose function is to establish consensus among its members, and between its members and the government and/or society.[42] Unlike the Church Partnership Body, the Organisation for Interchurch Consultation was established by its members, who come from Protestant denominations in Surabaya, whether registered or not in national ecumenical organisations. Even though some Surabaya churches have not joined this Organisation, many churches have found that they need its support, especially when they conduct major events with large crowds. To maintain harmonious interdenominational relations among churches around East Java, the Organisation for Interchurch Consultation holds a regular discussion every three months. One issue discussed during its sessions is membership shifts among Christian denominations. The Organisation usually advises churches to resolve these problems directly, but sometimes it is invited to mediate between the disputing churches, helping them to find a win-win solution.

---

41. Interview with Pastor Longgo Karosekali, chairperson of BKAG (Badan Kerjasama Antar Gereja), Medan. (Medan, 8 September 2011).
42. Interview with Eddie M Pattinasarane, chairperson of BAMAG Surabaya. (Surabaya, October 11, 2011).

The Organisation for Interchurch Consultation also routinely advises the local government to socialise its policies concerning living in religious harmony or building houses of worship—here by 'socialise,' the Organisation means 'better promote the common good.' In so doing, not only does the Organisation for Interchurch Consultation serve as the representative of Christians in local semi-governmental organisations, but it also represents the Christian voice to the Surabaya government itself. In a case when a local neighborhood rejects a plan to build a Christian house of worship, the Organisation for Interchurch Consultation is the private organisation that supports churches conducting discussions with either the local government and/or the neighborhood community. The success of the Organisation for Interchurch Consultation in Surabaya has made it a model for other churches in other places to imitate by founding similar organisations.

There are also organisations with an interreligious as well as an ecumenical membership. Such organisations are imperative for strengthening and building partnershipsnot only among churches but also between different religions within the extreme religious diversity that characterises Indonesia. The Interreligious Co-operation Body, *Badan Kerjasama Antar Umat Beragama* (BKSAUA), is an organisation in North Sulawesi that nurtures good interreligious relations. Unlike the Forum for Interreligious Harmony, *Forum Kerukunan Umat Beragama* (FKUB), the religious council established by the central government which advises local governments on issuing building permits for houses of worship, the Interreligious Co-operation Body was locally established by the provincial government with a presidium consisting of representatives of the five different religions: Christian Protestant, Christian Catholic, Islam, Hinduism and Buddhism. Located in a majority Christian area where mainstream Protestants are dominant, but with significant numbers of P/C, Evangelical and Catholic churches, the Interreligious Co-operation Body also focuses on internal relations among Christians in North Sulawesi.

There are some similar forums established in other places. In Medan, responding to the needs of unity among churches in Medan, Christians established the Prayer Fellowship of Churches in Medan, *Gereja Sekota Medan Berdoa* (GSMB) in 2002. This Prayer Fellowship was said to be open to all Christians, but thus far it appears to consist of exclusively P/C communities. Its principal activities are meetings to pray for the locality, planning social activities, and planning around permits for building houses of worship.[43]

In Solo, the local forum is called the Interchurch Body of Solo, *Badan Antar Gereja Kota Solo* (BAGKS),which focuses on building goodwill and dialogue among churches, including a dialogue between mainstream churches and P/C churches. One of its roles is to recommend representatives to join the local Forum for Interreligious Harmony, which chiefly deals with recommending to local government permits for building houses of worship. In Semarang, there is the Fellowship for Churches in Semarang, *Persekutuan Gereja-gereja Kota Semarang* (PGKS), which was established by the Semarang City Council to accommodate all churches in Semarang.[44]

All these forums, established either by government or churches, are meant to bridge and build goodwill among churches in Indonesia, and especially to mend relations between P/C churches and mainstream churches, as well as facilitate the life of all the churches in a diverse society.

National Level. At the national level, countless efforts to build understanding between P/C and mainstream churches have been made. Between 2009-2014, the Indonesian Communion of Churches and individual churches in Indonesia continued efforts to create dialogue and joint activities in cooperation with other national Christian organisations such as the Indonesian Bishops Conference, the Indonesian Pentecostal Church Fellowship, the Evangelical Fellowship of Indonesian Churches and Institutions, the Salvation Army, and many others.[45] This initiative and other efforts made by associates of the Protestant Church of The Netherlands seem to be breakthroughs toward building understanding in the future.

In addition, on October 7, 2011, representatives of a number of national organisations including the Indonesian Bishops Conference, the Communion of Churches, Fellowship of Pentecostal Churches,

---

43. Interview with Pastor David Silalahi, chairperson of GSMB (Gereja Sekota Medan Berdoa). (Medan, September 9, 2011).
44. Interview with Pastor Nathanel, GBI Gadjah Mada, Semarang. (Semarang, September 18, 2011).
45. *Dokumen Keesaan Gereja*, 59.

the Fellowship of Evangelical Churches and Institutions, the Baptist Fellowship of Indonesia, the Seventh Day Adventist Church in Indonesia and the Orthodox Church of Indonesia met in Manado and formed the Indonesian Christian Forum. This idea was reached after GCF II (Global Christian Forum II) was held in Manado on October 4-7, 2011. ICF is thus far a limited forum for pastors and leaders of each Christian group, yet it is an excellent stepping stone to respond to the need for unity among Christians, both among leaders and at the congregational level.

International Level. At the global level, all Indonesian ecumenical Christian organisations have made endeavors to establish connections within global Christianity. One of the forums and dialogues that strengthened bonds among Christians both regional and globally was the Global Christian Forum II conducted in Manado, Indonesia on October 4-7, 2011. The idea for this meeting came from Rev. Dr. Konrad Faiser, WCC Secretary General at the Eighth World Council of Churches congress in Harare, Zimbabwe in 1998, who proposed the importance of a public forum for all Christians, including non-members of the WCC.[46] The Global Christian Forum I was held in Luhuru, Kenya in 2007. As was the case at the first Global Christian Forum, the composition of GCF II in Manado consisted of half mainstream churches and half P/C and Evangelical churches, coming from Europe, North America, Africa, Asia, and Latin America.[47]

GCF II was attended by about 300 representatives from 65 countries with different Christian backgrounds including Anglican, African Churches, Charismatic, Evangelical, Roman Catholic, Orthodox, Protestant, mega-churches, and meditative communities. Christian leaders present represented twelve World Christian Communions and nine global ecumenical organisations, including the World Council of Churches, the World Evangelical Alliance, the Pentecostal World Fellowship, as well as national leaders of church fellowships, evangelical organisations, mega churches around the world, and the Pontifical Council for Promotion of Christian Unity from the Vatican, with special support from the Archbishop

---

46. *Global Christian Forum News,* 2013 Edition 02, p 2.
47. Brendan Leahy, 'Where is Ecumenism at Today?' *The Furrow*, Vol 60, No 1 (January 2009): 25-31.

of Canterbury. Leaders from The Salvation Army, Seventh Day Adventists, the Society of Friends and the Syrian Orthodox Church were also present.[48] It was this meeting in Manado that led to the establishment of the Indonesian Christian Forum (ICF) on October 7, 2011, supported by seven major national ecumenical Christian organisations in Indonesia.

To conclude, at the international level, P/C groups have received recognition as a major component of Christianity. In Indonesia, all the efforts to bridge the gap between mainstream and Pentecostal churches have been largely successful on both sides, though member shifts and re-baptism are in some places still obstacles to unity. Bilateral agreements and partnership, national and regional forums, and ecumenical organisations are imperative in creating and maintaining understanding among churches.

---

48. Global Christian Forum website. http://www.globalchristianforum.org/participants.html (Retrieved in February 2013).

Chapter Eight
Pentecostal-Muslim Relations in Indonesia: Indifference, Potential for Conflict and Prospects for Harmony

Zainal Abidin Bagir

In Indonesia, a country with a majority Muslim population (more than 200 million Muslims out of the total population of 237 million), it would not be an exaggeration to say that the growth of Pentecostalism depends rather significantly on its relations with Muslim communities. However, the existence of different majority religions in different parts of Indonesia also means that there can be more than one pattern of growth in this regard. In areas with Christian majorities, the challenge to Pentecostalism would be more likely to come from mainstream Christians, as is the case with Manado, Nusa Tenggara Timur, Papua, or Ambon. In these areas, the Pentecostals are a non-mainstream group which may not always go along with the mainstream—and its growth may be hindered because of that. While in areas with Muslim majorities, the Pentecostals are a minority which must consider Muslim sensitivities.

This chapter looks at Pentecostal relations with Muslims, especially focusing on the five areas which are the concentration of the larger research on which several chapters of this book are based. The first question is how do Muslims recognise the Pentecostals and what does it mean to study Muslim-Pentecostal relations? This chapter then starts with giving the historical-political background of the relationship of Christians in general to the state and to Muslim groups. Underneath the seemingly good relations, this is a history of mutual suspicions, ie Muslims' suspicions of aggressive Christian proselytisation ('Christianisation') and Christians' suspicion of Muslims' attempted 'Islamisation' of Indonesia. Today's problems in Muslim-Christian relations in general are to a significant extent a continuation of such mutual suspicions, but now in the context of democratisation. With regard to Muslim relations with Pentecostals, discussed in the next session, drawing mostly on the results of our research, we find that the issue of proselytisation (and, related to it, the building of churches which are suspected as vehicles or consequences of successful proselitysation) is a stumbling block that has not ceased to haunt Pentacostal relations with Muslims. While this issue applies to the relation of Muslims with Christians in general, there are a few different twists to the problem when it comes to the Pentecostals.

The whole portrait, however, cannot be simplified into a description of this stumbling block, because it is more complex. While in general this research finds a general attitude of indifference among the two parties, there are indications that a harmonious relation may be forged, despite the historically grounded tensions. There are also interesting findings related to Pentecostal social engagement and what appears to be a moral affinity with Muslims which may give us some insights in assessing whether there can be a better relationship in the future. A brief comparison with the case of Nigeria reminds us that things actually could be much worse in Indonesia, but are not. The last section will look further into the future, based on developments within Indonesian Pentecostalism.

Knowing the Pentecostals

As far as relations with Muslim communities are concerned, the history of Pentecostal/Charismatic (P/C) churches in Indonesia did not seem to diverge significantly from that of other Christian churches/denominations. The P/C movement has grown in the same historical context as other Christian churches, so its challenges were quite similar. Moreover, most Muslims, as shown by our research, could not easily distinguish P/C churches or members from other Christian groups, sometimes even from Catholics. Where it stands out is, in some cases, in its energetic or enthusiastic activities, whether in worship or proselytisation.

In general, only the old Pentecostal churches, which use 'Pentecostal' in their names, can be immediately recognised. For the Muslim respondents who can recognise other P/C churches, the use of music and loudspeakers are among the characteristics mentioned. In some places, the fast growth of the churches (in terms of its members who come to the churches—indicated by the need for larger parking space) is mentioned in comparison to smaller churches which did not attract much attention. Beyond those apparent characteristics, none of the respondents in the five cities could confidently say that they know the difference between P/C and other churches. Asked by the interviewers, they only made guesses. Suspecting that Pentecostalism is unorthodox, a respondent in Medan, for example, asked, 'Are the Pentecostals the same as Jehovah Witness?' Among a few who said that they knew the Pentecostals/Charismatics, none knew their main teachings or theology.

Some respondents who are members of the Forum for Interreligious Harmony (*Forum Kerukunan Umat Beragama—FKUB*) knew Pentecostalism from discussions among Christian representatives in the Forum. Some actually said that they only came to know that there are many denominations in Christianity after they joined the FKUB. In this Forum, which has the authority to issue a letter of recommendation for a proposed house of worship which is a requirement of getting a building license from the local (district or city level) government offices, apparently there have been quite a number of proposals from the P/C communities to build new churches.[1]

A Muslim in Surabaya, who lived close to a Bethany Church, said that he did not know anything about Pentecostal Chistianity and did not bother to know internal differences within Christianity in Indonesia. He never cooperated with them, but he was also never in conflict with them. Another Muslim, who occupies an important structural position in the Surabaya branch of Nahdhatul Ulama, the

---

1. Forums for Inter-religious Harmony (Forum Kerukunan Umat Beragama--FKUB) have gradually come into existence since 2006 in most provinces and districts in Indonesia. They are partly funded by the government (Ministry of Religious Affairs, Interior Ministry and local governments), and consist of representatives of religions in the area. Each religion has to be represented by at least one representative; beyond that the representation is proportional to the number of adherents of religions in the area, yet in its bylaws they are not supposed to reach a decision by voting. Their main task is to maintain religious harmony, but their authority mostly consists in giving recommendations to the local government on whether to issue a license to build houses of worship. The final authority in the issuance of the license lies with the local government—with an obligation for the local government to make sure that each religious community is able to perform their worship. See *Annual Report on Religious Life in Indonesia 2010*.

largest Islamic societal organisation, said that he could distinguish a Pentecostal church, but does not know the theological differences at all. However, he took notes of a particular church in Surabaya which grew very fast in the past few years, as indicated by the number of vehicles parked around the church when it holds services.

In Medan and a few other places, respondents, with the help of interviewers, could identify some Pentecostal churches as ones with more emotionally intense worship, using loud music and songs. Many of the Muslim respondents did identify the Pentecostals with louder sounds coming from the church, compared with other churches, though, drawing a parallel with mosques which use loudspeakers for broadcasting calls to prayer and sometimes for sermons as well, most local Muslim leaders interviewed said that they did not really care about the loud voices.

How Muslims identify the Pentecostal churches could be significant. But, from the other direction, how the Pentecostals look at Muslims would also be important. While identification of a Christian group as P/C may not be a central factor, it does not mean that Pentecostalism, in terms of its relation with religious others, could simply be subsumed under the large umbrella of Christianity. The higher visibility of the P/C churches sometimes does make a difference in how Muslims relate with them. Day-to-day relations seem to matter more than theology. On the other hand, Pentecostals' response to Muslims (including certain Muslim groups' political agenda) present a different picture, too. Before discussing these further, however, some historical background is necessary to understand why certain issues became more prominent in Muslims' relation with the Pentecostals/Charismatics, or, in many cases, Christians in general.

Muslim-Christian Relations and the Consequences of Democratisation

The development of the Christian churches has taken place within in the context of both official state policies on religion and the social space which constitutes the arena of Muslim-Christian encounters. Many of the contentious issues between certain Muslim and Christian groups today can only be understood by looking at the history that stretches back into the 1960s, or even to the time of Independence in 1945. Indonesian Christianity developed within the constraints of state policy on religions as well as political contestation between different religious groups and groups within the religions. The 1945 constitutional debate marked the first such encounter in the history of independent Indonesia. 1945 marked a historic political agreement between different political and religious factions on the foundations of Indonesian state. The decision was to make Indonesia a country based not on a specific religion, though the majority of Indonesians was overwhelmingly Muslim. However there was one prominent hurdle regarding the famous phrase which follows one of the five pillars (Pancasila) regarded as the foundation of Indonesian state ideology. 'The belief in one God' became the first pillar, after the controversial words ('with the obligation for Muslims to follow Islamic shari'a') were dropped. The political compromise which resulted in the dropping of this phrase was followed by certain Muslim groups' attempts to get political compensation in the years that followed.[2] It is important to understand that the contestation was not between Muslim and Christian (or other religious) groups per se. But it was also prominently between different Muslim groups, including those who are regarded as Muslims with a syncretic bent (*abangan*).

Another important historical moment was the failed *coup d'etat* which implicated the Indonesian Communist Party in 1965. The party was the third largest Communist Party in the world after Russia and China. The new regime, which was then known as the New Order regime that ruled until 1998, mobilised religious groups to fight the suspected Communists and opened a wide space for proselytisation of the allegedly atheist Communists. Successful Christian proselytisation of communists and suspected communists planted seeds of suspicion among Muslims.[3]

In 1967, an important event took place in Aceh which was repeated with much of the same arguments even today. Aceh is a majority Muslim area known for its strong Islamic identity. That year there was a rejection by some Muslim groups toward the building of a Methodist church. This quickly became a national issue which was brought to the parliament, first by a Christian member who used the argument of religious freedom to defend the church. A Muslim member of the parliament folllowed this by bringing up the issues

---

2. Nadirsyah Hosen, 'Religion and the Indonesian Constitution: A Recent Debate,' *Journal of Southeast Asian Studies* 36.3 (2005): 419–440.
3. A source which is frequently cited is Avery Willis, *Indonesian Revival: Why Two Million Came to Christ* (Pasadena, Ca: William Carey Library, 1977).

of foreign aid for religious organisations, which he said should be controlled by the government.[4] The logic underlying this quarrel was that the Christians were building churches as a way to proselytise—or at least, as an indication of successful proselytisation—and they were successful because they were helped by foreign aid. So the core of the issue was proselytisation, which was termed by the Indonesian Muslims as 'christianisation' (*kristenisasi*). Some developments that follow, especially the failure of a government-sponsored inter-religious consultation on November 1967, gave confirmation to Muslims that the Christians indeed wanted religious freedom to proselytise Muslims.[5] One point of contention which brought the consultation to an impasse was proposed restriction of proselytisation which was not accepted by the Christian delegations.[6]

This allegation of missionary works converting Muslims to Christianity remained a central theme in Muslim-Christian relations until today. The concern about possible conversion to Christianity was one of the reasons for making inter-religious marriage illegal for Muslims in the 1974 Marriage Law.(7) While religious conversion is not illegal, what could be restricted was proselytisation and foreign aid. Thus in 1979 the government officially issued such restrictions. Such a measure probably was needed to alleviate the tension, but the regulations might have also preserved, rather than defused, the mutual suspicions. Restriction of 'christianisation' would later also be one of the reasons for making inter-religious marriage (mostly this refers to couples of Muslims and non-Muslims) illegal in the 1974 Marriage Law.[7]

Indeed, it is difficult to deny that there are some Christian groups which carried out aggressive proselytisation by buying the converts (the so-called 'rice Christians') or through other means.[8] Similarly, though the idea of an Islamic state has never found majority support

---

4. Mujiburrahman, *Feeling Threatened: Muslim-Christian Relations in Indonesia's New Order* (Leiden: ISIM/Amsterdam: Amsterdam University Press, 2006), 29-38.
5. Cf Mujiburrahman, 41-48.
6. Cf Theodore van den End and Jan S.Aritonang, '1800–2005: A National Overview.' Jan S Aritonang and Karel Steenbrink, eds *A History of Christianity in Indonesia* (Leiden and Boston: Brill, 2008), 207-208.
7. Cholil, Suhadi. *Kawin Lintas Agama* (Yogyakarta: LKiS, 2006).
8. International Crisis Group. 'Indonesia: 'Christianisation' and Intolerance.' *Asia Briefing No. 114*. Jakarta/Brussels, 2010.

(as shown by the results of elections through 2009, in which Islamic political parties aspiring for more Islamic influence in the state, if not an Islamic state, never got significant votes), some *sharia*-aspiring groups managed to keep an exclusivist 'Islamisation' agenda alive. 'Christianisation' and 'Islamisation' had become symbolic tools in the political competition.

For the minority Christians in general, this created a situation of insecurity and led them to find protections wherever possible. Most Christians, as noted by Budijanto,[9] always felt that they needed to have representatives or protectors within the state system by working with the ruling or dominant party, or the government. Throughout the history of Christianity in Indonesia, 'The church's relationship to power changed little: a patron-client relationship with the Dutch colonial government, a feudalistic relationship with Soekarno, and opportunism practiced in the New Order era. The reasons varied— theological pietism, sociocultural patterns, survival strategy—but the basic attitude remained constant.'[10]

The last important historical turning point in the recent history of Indonesia is the 1998 *Reformasi*, which marked a transition to democratisation after 32 years of Soeharto's authoritarian ruling. This drastic change inevitably affected all parts of Indonesian politics, including the relation between the state and religions, as well as Muslim-Christian relations in general. Some Muslim groups, both new groups and old groups which were suppressed during the Soeharto era, consistently struggled for 'Islamisation' by attempting to influence policy making with *sharia*. An early attempt after 1998 was to insert the *sharia*-phrase back to the 1945 Constitution during its amendment (1999-2002). This controversial attempt, however, ended with another failure. Interestingly, as a matter of fact, one significant result of the Amendment was the insertion of explicit human rights articles, derived from Universal Declaration of Human Rights, including religious freedom (second amendment, 2000).

Failing in changing the Constitution, the struggle for *sharia* took a different turn. At the national level, there have been attempts to

---

9. Bambang Budijanto, 'Evangelicals and Politics in Indonesia,' in *Evangelical Christianity and Democracy in Asia*, ed David Halloran Lumsdaine. Oxford and New York: Oxford University Press, 2009.
10. Budijanto, 160.

bring certain interpretations of *shari'a* or Islamic morality to national laws, such as in the case of laws on pornography, liquor, *halal* products as well as education, with different results. What emerged more clearly was attempts to enact *shari'a*-inspired local bylaws, thanks to the ongoing decentralisation. Decentralisation is another consequence of democratisation which gives local governments from provinces down to districts more authority and autonomy from the central government. Increased local authority led to enactment of discriminative bylaws with, so far, no effective control from the central government.[11]

While debates on such laws in general were conducted in a civil, albeit polarising, manner, the main source of insecurity for Christians after the Reformasi came mainly from horizontal conflicts with certain groups in society at a time when the state has been weakened—another consequence of democratisation. The weakened state has been an issue not only with regard to Christians, but also other religious minority groups (including non-mainstream Muslim groups). The weakened state has been a factor not only with regard to religious issues, but also in cases such as corruption and environmental degradation, which became worse after 1998. The big issue here is the state's weakness vis a vis increasingly more aggressive uncivil social organisations. Several such organisations, especially those that take on a religious political agenda, could not have even existed during the previous authoritarian regime, but now claim a significant space in the public sphere. The tensions that accompanied debates on some controversial public policies were mostly between groups in society, while the state remained ambivalent and passive in many controversial cases.

At the societal level, democracy opened up space for both uncivil and civil society organisations, including progressive religious groups; in this now more crowded public space, competitions sometimes become conflicts. A significant change which impacted the Muslim-

---

11. Robert Hefner. 'Indonesia: Shari'a Politics and Democratic Tradition.' Robert Hefner, ed, *Shari'a Politics: Islamic Law and Society in the Modern World*. Indiana University Press, 2011. 146-178; Robin Bush, 'Regional Sharia Regulations in Indonesia: Anomaly or Sympton?' in Greg Fealy and Sally White, Eds, *Expressing Islam: Religious Life and Politics in Indonesia* (Singapore: Institute of Southeast Asian Studies, 2008), 174-191.

Christian relationship was the emergence of aggressive groups which in some cases use violence, such as the Defender of Islam Front (*Front Pembela Islam* or DIF). The dissension that has come up frequently concerns the building of churches. In the new transparent, democratic country this difficulty, which actually had been present since the 1960s, became much more visible. Several cases went public, widely reported by the media, and became international issues. It needs to be mentioned at the outset, however, that such problems do not affect the churches uniformly across Indonesia. Several reports on religious freedom that have appeared in the past five years or so show some such problems to be concentrated in specific areas. In general, Java, the most populous island, is where many such problems take place. As an illustration, in 2011, there were 36 cases against houses of worship, 24 of which concerned churches targeted by some Muslim groups (the others concern churches problematised by Christians of different denominations, Ahmadi mosques attacked by Muslim groups, and one mosque in Kupang protested by a group of Christians).[12] The concentration of the problems concerning houses of worship is in West Java. Yet, it has now also spread to other areas of Indonesia, including, more prominently in 2012, the forced closure of sixteen Protestant churches in a district in Aceh.[13]

What also needs to be mentioned is that those uncivil groups that are involved in attacks on churches were also in conflict with the majority moderate Muslim groups, as well as non-mainstream Muslim groups such as the Ahmadiyah, a Muslim sect considered heretical by most Muslims. Ahmadiyah had been an issue of contention for a

---

12. CRCS (Center for Religious and Cross-cultural Studies), *Laporan Tahunan Kehidupan Beragama di Indonesia (Annual Report on Religious Life in Indonesia) 2012*. Yogyakarta, Indonesia: Center for Religious and Cross-cultural Studies, Gadjah Mada University. (Available for download at http://crcs.ugm.ac.id/annual-report-top). Also, reports published by The Wahid Institute, Setara Institute, and Jakarta Christian Communication Forum give different numbers of incidents because of different methods of counting. For example, CRCS Report counts the number of houses of worship in a given year, not the number of incidents. Another source of possible inaccuracy is the limited scope of research. There were more incidents reported by different reports or media all over Indonesia, but not all of them can be verified.
13. CRCS 2013, 31, 36-39.

long time, but only recently were deliberate and highly visible attacks launched against them.

We have thus seen several issues that define the relationship between Indonesian Christians and the state as well as Muslim groups. Among the concrete issues which can be used as a measure of the relationship is the issue the building of churches, closely related to suspicion of proselytisation, and Muslim aspiration to insert *sharia* into public policies. These are some of the issues on which we questioned respondents in surveys and interviews, in addition to a few other questions on day-to-day relationship.

Points of Contention: Proselytisation and Growth of Churches

One of the Muslim respondents who is a member of the FKUB mentioned that he knew that Pentecostal churches had frequently proposed to the Forum getting a license to build new churches. For some Muslim groups, any declared need for more churches is regarded as an indication of successful proselytisation that has converted Muslims—historically a major issue in Muslim-Christian relations. In interviews with Muslin respondents one issue that emerged frequently was precisely this subject of 'christianisation.' And in spite of Muslims' general ignorance of the characteristics which distinguish Pentecostal from other Christian churches, one Muslim respondent in our research mentioned aggressiveness in proselytisation as a Pentecostal characteristic. As a matter of fact, it is not only Muslims, but mainstream, non-Pentecostal Christians who also voice their concern at what they regard as Pentecostal aggressiveness at proselytisation. Is this a fact?

The suspicion is not entirely unfounded, though we do not know for sure what actually is the magnitude. The survey results, as well as a few other sources, do show that there is a strong zeal to proselytise among the Pentecostals—though this conclusion may have to be qualified by what is meant by 'proselytisation' in this case. In our member survey, 82% of the respondents say that it is important for the church to grow its membership, and 16.3% say somewhat important. When asked whether they try to spread gospel among family members, friends or neighbors, 91.8% answer affirmatively. For most lay members, this may simply mean the obligation to spread the good news, and not necessarily systematic efforts at conversion, as suspected by some Muslim groups. The survey did not make this distinction. Some church leaders interviewed in this research openly acknowledge that proselytisation for conversion is a religious obligation. A Pentecostal author[14] regards that a positive Pentecostal contribution within Christianity is precisely its zeal to plant churches and make converts.

However, if the answer to those questions on proselytisation is regarded as an indicator of successful conversion to Pentecostalism, then the data shows that it is actually directed more to non-Pentecostal Christians rather than Muslims, as will be shown below.

The survey reveals that 43.8% of the respondents were members of the Pentecostal church for all their life; 28.6% were members of non-Pentecostal Protestant churches before they become Pentecostal, 8.7% were Catholics and 6.4% were Buddhists and only 3.9% were Muslims.

Therefore, it is not surprising that complaints regarding Pentecostal aggressive proselytisation have come from mainstream churches. As mentioned by Aritonang and Steenbrink, Pentecostal churches quite often do not respect comity, that is, in this case, 'mutual understanding not to invade the other mission or church fields.'[15] In Indonesia, the issues with Pentecostal conversion attempts may not only be related to the mainstream churches' loss of members; it may also have an impact on their relations with majority Muslims. Precisely because Muslims in general do not and cannot differentiate denominations of Christian churches, Pentecostal aggressiveness may give the impression simply of 'Christian aggressiveness.' This feeling seems to be shared by many mainstream Christians. They worry that the Pentecostals can damage—and sometimes are damaging—the good relationship and tolerance mainstream Christians have maintained with Muslims.[16] The worry actually is not only related to the issue of conversion, but to a general image of Pentecostal aggressiveness.[17]

---

14. 'A History of the Pentecostal Movement in Indonesia,' *Asian Journal of Pentecostal Studies*, 4: 1 (2001): 131-148. This is an anonymous article.
15. Jan S Aritonang and Karel Steenbrink, 'The Spectacular Growth of the Pentecostals in Indonesia,' in *A History of Christianity in Indonesia* (Leiden and Boston: Brill, 2008), 896.
16. This is also apparent in the article cited above, by Aritonang and Steenbrink (2008).
17. International Crisis Group's report (2008) has some detailed story about such incidents.

Specifically with regard to Muslims, it is difficult to assess how effective Pentecostal proselytising attempts actually are. That there are Muslims converted to Pentecostalism is difficult to deny. A prominent priest from Bethel Church (GBI), Jacob Nahuway, mentions conversion of Muslims to his church.[18] Aritonang and Steenbrink mention that several Evangelical-Pentecostal seminaries encourage their students to recruit people of other faiths from other religions as one of the requirements of completing their study;[19] this is also sometimes done through revival meetings. Our own survey reveals that among all Pentecostals, only 3.9% were Muslims. While conversion is legal in Indonesia (that is, there is only a regulation that restricts proselytisation, but no regulation about conversion), more problematic is the general impression that 'Christians are converting Muslims', or worse, that they do it in unethical, 'rice Christian' manners.

Apparently, this suspicion of aggressive proselytisation is held not only by conservative Muslims. An open-minded Muslim interfaith figure, who is close to Christian groups, complained about this in our interview. He saw that many churches had grown very quickly and aggressively before they had sufficiently strong social roots, but because they got international aid. This is an attitude which he calls, originally in Javanese, 'you have money [implicated from foreign aid], you build church'—without considering other factors. For him, it is important to first build good communication with the neighbors, which he himself tried to facilitate.

The issue of the growth of churches is a potential source of conflict, especially when it is connected with Muslims' not understanding why Christians need new churches and suspicion that the new churches are being built for growth in members resulting from conversion. In this regard, the establishment of new churches that separate themselves from their parent churches could be another source of misunderstanding. In Manado, a Muslim representative of FKUB referred to a Pentecostal representative's statement that they cannot worship in other churches. He then compared this with Muslims, whether belonging to the Muhammadiyah or Nahdhatul Ulama, the two largest Muslim organisations, who *can* worship together (he

---

18. Quoted from Adiprasetya 2011, 6
19. Aritonang and Steenbrink, 898.

also mentioned Muslims' disappointment with the Ahmadiyah who have refused to pray together with other Muslims). This comparison with the two Muslim organisations shows the difficulty for Muslims in understanding the existence of many churches or synods in the Christian case.

In Surabaya, a respondent regrets the tendency of 'too many sects in Christianity', each of which wishes to have its own church. 'This is a troubling trend,' he said. 'East Java is 97% Muslim; there are not many Christians, but there are so many churches.' Moreover, Muslims have been accused of violating human rights when they voice their disagreement with the numbers of churches. A number of respondents expressed the same feeling, but it was not shared by all. Many Muslims actually take an indifferent attitude. Another respondent in Manado, who lived close to an Old Pentecostal church said that he heard that the reason for the splitting up of churches has to do with the tithes and church assets. This was interesting, because it was confirmed by a Christian respondent from a mainstream church who said that, in a change from the past, today's growth of new churches was more often related to issues of asset management rather than theological difference.

A church that grows quickly means that it needs more facilities, including more parking space for members. Another Muslim in Manado who lived in a majority non-Muslim housing complex and was a neighbor of a Bethany church observed how the building of the church was initially protested by the people in the area. Then the building changed into a nursing home, but then it became a church again during the time of Abdurrahman Wahid's presidency, and its security was guarded by NU (Muslim) youth.[20] According to this respondent, Muslims in the area were never in conflict with the Christians, but neither did they cooperate with them. The big issue was land. There was, among other things, a lack of adequate parking space which forced the congregation to encroach on public facilities. There was also a concern that lands in the area would be bought and made into a Christian housing complex.

---

20. Abdurrahman Wahid, one of the most prominent NU leaders, was elected to become the president of Indonesia (1999-2001). He was well known as a liberal Muslim and defender of minority religions.

This seems to be one of the patterns that is repeated in different areas. A Muslim in Surabaya, who held a high position in one of the largest Islamic organisations, gave an example of a church close to his house. The building of the church in the area was initially protested and stopped because of the protests. However, when the area became a housing complex the church finally could be built again. He regretted it, but took an indifferent attitude, because 'my house is far from the church, anyway, so it doesn't disturb me.' Interestingly, the church once tried to approach the Muslim neighbors through a Christmas gathering, which was then forbidden by the leader of the church itself.

Houses of worship continue to be one of the thorny issues in inter-religious, especially Muslim-Christian, relations in Indonesia. In many cases, the tension did not always begin from suspicion of proselytisation, but rather from local politics or even business interests, yet it it was easy for it to become an issue of proselytisation, wrapped as a problem related to the lack of legal building permits. Tensions related to the building of churches sometimes end up in threats or even actual attacks. Among the P/C pastors interviewed, almost half of them said that their churches had an experience of being threatened. The real number may be higher, since several pastors of the churches which were publicly threatened in the past, denied that they had ever received threats. Using the data reported in CRCS' *Annual Report of Religious Life* from 2008 to 2010, P/C churches were *not* more likely than other churches to be attacked. But the *2011 Report* is surprising since it shows that 11 out of 25 churches which were disturbed were P/C.

Nevertheless, considering that Muslims in general could not distinguish churches' denominations, we can't say whether such attacks were deliberately targeted at the Pentecostals. What Muslims do identify is the fact that (new) Pentecostal churches tend to be more visible. This is indicated, among other things, in the use of loud music in the churches or services held in shopping malls. But even here, as shown by interviews with Muslims, not all Muslims are hostile; most tend to be indifferent.

In Surabaya, for example, a respondent considers Pentecostal services in the malls as another sign of their aggressiveness, but many other Muslim respondents are simply indifferent—they do not question whether there is a license to perform such religious services in the malls. A Muslim respondent in Jakarta imagined the function of church as *mushalla* (Muslim's place for praying which usually is smaller, not holding all regular functions of a mosque, and now exists in many shopping malls in Indonesia) and Christian worship as similar to Muslim five daily prayers. Thus, for him, just as *mushalla* in malls are needed so that Muslims who do shopping have the facility to pray, it is also good if Christians can do their worship in malls. 'They can shop and worship, so it is more practical and efficient.'

With regard to the use of loud music, though it may be a problem, many Muslim respondents similarly understood it in the same way they understand the use of loudspeakers in mosques. It may seem too excessive to have an official regulation on the use of loudspeakers in houses of worship, but this issue emerged in the national conference of FKUB in 2011. In some places what has existed is mutual agreement not to make the use of loudspeakers disturbing to the neighbors. Small though this issue may seem, a Muslim leader in Manado said that at the grassroots level, this may be a source of conflict. However, he also criticised mosques which broadcast not only the call to prayer but also supplementary prayers when it was still very early in the morning.

What we see from the member surveys and interviews with P/C as well as Muslim leaders is the sensitivity on the issue of proselytisation. Houses of worship are an issue insofar as they are related to the issue of proselytisation, and usually only after instigation by Muslim groups such as DIF. Otherwise, many Muslims seem indifferent to the growth of churches. As this issue has been present for a long time, we could not say that this is specific to Pentecostals/Charismatics. Especially looking at churches disputed by some Muslim groups, the P/C churches are not a special case. Where Pentecostals are special is in their being more visible.

A Meeting Point: Social Service

While proselytisation is a crucial issue, it does not wholly define the relation between Muslims and Pentecostals/Charismatics. This section will look at several other avenues of interaction as well as Pentecostal reactions to the presence of Muslims or the Muslim political agenda. In these cases the relationship is not actually as tense as in the case of proselytisation. Another way Muslims and

Pentecostals/Charismatics interact is through the latter's social services. In addition to that, P/C churches somehow have to respond to Muslims, including their political agendas. (When speaking of Muslims' political agendas, it is always important to remember that not all Muslims share the same agenda—history, as discussed above, showed this, and today's political landscape in Indonesia also presents very diverse and divergent political agendas of Muslims.)

From what has been gathered in this research, P/C social service in Indonesia has not been a striking feature compared with that of Indonesian mainstream churches, or P/C churches in some other countries (Miller and Yamamori, 2007). Yet one characteristic mentioned by Muslim respondents, especially those who live close to a Pentecostal church, is the church's social service. Indonesian Muslims notice P/C social service, though they do not see this as a feature which significantly defines the Pentecostal. Several Muslims interviewed were very careful in responding to the church's social service, but others are open. For a Muslim leader in Surabaya, there is nothing wrong in offering such a service or cooperating in it. In Medan, almost all Muslim respondents accept P/C social services, though they always gave a similar caveat: as long as there is no attempt to convert Muslims.

An interesting—and one should perhaps add, unlikely—story comes from Central Jakarta. In the area of Petamburan there is an Indonesian Bethel Church which has been there for a long time,[21] located quite close to the headquarters of the Defender of Islam Front (DIF). The church has been in existence since the 1970s, and many of the local Muslim children went to the Bethel schools, including Riziq Shihab, leader of the Front. Shihab is known as a firebrand preacher and was once jailed because he was held responsible for an attack by his 'Defender of Islam Army' on a group who demonstrated for tolerance, religious freedom and defending the Ahmadiyah. The DIF is notorious for its regular attacks on cafes and bars to get rid of what they regard as social vice. Some churches and non-mainstream Muslim groups, such as the Ahmadiya, have also occasionally become their targets—the former on the pretext of their having no building permit

---

21. The Indonesian Bethel Church in Petamburan was the first Bethel church in Jakarta, founded by the founder of the church, Rev HL Senduk.

for a house of worship, the latter because the group was regarded as heretical. The DIF was established not long after May 1998, when the former authoritarian regime was toppled and the transition to democracy began. The area in question is quite close to the heart of metropolitan Jakarta. Interestingly, things that become problems in other places, including the use of loudspeakers or parking space, did not become a problem here. They tried to co-exist well.

Ever since this Bethel church was established, according to the people living in the area, many of members of the church have not been from the area; a significant portion of them are of Chinese descendants. The church grew relatively fast, such that on Sundays now they offer several worship services starting at 6 AM, for general audiences: children, teenagers and adults. Muslims in the neighborhood who were interviewed could not differentiate it from a non-P/C church and did not seem to care. What matters is, according to them, that it does not try to proselytise or convert the Muslims, it offers regular social service and it is tolerant. They also mentioned that the local (Muslim) people there are tolerant—they had not objected when some lands were bought to expand the church.

Besides education, health is another service provided by the Bethel church. For a long time, many Muslim neighbors enjoyed a Bethel health service regarded as combining quality with low costs, until a government-funded public health center was established—even then many of its doctors came from the Bethel clinic. Of the Bethel health clinic, a minister of the church remarked, 'Even women in *hijab* came here.' Confirming that there is no mutual suspicion, a leader in the mosque explained that 'the service they gave is humanitarian,' not religiously-motivated for conversion. Even during the Idul Adha festival, when Muslims slaughter sheep and cows, local Muslims accept animals contributed by church members, as long as the animals are not intended as an aid from the church itself. Furthermore, Muslims who attend the mosque sometime have cooperated with the church. For example, when there was a flood in the area, mosque members and Bethel members worked together. During the general election, the Church was also used as a location for a voting booth.

The good relationship that had been maintained for many years is the reason why issues which became serious problems in other places did not become problems here. The principle mentioned several times by the people there is that there is a mutual understanding and neither party disturbs the other. The sound of church music which can be heard on the outside is tolerated because the voice from the mosque must have reached the church, too, because of the loudspeaker. 'We do our worship, they do theirs.' A neighbor said that actually when some of the nearby lands were bought, the people who sold them did not know that it was for the church, yet this did not develop into a problem. Some members of the mosque now even work as parking officers on Saturdays and Sundays when the church holds its services.

This story is very interesting, especially because it relates to the notorious militia such as the DIF. However, it does not seem to be a unique exception. In many places the situation is very similar. Most Muslims interviewed are open to cooperate with the church and become part of the church's social service, but there is almost always an added caveat: so long as there is no intention to convert Muslims.

From the P/C side, with regard to how they perceive Muslims, there is a similar impression with the way Muslims see the members of P/C churches. That is, they do not know much about Muslims, they seem to be indifferent, as long as their interests are not disturbed. The pastor in the Bethel church in Jakarta said that in general the situation is peaceful. There is no tension with the DIF, but there is not much communication with them either. Because the church there is relatively old, people working in the church know well their neighbors, many actually were childhood friends. But otherwise there is no attempt to know them better.

Another Meeting Point: Moral Affinity

An interesting finding of the survey of P/C members shows that insofar as questions about morality are concerned, there seems to be a close moral affinity with Muslims. In the interviews with the pastors, moral issues such as honesty, restriction of alcoholic beverages or even smoking are considered important. In several studies in other countries, it appears that in general the Pentecostals do pay great attention to issues of morality. One of the questions in the survey is about how often they bribe officers in taking care of documents such as ID cards, driving licenses or traffic violation tickets. Seventy percent of the P/C respondents say that they have never bribed; if this number is added with those who bribed only once, the total is almost

90%. While there is no comparative data to know the significance, we can surmise that if that is the case, considering the situation of bureaucracy in Indonesia, this is an exceptionally high percentage.

When asked about whether the government should restrict pornography, 67% said yes. This is significant, considering that the Pornography Law enacted in 2008 was the subject of very heated controversy, and a trademark of Muslim political agendas. What may even be more surprising is that 44% of respondents said that they agree on local bylaws which regulate alcoholic beverages, women's dress, etc. The reason for their support is that such bylaws protect important moral values. Other than that, 11% said that such bylaws are acceptable if they are only applied to Muslims. Only 22% said that they disagreed because the bylaws are discriminative, while 23% said that they have no opinion on this issue.

Even if the agreement could be explained by reference to the content of the bylaws which are said to protect moral values, and are regarded as important for Pentecostals too, it is surprising because such bylaws were so strongly associated with conservative Muslim political agendas. Does it mean that attention to morality issues is so very high such that it relativises for P/C members the political aspirations of Muslim conservatives? It is important to note that many mainstream Christian leaders are openly critical of the trend toward 'shari'a-inspired bylaws' as well as to the pornography law. When this survey result was conveyed to Muslim respondents, none was surprised. Some Muslims simply said that it is natural and as it should be that all religious believers should pay attention to those moral issues.

Last but not least, there is one question, formulated in a standard survey question about tolerance, on which group of people different from one's own religious tradition that one is most comfortable with. The question asks: if the teacher of your child is not a Pentecostal, with teachers of which religious group are you most comfortable or most uncomfortable? For these questions, 60% of Pentecostal respondents say that they do not have an issue with teachers from any religious group. However, when several religions are compared, it turns out that they are least comfortable with Muslim teachers, and 20% of them said that they are most uncomfortable with Muslim teachers. (The religious groups with which they are most comfortable is non-Pentecostal Christians.)

Future Relations: Dialogue and Theological Maturity?

A better assessment of Muslim-Pentecostal relations in Indonesia could be made with comparison with other countries. Unfortunately, Muslim-Pentecostal relations have not been studied widely, so there are not many choices for comparison. An exception is Nigeria.[22] Comparing the situation in Nigeria and Indonesia may be not appropriate, because of the important differences in the history of both, as well as the demographic composition. Nevertheless, if one has to made such a comparison, it is not difficult to say that the relation between Muslims and the Pentecostals in Indonesia is much better—if not for anything else, this is a reflection of the fact that Muslim-Christian conflicts in Nigeria have reached a much stronger intensity and magnitude.

In any case, there is an important similarity: the new context of democratisation. In Nigeria, the 1999 democratic experiment was quickly followed up with stronger and revitalised assertion of *shari'a* aspirations among Muslim fundamentalists, which created much higher tensions, especially in the northern states of the country.[23] In Indonesia, the 1998 democratisation also opened up space for fundamentalist Muslims, one of whose prominent agenda items is implementation of *shari'a*, which many (Muslims and non-Muslims) are worried would be discriminative.

While in local elections there have been strong temptations to use *shari'a* as a vote-getter—and conservatives in some areas were successful in enacting discriminative '*shari'a*-inspired' bylaws—this trend does not seem to be continuing.[24] In the first few years after the start of 1998 democratisation, when a number of communal conflicts between Muslims and Christians took place, there were

---

22. See Matthews A Ojo, 'Pentecostal Movements, Islam and the Contest for Public Space in Northern Nigeria.' *Islam and Christian–Muslim Relations*, 18:2 (2007): 175-188; Matthews A Ojo & Folaranmi T Lateju, 'Christian-Muslim Conflicts and Interfaith Bridge-building Efforts in Nigeria.' *The Review of Faith & International Affairs*, 8:1 (2010): 31-38; Cyril Imo, 'Evangelicals, Muslims, and Democracy: With Particular Reference to the Declaration of Sharia in Northern Nigeria.' Terence O. Ranger, Ed, *Evangelical Christianity and Democracy in Africa* (London: Oxford University Press, 2008), 37-66.
23. Imo, 38.
24. Cf Bush; Hefner.

actually similar worries that interreligious clashes would become more common. But, again, the fact is that the number of large-scale incidents of Muslim-Christian communal violence has abated. In some places, hardline Muslim groups would restrict the movement of Christians, attack churches, and use the local governments to resist the building of churches (as they also did with non-mainstream Muslims). Clashes, a few of which are described here, did happen, but the larger pattern could hardly be described as dominated by violence.

In this regard, while the portrait of a clash of fundamentalisms such as drawn by Philip Jenkins may be accurate in the case of Nigeria, Muslim-Pentecostal relations in Indonesia defies Jenkins' general description.[25] The relations between Indonesian Muslims and the Pentecostals (and to an important extent this applies to Christians in general, too) could probably be summarised in a statement from a Muslim respondent who lives close to the Bethel Church in Petamburan Jakarta, and at the same time close to the headquarter of DIF:

> Here we have our separate businesses; the church has its own business, we do too. Our neighborhood is safe, so even without a forum for inter-religious harmony, we already lived in harmony. I have lived beside the church for 70 years and there has never been a a conflict. When there is a free health service, I come. When there is a bazaar, we shop there. But I don't become a Christian. We have our own *aqida* (theological priciples), they have their own *aqida*. The issue of christianisation does not exist here. This neighborhood is their basis and our basis too.

The main principle at work here, and this is shared by many Muslim as well as Pentecostal leaders, is 'not disturbing each other.' Despite all the stories of harmonious relationships in many places, both Muslims and Pentecostals said that communication between the leaders is rare, and that there is no special forum for it.

---

25. Jenkins, Philip. *The Next Christendom : The Coming of Global Christianity*. Oxford, UK: Oxford University Press, 2002.

This is a kind of tolerance which borders on indifference but has given birth to a situation of relative harmony in many places.[26] The use of public space for church members' parking or the use of loudspeakers are examples in which a common area is used for the interest of one group, which could be tolerated. Can the communities move further than this kind of relationship? For Muslims, any further move of cooperation could only be taken after a clear boundary, whether based on fact or suspicion, is drawn: no attempt to proselytise or convert. For the Pentecostals, though there are some moral affinity with conservative Muslims, who otherwise may be the group with which they are more likely to be in conflict on issues such as building of churches and proselytisation, there has also not been much effort to engage more deeply with Muslims except for pragmatic interests.

This situation of 'harmony' may not be the ideal of a civic pluralist society. Tolerance without an attempt to know each other better, while suspicion or fear is kept at bay, could quickly degenerate into tension. In a plural society, tensions can't be avoided and disputes happen, but do not necessarily escalate into unwanted conflicts. However, this situation may be fertile soil for conflict when it is seized for the sake of local political competition, for example, which has happened a lot recently in democratising Indonesia. If one adds to this mix the vested interests of some conservative or even militant religious groups and the indifference of law enforcement, this is a volatile formula. Furthermore, the perception that Pentecostals are relatively aggressive compared to mainstream Christians may make the apparent harmony more vulnerable. Coupled with Muslims' ignorance of the difference between Protestant and even Catholic churches, suspicion could be easily generalised. Even though some Muslims benefit from Pentecostal social services, especially from the older churches, a deeply grounded suspicion is still there and partly, but significantly, defining their relationship.

---

26. Of course, this does not deny the well-documented attacks on churches, as illustrated in the second section of this chapter. While such attacks have become increasingly visible in the recent years, they do not affect all parts of Indonesia, but are concentrated in some areas in Java. Not discounting the more widespread fear which may be the effect of such attacks, the majority of Christians can still be said to be free to worship. Cf Franz Magnis-Suseno, SJ, 'Will Religious Tolerance in Indonesia Continue?' http://www.commongroundnews.org/article.php?id=30731&lan=en&sp=0 (29 November 2011).

From the Pentecostal side, Miller and Yamamori mention the emergence of what they call 'progressive Pentecostals' in some countries. The emergence of such a community could open up a better relation of Muslims with Christians, especially the Pentecostals. A more intensive social engagement may to some extent depend on softening existing suspicion, but it could also function to overcome suspicions.

Is there a possibility for 'progressive Pentecostalism' in Indonesia? This research as well as Budijanto's research in Surakarta shows that the hope lies in the younger generation of the Pentecostals. This new generation is growing up in the atmosphere of democratisation, which also shows more transparently the difficulties experienced by Christians. Budijanto's characterisation of this new Pentecostal and evangelical generation is similar to Miller and Yamamori's progressive Pentecostals. They advocate a more progressive interpretation of the Bible and are more open to civic and interfaith engagement, beyond the older generation's pragmatism that only seeks protection of themselves as minority. [27] This shift becomes more significant when it is combined with the maturing of their theology. This is the path of the Pentecostal development in the Philippines, following the mid-1980s anti-Marcos democratisation movement, which became a turning point for the church's political stand. This event helped the development of a new theology that does not strictly separate the sacred and the profane.[28]

Joas Adiprasetya uses the example of the Church of Jesus Christ (*Isa Almasih*-GIA) Pringgading, Semarang, which he sees as a unique Pentecostal example of an initiative to open to other churches and other religions and develop interfaith dialogue.[29] However, Adiprasetya sees that this opening was possible because of the central position of its leader; there is a question as to whether the Church members share this aspiration. Another point he raises is that in its doctrine, there

---

27. Budijanto, 173-175. A similar observation was made in an interview with one of the young staff of a Christian online media.
28. Miller and Yamamori, 126.
29. Joas Adiprasetya, 'Pentakostalisme di Indonesia dan Sang Lain Religius' (Pentecostalism in Indonesia and the Religious Others), forthcoming in a book on Pentecostalism published by the Center for Religious and Cross-cultural Studies, Gadjah Mada University, Yogyakarta, 2014.

is no unique Pentecostal theological construct that can adequately sustain such interfaith initiative. Interestingly, very recently (2012) the Church's Commission of Interfaith Dialogue, in cooperation with the Abdiel Theological School that it supports, published a book which is the result of a series of workshops that tried to answer this precise challenge.[30] Besides debating a Pentecostal theological foundation of interfaith dialogue, the book includes a very critical reflection by a young Pentecostal theologian, Rony C Kristanto (the editor of the book), which pointedly tries to move Pentecostalism beyond its exclusiveness to speak in the language of universal human rights for universal humanitarian concerns. Kristanto confidently says that what used to be an oxymoron—Pentecostals (considered uneducated and intolerant) and enlightened interfaith dialogue—has now started to become a reality. If this indeed becomes a reality, the next episode of the Pentecostal growth will be very interesting to observe.

---

30. Minggus M Pranoto and Rony C Kristanto, editors, *Melampaui Sekat: Pentakostalisme dan Dialog Antar Agama* (Overcoming the Barriers: Pentacostalism and Interfaith Dialogue), Komisi Diaolog Antar Agama Sinode GIA, dan eLSA, 2012.

Appendix A

Pentecostal and Charismatic Churches of
Jakarta, Yogyakarta, Surabaya, Medan and Manado
in which Our Team Observed, Interviewed Pastors
and/or Surveyed Members

The research was conducted in 2010 – 2012 in five cities by a team consisting of Christine Gudorf, Zainal Abidin Bagir, Marthen Tahun, and five other fieldworkers based in the five cities: Johanes Lengkong (Jakarta), Haryani Saptaningtyas (Yogyakarta), Ubed Abdillah (Surabaya), Agus Heru (Medan), Angie Wuysang (Manado).

[1] JAKARTA

Abbalove	Abbalove Ministry Southern Jakarta Area
AOC	Alpha Omega Community
GKTT	Gekari Kota Tanpa Tembok (GKTT)
GBAP	Gereja Bethel Apostolik & Profetik (GBAP) Bunga Bakung
GBI	Gereja Bethel Indonesia (GBI) Mawar Saron
GBI	Gereja Bethel Indonesia (GBI) Praise Revival for Jesus (PRJ)
GBI	Gereja Bethel Indonesia (GBI) 'Ebenhaezer' Wahid Hasyim
GBI	Gereja Bethel Indonesia (GBI) GLOW Fellowship Centre
GBI	Gereja Bethel Indonesia (GBI) Kerajaan Allah
GBI	Gereja Bethel Indonesia (GBI) Petamburan
GDI	Gereja Duta Injil (GDI)

GIA	Gereja Isa Almasih (GIA) Kelapa Gading
GIA	Gereja Isa Almasih (GIA) Lokaindah
GIA	Gereja Isa Almasih (GIA) Pegangsaan – Jakarta Pusat
GPdI	Gereja Pantekosta di Indonesia (GPdI) Kana – Kampung Melayu
GPdI	Gereja Pentakosta di Indonesia (GPdI) Ketapang
GSJA	Gereja Sidang Jemaat Allah (GSJA) Batu Tulis
GSJA	Gereja Sidang Jemaat Allah (GSJA) Calvary Ministry
Gereja Tiberias Indonesia	Gereja Tiberias Indonesia (GTI) Balai Sarbini
GKSI	Gereja Kristen Sangkakala Indonesia (GKSI) Betlehem
IFGF GISI	International Full Gospel Fellowship - Gereja Injil Seutuh Internasional (IFGF GISI) Keluarga Allah
JPCC	Jakarta Praise Community Church (JPCC)
MSI	Morning Star Indonesia (MSI) Kuningan Branch

[2] YOGYAKARTA, SOLO and SEMARANG

GBI	Gereja Bethel Indonesia (GBI) Bethesda Maguwoharjo
GBI	Gereja Bethel Indonesia (GBI) Aletheia
GBI	Gereja Bethel Indonesia (GBI) Keluarga Allah
GBI	Gereja Bethel Indonesia (GBI) Teleios
GBI	Gereja Bethel Indonesia (GBI) The Rock
GBI	Gereja Bethel Indonesia (GBI) Keluarga Allah Widuran, Solo
GBI	Gereja Bethel Indonesia (GBI) The seed
GBIS	Gereja Bethel Injil Sepenuh (GBIS) Kepunthon Solo
GBAP	Gereja Bethel Apostolic & Profetik (GBAP) Jemat Bunga Bakung, Solo
GIA	Gereja Isa Almasih (GIA) Kolombo
GKKI-IBC	Gereja Kasih Kristus Indonesia International Blessing Community (GKKI-IBC) Yogyakarta
GKA	Gereja Keluarga Allah (GKA) Stock Well
GKKD	Gereja Kristen Kemah Daud (GKKD)
GKT	Gereja Kristen Tabernakel (GKT)

GKT	Gereja Kristen Tabernakel (GKT) Mentari Pagi
GMS	Gereja Mawar Sharon (GMS) Yogyakarta
GPdI	Gereja Pantekosta di Indonesia (GPdI) Elim Kadipiro
GPdI	Gereja Pantekosta di Indonesia (GPdI) Hayam Wuruk
GPdI	Gereja Pantekosta di Indonesia (GPdI) Jatimulyo
GPdI	Gereja Pantekosta di Indonesia (GPdI) Sleman
GPdI	Gereja Pantekosta di Indonesia (GPDI) Sosrowijayan Hagios Family
GPT	Gereja Pentakosta Tabernakel (GPT)
GSPdI	Gereja Sidang Pentakosta di Indonesia (GSPdI)
GTJ	Gereja Tahta Jesus (GTJ)
Gereja Bethany Indonesia	Graha Bethany Ex Mataram
Gereja Bethany Indonesia	Gereja Bethany Salatiga

SEMARANG:

GBI	Gereja Bethel Indonesia (GBI) Gadjah Mada
GBT	Gereja Bethel Tabernakel (GBT) Alfa Omega Kristus Raja
IFGF GISI	International Full Gospel Fellowship – Gereja Injil Seutuh Internasional (IFGF GISI) Kasih Allah
GIA	Gereja Isa Al Masih (GIA) Pringgading
GIA	Gereja Isa Al Masih (GIA) Jemaat Dr. Cipto
JKI	Jemaat Kristen Indonesia (JKI) Injil Kerajaan

[3] SURABAYA

Gereja Bethany Indonesia	Bethany Indonesia SIER
GBI	Gereja Bethel Indonesia (GBI) Altar Filadelfia
GBI	Gereja Bethel Indonesia (GBI) Diaspora
GBI	Gereja Bethel Indonesia (GBI) Graha Famili
GBI	Gereja Bethel Indonesia (GBI) House of Miracle (HoM)
GBI	Gereja Bethel Indonesia (GBI) Rehobot

GBI	Gereja Bethel Indonesia (GBI) ROCK Plaza Marina
GBI	Gereja Bethel Indonesia (GBI) ROCK Satelit Atlas
GBT	Gereja Bethel Tabernakel (GBT) Air Hayat
GBT	Gereja Bethel Tabernakel (GBT) Pelangi Kasih
GBT	Gereja Bethel Tabernakel (GBT) Kristus
Gereja Bethany Indonesia	Gereja Bethany Indonesia 'Family Blessing' Wiyung
GBdI	Gereja Bethany di Indonesia (GBdI)
Gereja Bethany Indonesia	Gereja Bethany Indonesia 'Puncak Permai'
Gereja Bethany Indonesia	Gereja Bethany Indonesia 'Sumur Welut'
Gereja Bethany Indonesia	Gereja Bethany Indonesia Pusat Surabaya
Gereja Bethany Indonesia	Gereja Bethany Pakuwon Trade Center/Pitstop Transform Church (PTC)
GBI	Gereja Bethel Indonesia (GBI) ROCK (Representative of Christ Kingdom)
GET	Gereja Elim Tabernakel (GET)
GKKA	Gereja Kasih Karunia Allah (GKKA)
MDC	Gereja Masa Depan Cerah (MDC)
GMS	Gereja Mawar Sharon (GMS)
GPT	Gereja Pantecosta Tabernakel (GPT) 'Kristus Penolong'
GPT	Gereja Pantakosta Tabernakel (GPT) 'Manyar Tegal'
GPPS	Gereja Pentakosta Pusat Surabaya (GPPS)
GMS	Gereja Satu Jam Saja-GBT Mawar Saron-Gereja Menara Kota
GSJA	Gereja Sidang Jema'at Allah (GSJA) 'Imanuel'-Wiyung
GSJA	Gereja Sidang Jemaat Allah (GSJA) 'Anugerah'
GSJA	Gereja Sidang Jemaat Allah (GSJA) Kristus Raja
GSJPdI	Gereja Sidang Jemaat Pantekosta di Indonesia (GSJPdI) 'Adityawarman'
GSJPdI	Gereja Sidang Jemaat Pentakosta di Indonesia (GSJPdI) 'Baetisda'
GTI	Gereja Tabernakel Indonesia

GUPdI	Gereja Utusan Pentakosta di Indonesia (GUPdI)
GPdI	Gereja Pantekosta di Indonesia (GPdI) Alfa Omega
GPdI	Gereja Pantekosta di Indonesia (GPdI) Efrata Perum Pratama
GPdI	Gereja Pantekosta di Indonesia (GPdI) Jemaat CORNELIUS
GPdI	Gereja Pantekosta di Indonesia (GPdI) Victory
IFGF GISI	International Full Gospel Fellowship - Gereja Injil Seutuh Internasional (IFGF GISI) CENTER
IFGF GISI	International Full Gospel Fellowship – Gereja Injil Seutuh Internasional (IFGF GISI) Imamat Radjani
IFGF GISI	International Full Gospel Fellowship – Gereja Injil Seutuh Internasional (IFGF GISI) Satelit Kenjeran
IFGF GISI	International Full Gospel Fellowship – Gereja Injil Seutuh Internasional (IFGF GISI) Perum Babatan Mukti
MSC	Morning Star Church (MSC)

[4] MEDAN

CCA	Church of Christians Assembly (CCA)
GPdI	Gereja Pantekosta di Indonesia (GPdI) Elsaddai
GBI Anthiokhia	Gereja Berita Injil 'GBI Anthiokhia' Medan
Gereja Bethany Indonesia Setia Budi	Gereja Betanny Indonesia Yerusalem Baru Cabang
Gereja Bethany Indonesia Simalingkar	Gereja Betanny Indonesia Yerusalem Baru Ranting
Gereja Bethany Indonesia	Gereja Bethany Corner Stone
Gereja Bethany Indonesia	Gereja Bethany Indonesia Yerusalem Baru Medan
GBI	Gereja Bethel Indonesia (GBI) 'Immanuel'
GBI	Gereja Bethel Indonesia (GBI) AVIA Mandarin service
GBI	Gereja Bethel Indonesia (GBI) Bukit Zaitun
GBI	Gereja Bethel Indonesia (GBI) Medan Plasa

GBI	Gereja Bethel Indonesia (GBI) Sie Wampu
GBI	Gereja Bethel Indonesia (GBI) Sumber
GBI	Gereja Bethel Indonesia (GBI) Sunggal
GBI	Gereja Bethel Indonesia (GBI) Tiberias
GEKI	Gereja Elim Kristen Indonesia (GEKI)
GKII	Gereja Kemenangan Iman Indonesia (GKII)
GKB	Gereja Kristen Baithani (GKB)
GK Bersinar	Gereja Kristen Bersinar (GK Bersinar)
GKMI	Gereja Kristen Maranatha Indonesia (GKMI)
GKPB	Gereja Kristen Perjanjian Baru (GKPB) Masa Depan Cerah
GKSI	Gereja Kristen Sangkala Indonesia (GKSI)
GMS	Gereja Mawar Saron (GMS) My Home
GPdI	Gereja Pantekosta di Indonesia (GPdI) Ebenhaeser
GPdI	Gereja Pantekosta di Indonesia (GPdI) Filadelfia
GPdI	Gereja Pantekosta di Indonesia (GPdI) Jemaat Maranatha
GPPS	Gereja Pantekosta Pusat Surabaya (GPPS)
GPT	Gereja Pantekosta Tabernakel (GPT) Kristus
GPT	Gereja Pantekosta Tabernakel (GPT) Rehobot
GPI	Gereja Penyebaran Injil (GPI)
GESBA	Gereja Segala Bangsa (GSB)
GSJA	Gereja Sidang Jemaat Allah (GSJA) Anugerah
GSJA	Gereja Sidang Jemaat Allah (GSJA) CWS
GSJA	Gereja Sidang Jemaat Allah (GSJA) Tanjung Sari
GSYI	Gereja Sungai Yordan Indonesia (GSYI)
GTdI	Gereja Tuhan di Indonesia (GTdI)
IRC	Indonesia Revival Church (IRC)
IFGF GISI	International Full Gospel Fellowship – Gereja Injil Seutuh Internasional (IFGF GISI) Jl. Monginsidi Medan
IFGF GISI	International Full Gospel Fellowship - Gereja Injil Seutuh Internasional (IFGF GISI) Grand Aston
RPC	The Royal Priesthood Community (RPC)

[5] MANADO

Gereja Bethany Indonesia	Gereja Bethany Indonesia Jemaat Betania
Gereja Bethany Indonesia	Gereja Bethany Indonesia Jemaat House of Joy
GBI	Gereja Bethel Indonesia (GBI) Anugerah
GBI	Gereja Bethel Indonesia (GBI) City Worship
GBI	Gereja Bethel Indonesia (GBI) Gilgal Ministries
GBI	Gereja Bethel Indonesia (GBI) ROCK
GBI	Gereja Bethel Indonesia (GBI) Shower of Blessing
GBI	Gereja Bethel Indonesia (GBI) Sion Zebaoth
GBI	Gereja Bethel Indonesia (GBI) Jemaat Jehuda, Manado
GBI	Gereja Bethel Indonesia (GBI) Tanjung Batu
GGP	Gereja Gerakan Pentakosta (GGP) Pinksterbeweging
GPdI	Gereja Pantekosta di Indonesia (GPdI) Berea
GPdI	Gereja Pantekosta di Indonesia (GPdI) Jemaat Imanuel
GPdI	Gereja Pantekosta di Indonesia (GPdI) Jemaat Karmel
GPdI	Gereja Pantekosta di Indonesia (GPdI) Jemaat Kineret
GPdI	Gereja Pantekosta di Indonesia (GPdI) Jemaat Hosana, Manado
GPdI	Gereja Pantekosta di Indonesia (GPdI) Jemaat Kuranga
GPPS	Gereja Pantekosta Pusat Surabaya (GPPS) Betlehem
GPT	Gereja Pantekosta Tabernakel (GPT) Filadelfia
GPT	Gereja Pantekosta Tabernakel (GPT) Jemaat Bukit Hermon
GPT	Gereja Pantekosta Tabernakel (GPT) Kristus Gembala
GSPdI	Gereja Sidang Pantekosta di Indonesia (GSPdI) Tomohon
GESBA	Gereja Segala Bangsa (GESBA) Jemaat Koya

GSJA	Gereja Sidang-Sidang Jemaat Allah (GSJA) Agape
Gereja Tiberias Indonesia	Gereja Tiberias Indonesia Manado
Gereja Tiberias Indonesia	Gereja Tiberias Indonesia Tomohon
MSI	Morning Star Indonesia: A Generational Church (MSI) Manado

Appendix B

The Member Survey

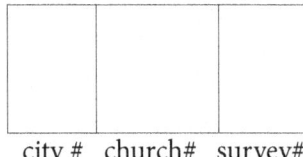

Introduction and contact   city #   church#   survey#

I. Would you describe yourself as Pentecostal, Charismatic, Evangelical, or Other?
   1. Pentecostal 2. Charismatic 3. Pentecostal and Charismatic
   4. Evangelical 5. Other

II. Your age (recoded)
    1. 15-19   2. 20-29   3. 30-39   4. 40-49   5. 50+

III. Your sex
     1. Male   2. Female

IV. How long have you lived in this city?
    1. Since birth   2. Less than five years   3. 5-10 years
    4. 11-15 years   5. 15+ years

V. Do you have any ancestry from the following groups?
   1. No   2. European   3. American   4. Indian   5. Chinese
   6. Middle Eastern   7. Other non-Indonesian areas

VI. Marital Status
    1. Married   2. Single   3. Divorced

VII. What is the highest level of education you have?
1. No certificate or elementary level   2. junior high school certificate   3. senior high school certificate   4. associate degree   5. university degree   6. postgraduate degree

VIII. Are you employed?
1. Yes   2. No   3. Student

IX. Your total household or parental income is closest to which of the following
1. equal to or less than MW   2. 1-1.5 MW   3. 2-2.5 MW   4. 2-2.5 MW.   5. 3-5 MW   6. 6-10 MW   7. 11+ MW

X. Are you registered in this church?
1. Yes   2. No

XI. How long have you attended this church?
1. Visitor (less than 6 months)   2. 6 months- 1 year   3. 1-3 years   4. 3-5 years   5. 6-10 years   6. 11+ years   7. All my life

XII. If you are married, is your spouse a member of this church?
1. Yes   2. No   3. Not married

XIII. How many members of your family of origin belong to this or a similar church?
1. All my family   2. Most of my family   3. Some of my family   4. None of my family

XIV. Are you a member of any other church or religion besides this one?
1. No, only this one   2. Yes, one other   3. More than one other

XV. How many different churches did you attend in the previous year?
1. Only this one   2. 2   3. 3   4. 4   5. 5 or more

XVI. If you belonged to another church or religion before this one, which of the following categories comes closest to describing it?
1. Pentecostal 2. Catholic 3. Non-Pentecostal Christian
4. Hindu 5. Muslim 6. Buddhist 7. Confucian
8. No other church/religion

XVII. Do you practice any elements of other religious traditions (eg, yoga, devotion to Mary or saints)
a. Yes b. No

Indicate which of the following are important in attracting you to, or keeping you in, this church:

XVIII.	preaching	1. Yes 2. No
XIX.	support from the church community	1. Yes 2. No
XX.	access to healing and miracles	1. Yes 2. No
XXI.	opportunity to exercise leadership	1. Yes 2. No
XXII.	influence of spouse or friends	1. Yes 2. No
XXIII.	lively music	1. Yes 2. No
XXIV.	fellowship	1. Yes 2. No

XXV. Have you encountered any hostility or prejudice in others as a result of your membership in this church?
1. No, none   2. Yes, from family members
3. from neighbors   4. from local officials
5. from members of other religions
6. from members of other churches

XXVI. About how often do you attend church services or other church programs at this church?
1. Three or more times a week   2. Twice a week
3. Once a week   4. Two or three times a month
5. Once a month or less

XXVII. Which of the following statements describes you?
1. I am not baptised   2. I was baptised in this church
3. I was baptised in another church
4. I was baptised in another church and later rebaptised

XXVIII. Do you belong to any ministry or service group in your church (choir, home visitors, youth group, cell group, bible study group, etc)?
1. Yes, as a member   2. Yes, as a leader   3. No
4. Not now, but in the past   5. Not now, but would like to

XXIX. Do you receive any material support from your church or its members?
1. No   2. Not now, but yes in the past   3. Yes

If you have been baptised in the Holy Spirit, did you receive any of the following gifts?

XXX.	I have been baptised in the Holy Spirit	1. Yes 2. No
XXXI.	Speaking in tongues	1. Yes 2. No
XXXII.	Power to interpret/understand tongues	1. Yes 2. No
XXXIII.	Prophecy	1. Yes 2. No
XXXIV.	Was healed or enabled to heal others	1. Yes 2. No
XXXV.	Enabled to exorcise demons/evil spirits	1. Yes 2. No
XXXVI.	Enabled to preach	1. Yes 2. No
XXXVII.	Given other gifts	1. Yes 2. No

If you have been baptised in the Holy Spirit, how did it affect you? (Others, do not answer)

XXXVIII.	Gave me strength to keep going	1.Yes 2. No
XXXIX.	Gave me hope for the future	1.Yes 2. No
XL.	Made me feel forgiven	1.Yes 2. No
XLI.	Made me feel God's love	1.Yes 2. No
XLII.	Healed me, made me whole	1.Yes 2. No
XLIII.	Made me more successful	1.Yes 2. No

XLIV. In this church:
1. only men can be helping, junior or senior pastors
2. only men can be junior or senior pastors
3. only men can be senior pastors
4. Both men and women can hold all positions, including pastor

XLV.   In this church:
1. there are no limitations on women's service
2. both men and women can preach, but only men lead communion services
3. women only work under men's supervision
4. women's ministry is limited to serving women

XLVI.   This church teaches that in the home
1. men are the heads of household, who love and care for women and children
2. men and women are equal partners in decision-making and parenting
3. Mothers have principle care for children
4. this church does not have a clear teaching on this

XLVII.   Have you attended a healing service in the last year?
1. Yes   2. No

XLVIII.   Have you or a member of your family been healed by a church service?
1. Yes   2. No

XLIX.   Do you believe that if you have true faith you will become more prosperous?
1. Yes, always   2. Yes, most of the time   3. Yes, sometime
4. No, I doubt

L.   How accepting of your ethnic or cultural heritage is this church?
1. Very   2. Some   3. A little   4. Not very

LI.   Do you think the government should restrict pornography?
1. Yes   2. No   3. I don't know

LII.   What is your attitude toward shari'a-inspired local laws? (regulations on alcohol, women's modesty, etc)
1. I strongly disagree because this is discrimination
2. I agree, so long as it only affects Muslims
3. I agree because it protects important moral values
4. I don't have an opinion

LIII. How serious a sin do you think the bribery is?
1. Serious for both takers and givers
2. Serious for takers, less serious for givers
3. Possibly not so serious for either takers or givers, depending on circumstances
4. Not clear that bribery is sinful

LIV. If the teacher of your child were not Pentecostal, with which following groups would you feel MOST comfortable as his/her teacher?
1. Non-Pentecostal Christians   2. Catholics   3. Muslims
4. Buddhists/Hindus/Confucians   5. No problem with any

LV. I f the teacher of your child were not Pentecostal/Charismatic, with which of the following groups would you feel LEAST comfortable as his/her teacher?
1. Non-Pentecostal Christians   2. Catholics   3. Muslims
4. Buddhist/Hindu/Confucian   5. No problem with any

LVI. How important do you think it is for this church to grow its membership?
1. Very important   2. Somewhat important
3. Not important

LVII. Are you involved in spreading the gospel?
1. Yes   2. No

LVIII. Do you think it is important to have a Christian party to represent your political views?
1. Very important   2. Somewhat important
3. Not important   4. I don't know

LIX. How does this church help you in the process of political elections?
1. it provides a variety of information
2. it guides me on issues relevant to religion
3. it suggests particular candidates or parties
4. it does not speak of politics

Appendix C

Frequencies for Member Survey

City

		Frequency	Percent	Valid Percent	Cumulative Percent
Valid	Jakarta	985	26.3	26.3	26.3
	Yogyakarta	775	20.7	20.7	47.0
	Surabaya	563	15.0	15.0	62.0
	Medan	658	17.6	17.6	79.5
	Manado	767	20.5	20.5	100.0
	Total	3748	100.0	100.0	

Church

		Frequency	Percent	Valid Percent	Cumulative Percent
Valid	1	66	1.8	1.8	1.8
	2	189	5.0	5.0	6.8
	3	35	.9	.9	7.7
	4	56	1.5	1.5	9.2
	5	130	3.5	3.5	12.7
	6	68	1.8	1.8	14.5
	7	50	1.3	1.3	15.8
	8	15	.4	.4	16.2
	9	59	1.6	1.6	17.8
	10	98	2.6	2.6	20.4
	11	366	9.8	9.8	30.2
	12	159	4.2	4.2	34.4
	13	174	4.6	4.6	39.1
	14	257	6.9	6.9	45.9

	Frequency	Percent	Valid Percent	Cumulative Percent
15	57	1.5	1.5	47.5
16	115	3.1	3.1	50.5
17	131	3.5	3.5	54.0
18	155	4.1	4.1	58.2
19	150	4.0	4.0	62.2
20	293	7.8	7.8	70.0
21	84	2.2	2.2	72.2
22	58	1.5	1.5	73.8
23	99	2.6	2.6	76.4
24	20	.5	.5	76.9
25	192	5.1	5.1	82.1
26	92	2.5	2.5	84.5
27	16	.4	.4	85.0
28	89	2.4	2.4	87.3
29	14	.4	.4	87.7
31	55	1.5	1.5	89.2
32	36	1.0	1.0	90.1
33	44	1.2	1.2	91.3
34	36	1.0	1.0	92.3
35	57	1.5	1.5	93.8
36	63	1.7	1.7	95.5
37	42	1.1	1.1	96.6
38	67	1.8	1.8	98.4
39	29	.8	.8	99.1
41	12	.3	.3	99.5
43	20	.5	.5	100.0
Total	3748	100.0	100.0	

How would you describe your religious identity?

		Frequency	Percent	Valid Percent	Cumulative Percent
Valid	Pentecostal	1153	30.8	30.9	30.9
	Charismatic	1180	31.5	31.6	62.4
	Both, Pentecostal and Charismatic	997	26.6	86.7	89.1
	Evangelical	149	4.0	4.0	93.1
	Other	258	6.9	6.9	100.0
	Total	3737	99.7	100.0	
	Missing	11	.3		
Total		3748	100.0		

Your sex?

		Frequency	Percent	Valid Percent	Cumulative Percent
Valid	Jakarta	985	26.3	26.3	26.3
	Yogyakarta	775	20.7	20.7	47.0
	Surabaya	563	15.0	15.0	62.0
	Medan	658	17.6	17.6	79.5
	Manado	767	20.5	20.5	100.0
	Total	3748	100.0	100.0	

How long have you lived in this city?

		Frequency	Percent	Valid Percent	Cumulative Percent
Valid	From birth	1422	37.9	38.0	38.0
	Less than 5 years	692	18.5	18.5	56.4
	5-10 years	447	11.9	11.9	68.4
	11-15 years	306	8.2	8.2	76.6
	15+	878	23.4	23.4	100.0
	Total	3745	99.9	100.0	
	Missing	3	.1		
Total		3748	100.0		

Do you have any ancestry from the following groups/areas?

		Frequency	Percent	Valid Percent	Cumulative Percent
Valid	No, Only Indonesia	2135	57.0	57.1	57.1
	Europe	55	1.5	1.5	58.6
	America	19	.5	.5	59.1
	India	24	.6	.6	59.7
	China	1272	33.9	34.0	93.7
	Middle East	20	.5	.5	94.3
	Mixed	206	5.5	5.5	99.8
	None of the above	8	.2	.2	100.0
	Total	3739	99.8	100.0	
Missing	System	9	.2		
Total		3748	100.0		

Your marital status?

		Frequency	Percent	Valid Percent	Cumulative Percent
Valid	Married	1844	49.2	49.2	49.2
	Single	1850	49.4	49.4	98.6
	Divorced	54	1.4	1.4	100.0
	Total	3748	100.0	100.0	

What is the highest level of education you have attained thus far?

		Frequency	Percent	Valid Percent	Cumulative Percent
Valid	No certificate or elementary school	202	5.4	5.4	5.4
	Jr HS certificate	528	14.1	14.1	19.5
	Sr HS certificate	1580	42.2	42.2	61.7
	Associate's degree	373	10.0	10.0	71.6
	BA/BS degree	951	25.4	25.4	97.0
	Post Graduate degree	110	2.9	2.9	100.0
	51	1	.0	.0	100.0
	Total	3745	99.9	100.0	
Missing	System	3	.1		
Total		3748	100.0		

Are you employed?

		Frequency	Percent	Valid Percent	Cumulative Percent
Valid	Yes	2286	61.0	61.0	61.0
	No	1461	39.0	39.0	100.0
	4	1	.0	.0	100.0
	Total	3748	100.0	100.0	

What is your average monthly household income? (in terms of the minimum wage)?

		Frequency	Percent	Valid Percent	Cumulative Percent
Valid	Equal or less than mw	654	17.4	17.8	17.8
	1-1.5 X mw	478	12.8	13.0	30.8
	1.5-2 X mw	505	13.5	13.7	44.5
	2-2.5 X mw	313	8.4	8.5	53.1
	2.5-3 X mw	355	9.5	9.7	62.7
	3-5 X mw	351	9.4	9.6	72.3
	5-10 X mw	404	10.8	11.0	83.3
	11+ X mw	37	1.0	1.0	84.3
	Not sure	578	15.4	15.7	100.0
	Total	3675	98.1	100.0	
Missing	System	73	1.9		
Total		3748	100.0		

Are you registered in this church?

		Frequency	Percent	Valid Percent	Cumulative Percent
Valid	Yes	3380	90.2	90.3	90.3
	No	360	9.6	9.6	99.9
	3	1	.0	.0	99.9
	7	2	.1	.1	100.0
	Total	3743	99.9	100.0	
Missing System		5	.1		
Total		3748	100.0		

How long have you belonged to this church?

		Frequency	Percent	Valid Percent	Cumulative Percent
Valid	Visitor, not member	336	9.0	9.0	9.0
	6 months to one year	310	8.3	8.3	17.3
	2-3 years	657	17.5	17.5	34.8
	4-5 years	556	14.8	14.9	49.7
	6-10 years	552	14.7	14.7	64.4
	11+ years	718	19.2	19.2	83.6
	All my life	615	16.4	16.4	100.0
	Total	3744	99.9	100.0	
Missing	System	4	.1		
Total		3748	100.0		

If you are married, is your spouse a member of this church?

		Frequency	Percent	Valid Percent	Cumulative Percent
Valid	Yes	2619	69.9	70.4	70.4
	No	476	12.7	12.8	83.2
	Not Married	623	16.6	16.8	100.0
	Total	3719	99.2	100.0	
	Missing	29	.8		
	3748	100.0			

How many members of your family of origin are members of this or a similar church?

		Frequency	Percent	Valid Percent	Cumulative Percent
Valid	All my family	1246	33.2	33.3	33.3
	Most of my family	666	17.8	17.8	51.0
	Some of my family	1081	28.8	28.9	79.9
	None of my family	753	20.1	20.1	100.0
	Total	3746	99.9	100.0	
Missing	System	2	.1		
Total		3748	100.0		

Do you belong to any other church?

		Frequency	Percent	Valid Percent	Cumulative Percent
Valid	No, only this one	2944	78.5	78.6	78.6
	Yes, one other	635	16.9	17.0	95.6
	More than one other	163	4.3	4.4	99.9
	4	1	.0	.0	100.0
	33	1	.0	.0	100.0
	Total	3744	99.9	100.0	
Missing	System	4	.1		
Total		3748	100.0		

How many different churches have you attended in the past year?

		Frequency	Percent	Valid Percent	Cumulative Percent
Valid	Only this one	1438	38.4	38.4	38.4
	2	1480	39.5	39.6	78.0
	3	529	14.1	14.1	92.1
	4	117	3.1	3.1	95.2
	5+	178	4.7	4.8	100.0
	Total	3742	99.8	100.0	
Missing	System	6	.2		
Total		3748	100.0		

If you belonged to another church or religion before this one, which of the following categories comes closest to describing it?

		Frequency	Percent	Valid Percent	Cumulative Percent
Valid	Other Pentecostal church	1643	43.8	44.5	44.5
	Catholic	325	8.7	8.8	53.2
	Non-Pentecostal Christian	1071	28.6	29.0	82.2
	Muslim	147	3.9	4.0	86.2
	Hindu	27	.7	.7	86.9
	Buddhist	189	5.0	5.1	92.0
	Confucian	55	1.5	1.5	93.5
	No other ch/rel	239	6.4	6.5	100.0
	Total	3696	98.6	100.0	
Missing	System	52	1.4		
Total		3748	100.0		

Do you practice any elements of other religious traditions (eg, yoga, devotion to Mary or saints)?

		Frequency	Percent	Valid Percent	Cumulative Percent
Valid	Yes	1163	31.0	31.0	31.0
	No	2581	68.9	68.9	99.9
	3	2	.1	.1	100.0
	Total	3746	99.9	100.0	
Missing	System	2	.1		
Total		3748	100.0		

How important was the preaching in attracting you to, or maintaining you in, this church?

		Frequency	Percent	Valid Percent	Cumulative Percent
Valid	Extremely important	2108	56.2	56.4	56.4
	Somewhat important	739	19.7	19.8	76.1
	No opinion either way	465	12.4	12.4	88.6
	Somewhat unimportant	195	5.2	5.2	93.8
	Not important at all	233	6.2	6.2	100.0
	Total	3740	99.8	100.0	
Missing	System	8	.2		
Total		3748	100.0		

How important was the possibility of support in attracting you to, or maintaining you in, this church?

		Frequency	Percent	Valid Percent	Cumulative Percent
Valid	Extremely important	1612	43.0	43.1	43.1
	Somewhat important	995	26.5	26.6	69.7
	No opinion either way	690	18.4	18.5	88.2
	Somewhat unimportant	228	6.1	6.1	94.3
	Not important at all	214	5.7	5.7	100.0
	Total	3739	99.8	100.0	
Missing	System	9	.2		
Total		3748	100.0		

How important was healing in attracting you to, or maintaining you in, this church?

		Frequency	Percent	Valid Percent	Cumulative Percent
Valid	Extremely important	1314	35.1	35.3	35.3
	Somewhat important	984	26.3	26.4	61.7
	No opinion either way	956	25.5	25.7	87.3
	Somewhat unimportant	273	7.3	7.3	94.7
	Not important at all	199	5.3	5.3	100.0
	Total	3726	99.4	100.0	
Missing	System	22	.6		
Total		3748	100.0		

How important were leadership possibilities in attracting you to, or maintaining you in, this church?

		Frequency	Percent	Valid Percent	Cumulative Percent
Valid	Extremely important	1120	29.9	30.1	30.1
	Somewhat important	1021	27.2	27.4	57.5
	No opinion either way	1000	26.7	26.8	84.3
	Somewhat unimportant	340	9.1	9.1	93.4
	Not important at all	245	6.5	6.6	100.0
	Total	3726	99.4	100.0	
Missing	System	22	.6		
Total		3748	100.0		

How important were spouse or friends in attracting you to, or maintaining you in, this church?

		Frequency	Percent	Valid Percent	Cumulative Percent
Valid	Extremely important	898	24.0	24.1	24.1
	Somewhat important	855	22.8	22.9	47.0
	No opinion either way	1039	27.7	27.9	74.9
	Somewhat unimportant	466	12.4	12.5	87.4
	Not important at all	469	12.5	12.6	100.0
	Total	3727	99.4	100.0	
Missing	System	21	.6		
Total		3748	100.0		

How important was the music in attracting you to, or maintaining you in this church?

		Frequency	Percent	Valid Percent	Cumulative Percent
Valid	Extremely important	1406	37.5	37.6	37.6
	Somewhat important	974	26.0	26.1	63.7
	No opinion either way	786	21.0	21.0	84.8
	Somewhat unimportant	326	8.7	8.7	93.5
	Not important at all	243	6.5	6.5	100.0
	Total	3735	99.7	100.0	
Missing	System	13	.3		
Total		3748	100.0		

How important was church fellowship in attracting you to, or maintaining you in, this church?

		Frequency	Percent	Valid Percent	Cumulative Percent
Valid	Extremely important	1905	50.8	51.0	51.0
	Somewhat important	787	21.0	21.1	72.0
	No opinion either way	600	16.0	16.1	88.1
	Somewhat unimportant	211	5.6	5.6	93.7
	Not important at all	233	6.2	6.2	99.9
	6	1	.0	.0	100.0
	11	1	.0	.0	100.0
	Total	3738	99.7	100.0	
Missing	System	10	.3		
Total		3748	100.0		

Have you experienced any hostility toward your membership in this church?

		Frequency	Percent	Valid Percent	Cumulative Percent
Valid	No, none	2842	75.8	75.9	75.9
	Yes, from family	358	9.6	9.6	85.4
	Yes, from neighbors	103	2.7	2.8	88.2
	Yes, from local officials	29	.8	.8	89.0
	Yes, from members of other religions	153	4.1	4.1	93.1
	Yes, from other church denominations	260	6.9	6.9	100.0
	Total	3745	99.9	100.0	
Missing	System	3	.1		
Total		3748	100.0		

About how often do you attend church services or other church programs at this church?

		Frequency	Percent	Valid Percent	Cumulative Percent
Valid	Three or more X a week	1432	38.2	38.4	38.4
	Twice a week	979	26.1	26.2	64.6
	Once a week	839	22.4	22.5	87.1
	2-3 X a month	231	6.2	6.2	93.2
	Once a month or less	252	6.7	6.8	100.0
	Total	3733	99.6	100.0	
Missing	System	15	.4		
Total		3748	100.0		

Have you been baptised?

		Frequency	Percent	Valid Percent	Cumulative Percent
Valid	No, I am not baptised	254	6.8	6.8	6.8
	Yes, I was baptised in this church	1533	40.9	40.9	47.7
	Yes, I was baptised in another church	1518	40.5	40.5	88.3
	I was baptised in another church and rebaptised here	440	11.7	11.7	100.0
	Total	3745	99.9	100.0	
Missing System	3	.1		
Total	3748	100.0		

Do you belong to a service group in this church?

		Frequency	Percent	Valid Percent	Cumulative Percent
Valid	Yes, as member	1648	44.0	44.0	44.0
	Yes, as leader	1079	28.8	28.8	72.8
	No, but I did in the past	525	14.0	14.0	86.8
	No, but I expect to in the future	450	12.0	12.0	98.8
	Total	3747	100.0	100.0	
	System Missing	1	.0		
	3748		100.0		

Have you received [material] support from this church?

		Frequency	Percent	Valid Percent	Cumulative Percent
Valid	No	2804	74.8	74.9	74.9
	No, not now, but yes in the past	315	8.4	8.4	83.3
	Yes	625	16.7	16.7	100.0
	Total	3745	99.9	100.0	
	Missing	3	.1		
		3748	100		

Have you received Holy Spirit baptism?

		Frequency	Percent	Valid Percent	Cumulative Percent
Valid	No	1163	31.0	31.0	31.0
	Yes	2585	69.0	69.0	100.0
	Total	3748	100.0	100.0	

In HS baptism, have you received the gift of tongues?

		Frequency	Percent	Valid Percent	Cumulative Percent
Valid	No	2299	61.3	61.4	61.4
	Yes	1448	38.6	38.6	100.0
	Total	3747	100.0	100.0	
Missing	System	1	.0		
	Total	3748	100.0		

RIn HS baptism, have you received the gift of interpreting tongues?

		Frequency	Percent	Valid Percent	Cumulative Percent
Valid	No	507	13.5	13.5	13.5
	Yes	3241	86.5	86.5	100.0
	Total	3748	100.0	100.0	

In HS baptism, have you received the gift of prophecy?

		Frequency	Percent	Valid Percent	Cumulative Percent
Valid	Yes	799	21.3	21.3	21.3
	No	2946	78.6	78.7	100.0
	Total	3745	99.9	100.0	
Missing	System	3	.1		
Total		3748	100.0		

In HS baptism, have you received the gift of healing?

		Frequency	Percent	Valid Percent	Cumulative Percent
Valid	Yes	1477	39.4	39.4	39.4
	No	2269	60.5	60.6	100.0
	Total	3746	99.9	100.0	
Missing	System	2	.1		
Total		3748	100.0		

In HS baptism, have you received the gift of exorcising demons?

		Frequency	Percent	Valid Percent	Cumulative Percent
Valid	Yes	1335	35.6	35.6	35.6
	No	2410	64.3	64.4	100.0
	Total	3745	99.9	100.0	
Missing	System	3	.1		
Total		3748	100.0		

IN HS baptism, have you received the gift of preaching?

		Frequency	Percent	Valid Percent	Cumulative Percent
Valid	Yes	1251	33.4	33.4	33.4
	No	2493	66.5	66.6	100.0
	Total	3744	99.9	100.0	
Missing	System	4	.1		
Total		3748	100.0		

In HS baptism, have you received other gifts of the Holy Spirit?

		Frequency	Percent	Valid Percent	Cumulative Percent
Valid	Yes	1640	43.8	44.0	44.0
	No	2084	55.6	56.0	100.0
	Total	3724	99.4	100.0	
Missing	System	24	.6		
Total		3748	100.0		

Being baptised in the Holy Spirit gave me the strength to keep going.

		Frequency	Percent	Valid Percent	Cumulative Percent
Valid	Yes	3294	87.9	88.8	88.8
	No	414	11.0	11.2	100.0
	Total	3708	98.9	100.0	
Missing	System	40	1.1		
Total		3748	100.0		

Being baptised in the Holy spirit gave me hope for the future.

		Frequency	Percent	Valid Percent	Cumulative Percent
Valid	Yes	3234	86.3	87.2	87.2
	No	474	12.6	12.8	100.0
	Total	3708	98.9	100.0	
Missing	System	40	1.1		
Total		3748	100.0		

Being baptised in the Holy Spirit made me feel forgiven.

		Frequency	Percent	Valid Percent	Cumulative Percent
Valid	Yes	3106	82.9	83.9	83.9
	No	597	15.9	16.1	100.0
	Total	3703	98.8	100.0	
Missing	System	45	1.2		
Total		3748	100.0		

Being baptised in the Holy Spirit made me feel God's love.

		Frequency	Percent	Valid Percent	Cumulative Percent
Valid	Yes	3275	87.4	88.4	88.4
	No	431	11.5	11.6	100.0
	Total	3706	98.9	100.0	
Missing	System	42	1.1		
Total		3748	100.0		

Being baptised in the Holy Spirit healed me, made me whole.

		Frequency	Percent	Valid Percent	Cumulative Percent
Valid	Yes	3149	84.0	85.1	85.1
	No	553	14.8	14.9	100.0
	Total	3702	98.8	100.0	
Missing	System	46	1.2		
Total		3748	100.0		

Being baptised in the Holy Spirit made me more successful.

		Frequency	Percent	Valid Percent	Cumulative Percent
Valid	Yes	3036	81.0	82.2	82.2
	No	659	17.6	17.8	100.0
	Total	3695	98.6	100.0	
Missing	System	53	1.4		
Total		3748	100.0		

In this church . . .

		Frequency	Percent	Valid Percent	Cumulative Percent
Valid	Only men can be helping pastors, junior pastors or senior pastors	128	3.4	3.4	3.4
	Only men can be junior pastors or senior pastors	97	2.6	2.6	6.0
	Only men can become senior pastors	157	4.2	4.2	10.2
	Both men and women can hold all positions, including senior pastor	3175	84.7	85.0	95.2
	Not sure	179	4.8	4.8	100.0
	Total	3736	99.7	100.0	
Missing	System	12	.3		
Total		3748	100.0		

Appendix C

In this church . . .

		Frequency	Percent	Valid Percent	Cumulative Percent
Valid	There are no limitations on women's service	2060	55.0	55.1	55.1
	Both men and women preach, but only men lead communion sercvices	1353	36.1	36.2	91.3
	Women work under men's supervision	84	2.2	2.2	93.6
	Women's ministry is only to other women	116	3.1	3.1	96.7
	Not sure	125	3.3	3.3	100.0
	Total	3738	99.7	100.0	
Missing	System	10	.3		
Total		3748	100.0		

This church teaches that in the home. . .

		Frequency	Percent	Valid Percent	Cumulative Percent
Valid	Men are heads of households, who care for women and children	2846	75.9	76.2	76.2
	Men and women are equal partners in parenting and decision-making	658	17.6	17.6	93.8
	Mothers have principal care for children	88	2.3	2.4	96.1
	This church does not have a clear teaching on this	144	3.8	3.9	100.0
	Total	3736	99.7	100.0	
Missing	System	12	.3		
Total		3748	100.0		

Have you attended a healing service in the last year?

		Frequency	Percent	Valid Percent	Cumulative Percent
Valid	Yes	2150	57.4	57.5	57.5
	No	1590	42.4	42.5	100.0
	4	1	.0	.0	100.0
	Total	3741	99.8	100.0	
Missing	System	7	.2		
Total		3748	100.0		

Have you or a member of your immediate family been healed?

		Frequency	Percent	Valid Percent	Cumulative Percent
Valid	Yes	2502	66.8	67.0	67.0
	No	1195	31.9	32.0	99.0
	Not sure	36	1.0	1.0	100.0
	Total	3733	99.6	100.0	
Missing	System	15	.4		
Total		3748	100.0		

Do you believe that if you have true faith, you will succeed?

		Frequency	Percent	Valid Percent	Cumulative Percent
Valid	Yes, always	2869	76.5	76.7	76.7
	Yes, most of the time	518	13.8	13.9	90.6
	Sometimes	227	6.1	6.1	96.6
	I'm not sure	126	3.4	3.4	100.0
	Total	3740	99.8	100.0	
Missing	System	8	.2		
Total		3748	100.0		

How accepting of your ethnic or cultural heritage is this church?

		Frequency	Percent	Valid Percent	Cumulative Percent
Valid	Very	1217	32.5	32.6	32.6
	Some	1571	41.9	42.1	74.8
	A little	503	13.4	13.5	88.3
	Not very	400	10.7	10.7	99.0
	Not sure	38	1.0	1.0	100.0
	Total	3729	99.5	100.0	
Missing	System	19	.5		
Total		3748	100.0		

Do you think the government should restrict pornography?

		Frequency	Percent	Valid Percent	Cumulative Percent
Valid	Yes	2508	66.9	67.1	67.1
	No	553	14.8	14.8	81.8
	Not sure	679	18.1	18.2	100.0
	Total	3740	99.8	100.0	
Missing	System	8	.2		
Total		3748	100.0		

What is your attitude toward shari'a-inspired local laws? (regulations on alcohol, women's modesty, etc)

		Frequency	Percent	Valid Percent	Cumulative Percent
Valid	I strongly disagree because this is discrimination	808	21.6	21.6	21.6
	I agree so long as this only affects Muslims	418	11.2	11.2	32.8
	I agree because it protects important moral values	1658	44.2	44.4	77.2
	I don't have an opinion	854	22.8	22.8	100.0
	Total	3738	99.7	100.0	
Missing	System	10	.3		
Total		3748	100.0		

How many times in the last year have you paid a bribe?

		Frequency	Percent	Valid Percent	Cumulative Percent
Valid	No times	2610	69.6	69.7	69.7
	Yes, once	666	17.8	17.8	87.5
	Yes, twice	187	5.0	5.0	92.5
	Yes, more than twice	279	7.4	7.5	100.0
	Total	3742	99.8	100.0	
Missing	System	6	.2		
Total		3748	100.0		

If the teacher of your child were not Pentecostal/Charismatic, with a person from which of the following groups would you feel MOST comfortable as his/her teacher?

		Frequency	Percent	Valid Percent	Cumulative Percent
Valid	Non-pentecostal Christian	1168	31.2	31.2	31.2
	Catholic	129	3.4	3.5	34.7
	Muslim	44	1.2	1.2	35.9
	Hindu/Buddhist/Confucian	47	1.3	1.3	37.1
	No problem with any	2301	61.4	61.6	98.7
	Not sure	49	1.3	1.3	100.0
	Total	3738	99.7	100.0	
Missing	System	10	.3		
Total		3748	100.0		

If the teacher of your child were not Pentecostal/Charismatic, with a person from which of the following groups would you feel LEAST comfortable as his/her teacher?

		Frequency	Percent	Valid Percent	Cumulative Percent
Valid	Non-Pentecostal Christian	263	7.0	7.0	7.0
	Catholic	67	1.8	1.8	8.8
	Muslim	832	22.2	22.3	31.1
	Hindu/Buddhist/Confucian	178	4.7	4.8	w35.9
	No problem with any	2325	62.0	62.3	98.2
	Not sure	67	1.8	1.8	100.0
	Total	3732	99.6	100.0	
Missing	System	16	.4		
Total		3748	100.0		

How important do you think it is for this church to grow its membership?

		Frequency	Percent	Valid Percent	Cumulative Percent
	Very important	3067	81.8	82.0	82.1
	Somewhat important	613	16.4	16.4	98.5
	Not so important	57	1.5	1.5	100.0
	Total	3738	99.7	100.0	
Missing	System	10	.3		
Total		3748	100.0		

Are you involved in spreading the gospel?

		Frequency	Percent	Valid Percent	Cumulative Percent
Valid	Yes	3437	91.7	92.1	92.1
	No	295	7.9	7.9	100.0
	Total	3732	99.6	100.0	
Missing	System	16	.4		
Total		3748	100.0		

Do you think it is important to have a Christian party to represent your political views?

		Frequency	Percent	Valid Percent	Cumulative Percent
Valid	Very important	860	22.9	23.0	23.0
	Somewhat important	1033	27.6	27.6	50.6
	Not very important	1047	27.9	28.0	78.5
	I don't know	803	21.4	21.5	100.0
	Total	3743	99.9	100.0	
Missing	System	5	.1		
Total		3748	100.0		

How does this church help you in the process of political elections?

		Frequency	Percent	Valid Percent	Cumulative Percent
Valid	Church suggests certain candidates or parties	260	6.9	7.0	7.0
	Church supports candidates from pentecostal backgrounds	279	7.4	7.5	14.4
	Church gives information on issues concerning religion	560	14.9	15.0	29.4
	Church does not speak of politics	2638	70.4	70.6	100.0
	Total	3737	99.7	100.0	
Missing	System	11	.3		
Total		3748	100.0		

Age (recoded)

		Frequency	Percent	Valid Percent	Cumulative Percent
Valid	14 and under	67	1.8	1.9	1.9
	15-19	481	12.8	13.5	15.4
	20-24	610	16.3	17.2	32.6
	25-29	489	13.0	13.8	46.3
	30-34	453	12.1	12.7	59.1
	35-39	399	10.6	11.2	70.3
	40-44	335	8.9	9.4	79.7
	45-49	232	6.2	6.5	86.2
	50-54	184	4.9	5.2	91.4
	55-59	132	3.5	3.7	95.1
	60-64	83	2.2	2.3	97.4
	65-69	53	1.4	1.5	98.9
	70-74	24	.6	.7	99.6
	75-79	5	.1	.1	99.7
	80-84	6	.2	.2	99.9
	85 and above	1	.0	.0	99.9
	33	1	.0	.0	100.0
	99	1	.0	.0	100.0
	Total	3556	94.9	100.0	
Missing	System	192	5.1		
Total		3748	100.0		

ATF Press Style Guide

1. Indented material: Indented quotations, of over 5 lines of material, or 30 words, should be indented on both sides. There should be a space of one line before and after the quotation. Quotations should not have quotation marks at the beginning or end and within the quotation there should be single quotation marks (exception: where *within* the indented quote there is a quote that is also quoting (. . . '. . . " . . . " . . . ' . . .).

2. Headings: Headings should not be numbered unless there is a particular need (for example, cross-referencing within the text, scientific or text-book style presentation. Capitals should be used for the initial letters only of headings and subsections (unless using proper nouns). Headings and subsections do not have punctuation at the end. (

3. Spelling: The general guide to spelling will be taken from *The Macquarie Dictionary*. We use '-ise' forms for words (and not '-ize') (so: realise, globalisation, modernise . . .). Hyphens should be used in words such as 'co-operate' and 'co-ordinate', except where the mathematical 'coordinate' is used. *The Australian Writers Dictionary* is a valuable tool for assisting with the use of hyphens. We prefer World War 1 (and not First World War). All Latin, Greek and all foreign words should be in italics and have an English translation. We prefer transliterations of biblical languages but if biblical languages are used then the English must be given in brackets.

4. Abbreviations and contractions
Abbreviations are generally not used: editor (rather than ed.), translated by (rather than trans.), volume (rather than vol.), number (rather than no.), for example (not e.g.). Those such as USA or UN do not have full points between the letters. Contractions, which end in the last of the whole word, should not be given a full point: Dr (Doctor), St (Saint).

5. *Personal initials* Do not insert a stop or space between personal initials, as for example: AN Simple.

6. *Dates and numbers* Avoid unnecessary punctuation: 24 June 1999 (and not 24 June, 1999, or June 24th, 1999). 1990s (not 1990's). Twentieth century (not 20th century). When referring to the age of a person, 'she was in her eighties', use the spelt-out form, but use figures in the hyphenated form when writing of an '80-year-old woman'. In text use of year span: 1991–8 with an en rule (not hyphen and no space) (not 1991-8), 1902–3 (and not1902-03), 1878–83. When in headings or subsections, use 1990–1992. Financial years are 1991/92. Spans of numbers: use as few digits as possible, with the exception of 11–19, where 1 is repeated. So: 112–13,103–8, 34–9, 145–53. Numbers up to ninety-nine are spelt out in the text, except where figures are needed in a string of hyphenated words (35-hour week) or where figures will assist with clarity (when several numbers are compared). Numbers over ninety-nine are usually written in numerals but can be spelt out (about a thousand people) where figures seem inappropriate in the text. When a date is the first word of the sentence, use the spelt out form. Use figures for sums of money, $1.24, but three cents. Times should be in words rather than numerals when precision is not intended. So: 'They had to leave at three o'clock'. But where a precise time is intended: 'The bus leaves at 10.23am'. Percentages should be spelt out in the text: ninety-three per cent (note 'per cent'). But 93% in footnotes and tables.

7. *Hyphens and dashes*: En rules (a short dash) should be used for spans of numbers: 182–3; for Christian biblical references for the verses: Mk 3:12–13; for expressions of time: May–June; expressions of distance: Adelaide–Melbourne; and where 'and' is meant. Em rules (a long dash) are used in parenthetical statements, with no gap either side. For example, 'To have wide lawns—and not any garden—is not necessary for a happy life'.

8. *Quotations*: Indented quotes do not have opening and closing quotation marks. Short extracts of less than 5 lines (or 30 words) may appear within the text, enclosed in single quotation marks. Quotation marks should go inside the final full point if there is any

comment within the sentence; that is, the full point belongs to the author as part of her/his sentence. Time and time again, 'people do not speak' was quoted by authors. Or Sally was known to have said that 'the weather at the Cape is fine all year round'. If the quotation begins within a sentence containing authorial comment but runs to more than one sentence, it is acceptable to place the closing quotation mark after the final full point. George Stephens wrote with glee 'about fifty men broke out of the prison yesterday evening. We expect to have them rounded up before the week is past.' When a sentence is entirely quoted material, then all punctuation belongs to the quotation; therefore, the final full point goes inside the closing quotation mark. Mary received the telegram at 10 am. 'I never knew a darker moment than when I read of John's death.' Double quotation marks are only used for quotes within quotes. Eggs were thrown at the 'vote "No" for a republic' banner.
Indicate any omission from a quotation by the use of an ellipsis (. . .), with a single space keyed in before and after each point. Do not insert an additional full point if the ellipsis occurs at the end of a sentence. Do not use editorial caps within square brackets as in '[I]t is then . . . ', but leave the lower close letter, or adjust the way the quote is used.

9. Footnotes
Notes should be used for sources you have used, published or unpublished, to a brief discussion of the sources, to develop a point out of the text, or to cross reference to other parts of the text. Footnotes in the text should be used as a superscript text and in Times.

9.1Books: First name (not initials) and surname, title of the book (in italics), place of publication, publisher and year (all in brackets), followed by page numbers. We do not use p or pp for footnote entries or in the text. In the text write word 'page' if necessary. In footnotes there is minimal punctuation: First reference:
Victor Pfitzner, *The Islands of Peru* (Adelaide: ATF Press, 1999), 21.
Second and subsequent references copy and paste name (surname only) and title of book (or abbreviated title), followed by page

number. Where a title is long a suitable shorter version should be used in second and subsequent references.
Pfitzner, *The Islands of Peru*, 28.

9.2 Articles in journals: First name, surname, title of article, (with single inverted commas), title of the journal (in italics), volume and number, year (year in brackets), followed by a colon and then the pages of the article. We do not uses p or pp in footnotes or in the text. First reference: Victor Pfitzner, 'Where To From Here?', in *Interface: A Pyschology Review*, 1/2 (1998): 22–3.
Second and subsequent references: Pfitzner, 'Where to From Here?', 38.

9.3 Articles in books: First name, surname, title of article (with single inverted commas), edited by, with first name first, title of the book (in italics), place of publication, publisher and year (all in brackets), followed by a colon and then page. Victor Pfitzner, 'Yesterday, Today And Tomorrow', in *Readings in Contemporary History*, edited by Victor Pfitzner (Adelaide: ATF Press, 2002), 22–56. *9.4 Web references*: First name, surname, title of article, web address enclosed in <…>, access date. Victor Pfitzner, 'Today and Not Tomorrow' at <www.newspoll.com.apost-au>. Accessed 20 July 2010. (No underlining).

10. Bibliography: We do not normally have a bibliography included with texts. But if one is to be used then, authors surname first, followed by initials and in alphabetical order of surname. Title of the book is in italics and with place of publisher, publisher and year in brackets. Pfitzner, V, *History of The New Time* (Adelaide: ATF Press, 2002).

Lightning Source UK Ltd.
Milton Keynes UK
UKOW04f1153051217
313901UK00002B/309/P